Fairytale and Gothic Horror

Laura Hubner

Fairytale and Gothic Horror

Uncanny Transformations in Film

Laura Hubner
Department of Media and Film Studies
University of Winchester
Winchester, UK

ISBN 978-1-137-39346-3   ISBN 978-1-137-39347-0 (eBook)
https://doi.org/10.1057/978-1-137-39347-0

Library of Congress Control Number: 2018934634

© The Editor(s) (if applicable) and The Author(s) 2018
The author(s) has/have asserted their right(s) to be identified as the author(s) of this work in accordance with the Copyright, Designs and Patents Act 1988.
This work is subject to copyright. All rights are solely and exclusively licensed by the Publisher, whether the whole or part of the material is concerned, specifically the rights of translation, reprinting, reuse of illustrations, recitation, broadcasting, reproduction on microfilms or in any other physical way, and transmission or information storage and retrieval, electronic adaptation, computer software, or by similar or dissimilar methodology now known or hereafter developed.
The use of general descriptive names, registered names, trademarks, service marks, etc. in this publication does not imply, even in the absence of a specific statement, that such names are exempt from the relevant protective laws and regulations and therefore free for general use.
The publisher, the authors and the editors are safe to assume that the advice and information in this book are believed to be true and accurate at the date of publication. Neither the publisher nor the authors or the editors give a warranty, express or implied, with respect to the material contained herein or for any errors or omissions that may have been made. The publisher remains neutral with regard to jurisdictional claims in published maps and institutional affiliations.

Cover credit: Mimadeo/Alamy Stock Photo

Printed on acid-free paper

This Palgrave Macmillan imprint is published by the registered company Macmillan Publishers Ltd. part of Springer Nature
The registered company address is: The Campus, 4 Crinan Street, London, N1 9XW, United Kingdom

Preface

The idea for this monograph originates in a Masters module I devised and began teaching in 2007, at the University of Winchester, called 'Fairytale and Gothic Horror'—a Film Studies module open to students from four other Masters degrees (English, Creative Writing, Cultural Studies and Religion: The Rhetoric and Ritual of Death) as well as Film students. The module examines fairytale and gothic horror traditions in a diversity of cultural forms, drawing on a range of theoretical modes of thought, such as postcolonial criticism, feminism and psychoanalysis. The dark undercurrents of fairy tale and folklore are explored, looking at the close links with gothic romance, gothic horror, fantasy and nightmare. Due to its open nature, the module also offers a broad cultural study that investigates a number of disciplinary perspectives, including art, film, literature, language, media, mythology and religion to shed light on the many faces of fairytale and gothic horror within the cinema. The challenge was to offer a module that, grounded in the field of film, at the same time presented themes that could interest and engage students from other disciplines.

This book is indebted to the students' monumental contributions to the module, and the disparate ways of thinking they inspired along the way.

Winchester, UK   Laura Hubner

Acknowledgements

I would like to thank the Faculty of Arts Research and Knowledge Exchange Committee at the University of Winchester for supporting this project through all its stages and for awarding the sabbatical that enabled the drafting of this book. Thanks also to the Faculty Head of Research, Inga Bryden, for her helpful guidance and encouragement, and to my colleagues in the Faculty, including Imruh Bakari, Jude Davies, Neil Ewen, Gary Farnell, Vanessa Harbour, Fran Mason and Andy Melrose. Special thanks are due to Steven Allen, for the valued and helpful suggestions on early drafts and ideas, Leighton Grist, whose inexhaustible knowledge and generosity helped galvanize a difficult chapter into better shape, Marcus Leaning, for the incredible support and boundless enthusiasm, and Dan Varndell, for the insightful and lively conversations that got me putting pen to paper many a time. I am also indebted to my valued research students, a constant inspiration, and MA students (given singular mention in the Preface).

My sincere thanks go to my editors at Palgrave Macmillan—Lina Aboujieb, Ellie Freedman, Karina Jakupsdottir, Chris Penfold, Felicity Plester and Hari Swaminathan—for their immense assistance and patience over the course of writing this book. I am very grateful to Steve Chibnall for the time given at the Hammer Film Archives (De Montfort University)—for the expertise and enthusiasm, as well as the special navigation through his personal collection. Thanks also to Jane Dipple for being the perfect research companion. I would like to thank the organizers (Kaja Franck, Samantha George, Bill Hughes) and delegates of the

'Company of Wolves Conference' held at the University of Hertfordshire (UK), especially Maggie Robb, who joined me there, and all those in attendance at the 'Supernatural in Literature and Film' Conference (North Unst, Shetland). I also gleaned vital information from the British Film Institute and the British Library exhibition 'Terror and Wonder: The Gothic Imagination,' thanks particularly to the knowledgeable and helpful staff. Singular thanks are due to Sue Short who provided supportive feedback on the draft manuscript, and helped me to see how the various strands linked together. Philippa Greening and Carl Davies are also due thanks for loaning the handy books on women, wolves and the work of Angela Carter, as are Owen Evans, Jane Foster, Francesca Froy, Pauline Greenhill, Beth King and James Walters for their whole-hearted encouragement of the research proposal and David Aldrich for the wonderful insights into 'framing the dark.' I am grateful to Zoe Ross for producing the index with dexterity and insight.

Exceptional thanks are due to my family for their ongoing support—in particular my parents, Anne and David, for their lifelong encouragement, kindness and inspiration and my sister, Clare, who has always been there by my side and is not afraid to walk through the woods at night. Thank you to Bob Bavister (the perfect outlaw) and Maggie Mclean for their warmth and enthusiasm. Last, but by no means least, I would like to thank Paul Bavister who has been a bountiful source of love, patience and good humour—thank you for helping me see through the haze, and for reading through every final draft.

I would like to dedicate this book to my sons, Daniel and Jason, whose magic and wonder persists.

CONTENTS

1 Introduction 1

2 Fairytale Roots and Transformations 13

3 Gothic Transgression, Horror and Film 43

4 Rebecca Returns: Death and Renewal Beyond the Door 75

5 Encountering the Werewolf—Confronting the Self: On and Off the Path to *The Company of Wolves* 117

6 The Horror in *Pan's Labyrinth*: Beneath the Rhetoric of Hope and Fear 159

7 Afterword: Uncanny Transformations in Film 191

Index 197

List of Figures

Fig. 3.1	The boundary is crossed; Corky slips out of control—*Magic* (Richard Attenborough, 1978)	63
Fig. 3.2	The camera comments on the horror of Fats taking over—*Magic* (Richard Attenborough, 1978)	64
Fig. 3.3	Innocence fuses with the sinister—*Let the Right One In* (Tomas Alfredson, 2008)	69
Fig. 4.1	The ending, just before the west wing goes up in flames—*Rebecca* (Alfred Hitchcock, 1940)	79
Fig. 4.2	In the beach cottage, when the telephone rings—*Rebecca* (Alfred Hitchcock, 1940)	80
Fig. 4.3	The heroine is at the door, about to leave—*Rebecca* (Alfred Hitchcock, 1940)	88
Fig. 5.1	The heroine smiles—*The Company of Wolves* (Neil Jordan, 1984)	127
Fig. 5.2	The werewolf sheds a tear—*The Curse of the Werewolf* (Terence Fisher, 1961)	134
Fig. 5.3	Voyeur on the outside world—*Werewolf of London* (Stuart Walker, 1935)	140
Fig. 5.4	Between the laboratory and the garden party—*Werewolf of London* (Stuart Walker, 1935)	141
Fig. 5.5	Encountering Dr. Yogami—confronting the self—*Werewolf of London* (Stuart Walker, 1935)	143
Fig. 6.1	The Resistance are spotted, framed by Vidal's binoculars—*Pan's Labyrinth* (Guillermo del Toro, 2006)	165

Fig. 6.2 Words and pictures flood Ofelia's body and the walls—*Pan's Labyrinth* (Guillermo del Toro, 2006) 169

Fig. 6.3 A white flower opens as the insect looks on—*Pan's Labyrinth* (Guillermo del Toro, 2006) 187

CHAPTER 1

Introduction

Fairy tales seep into filmmaking, projecting a simple articulation of hope as a force against fear. The spectre of gothic casts shadows over hope and fear, warning us to be less certain that they are poles apart. Looking initially at 'fairytale' and 'gothic' as independent concepts, as each acts adjectivally with 'horror,' this book explores how these seeming opposites respond to each other, share properties and merge as they find expression in film. In short, I am interested in both the distinctions and parallels between gothic and fairytale horror, as well as the new meanings created when certain elements are brought together. Fairytale and gothic horror contribute to films in rich and diverse ways. Their intersection in cinema is sometimes like oil and water—separating out or repelling each other—redefining their difference. Sometimes they amalgamate in the most unexpected and surprising ways. This book is motivated by the varying and idiosyncratic properties that are created as fairytale and gothic horror join, clash or merge in cinema.

Since the Age of Enlightenment, gothic thinking has shed light on the wild sensations that drive us and the pull between rational and irrational forces, asking us to reconsider the securities of home, our sense of self and our beliefs. Polarizations of good and evil are rife in the gothic tale, but often only so that their seeming oppositions with each other can be questioned, or broken down. Such polarizations tend to remain intact within the bounds of the fairy tale, but the candidness afforded by this fantastical realm exposes the complexities at stake in everyday life, via themes of jealousy, brutality, cruelty, desire and greed so that difficult subject matter can be addressed, including abuse in the home, child abandonment and rape.

While there might be a tendency to be sceptical of fairytale happy or restorative endings, they frequently signify the overcoming of trials, tasks or puzzles. As Sue Short argues:

> A happy ending is far from necessarily conservative. On the contrary, it grants us the imaginative power to rethink what is possible. Unlikely heroes who earn themselves a kingdom, imperilled heroines who put a difficult past behind them, fabulous beings and magical encounters that enable dreams to come true may all seem unbelievably far-fetched, yet a sense of wonder should also be valued for the creative freedom it allows to defy apparent restrictions and imaginatively reconceive reality. (2015: 167)

Gothic fictions tend to end very differently. Even though a sense of order is usually reinstated by the film's close, the gothic denies the final sanctuary of a 'happily ever after' resolution. Questions and tensions that are opened up through the course of the narrative create a sense of uncertainty that is unknown to fairy tales. Incorporating fairytale elements can help feed hope into films that are otherwise overwhelmingly bleak or horrific, or hope can stand in isolation, as an alternative vision or necessary illusion beyond the bounds of time and place. The use of hope can also enhance the horror, as the full force of the film's terrors or atrocities leak back in. As Maria Tatar (2003) has demonstrated, the forms that a fairy tale takes, and the intricate ways it is used and revised, challenge the notion of a primal, 'original' source. The bringing together of a number of fairy tales or versions of fairy tales with a variety of gothic elements and tendencies creates complex, enchanted effects.

My aim is to explore the convergences and deviations between fairytale and gothic horror as they are conveyed in film. Fundamental to this is an examination of cinema's lively embrace of fairytale horror, structures, motifs and themes and the need to locate a distinctively cinematic gothic horror that both draws on and is distinct from literary and other artistic forms. Underlying these objectives is an interest in the cultural and political functions of fairytale and gothic horror, and the levels of destabilization or social conformity at the heart of the films examined. Thus, the goal of this book is to provide insight into the films' elaborate, complex engagement with fairytale and gothic horror, rather than to impose any rigid structure of analysis or fixed theoretical framework.

I explore gothic and fairytale horror through a range of theoretical modes of thought, such as feminism and psychoanalysis. The dark undercurrents of fairy tales and folklore are analyzed, looking at the close links with gothic romance, gothic horror and fantasy. Through Chapters 2 and 3, debates are contextualized within a cultural study that briefly investigates a broad range of (art and literature) disciplinary perspectives to explore the many faces of fairytale and gothic horror in film. Because gothic is partly defined by tone and atmosphere, generated by film aesthetics, style, mise-en-scène and narrative techniques, I begin to uncover a cinematic gothic distinct from adaptation concerns.

Undertaking a close analysis of classical through to contemporary films, this book features detailed analyses of films made in North America, Latin America and Europe, with reference to a wider scope, identifying long-held traditions, important progressions and transgressions. Despite a fairly open scope, this book is also focused, and investigates key themes, ideologies, cultural values, pleasures and fears embedded within fairytale and gothic horror, as well as providing detailed insight into specific films, especially in the case studies (Chapters 4, 5 and 6). The process of putting together this book has necessarily involved selecting certain films for close critical investigation, and I have made no attempt for this to be a comprehensive study with respect to the scope of films discussed. My feeling is that the chosen films focus on issues in particularly compelling ways, but the omission or marginalization of other films does not imply they are not equally relevant to the debate. Where possible, attempts are made to acknowledge a wider scope; for example, where points relate to a number of films or to a much broader cinematic or cultural context.

The book begins (in Chapters 2 and 3) by tracing the geneses and evolution of fairy tales and gothic, as a means to articulate critical definitions of 'fairy tale' and 'gothic' over time, and across shifting cultural contexts, exploring the diverse ways these have been incorporated and developed by cinema and horror. Chapters 2 and 3 formulate the foundations for the analyses that follow in the case study chapters. Thus, the book moves on to a different stage with Chapters 4, 5 and 6 to investigate films close up, locating fairytale horror, motifs and themes as well as a distinctively cinematic gothic horror. The case study chapters are each ostensibly (and distinctively) framed by the analysis of a single film: *Rebecca* (Alfred Hitchcock, 1940) in Chapter 4; *The Company of Wolves* (Neil Jordan, 1984) in Chapter 5; and *El laberinto del fauno / Pan's Labyrinth*

(Guillermo del Toro, 2006) in Chapter 6. However, each of these films is used as a springboard to examine a wider range of films. Broadly speaking, there is a chronological development through these three chapters: beginning with 1940s films (Chapter 4), moving onto British werewolf films from 1935 to 1984 (Chapter 5), and ending with the more contemporary lens of *Pan's Labyrinth* (Chapter 6). While chronology helps shape the book, it is also thematically driven and attentive to cultural and political concerns. Each of the films used to frame the case study chapters has a central female protagonist whose dreaming is suggestive of an alternative journey that transgresses boundaries of the 'real' even if (ultimately) it does not attain full rein. Fundamental and cyclical concerns include: liminal zones and the spaces between; the boundaries of the human; death and rebirth; rational and irrational forces; fears and dreams; 'the uncanny'; and transitions between the wilderness and civilization. The key motivation of the book is to open up a space for further interest or study, rather than to attempt to be fully comprehensive or exhaustive.

Chapter 2 addresses the great paradox of the fairy tale. It is on the one hand perceived as a simple tale, concerned with overcoming challenges and attaining ultimate happiness. On the other hand, the fairy tale is seen as an allegorical window into an imaginary timeless land; it is able to give expression to the unspoken terrors and taboos of daily life. The richness and diversity of fairy tales are explored, together with their malleable application in a variety of contemporary forms of media. Communal knowledge of fairy tales means that films are able to draw upon the myths perpetuated by such stories, providing a shortcut to relationship and moral concerns—whether or not traditional visions or cautions are upheld or challenged. Chapter 2 investigates the diverse ways in which films make reference to and are inspired by specific and varying fairytale narratives, motifs and themes. Fundamental emotions (jealousy, greed, love) and motivations (curiosity, rivalry) carried across from the fairy tale, have a portable quality that appeals to a broad, international audience. Thus, films with more complex or historically situated narratives can embrace fairytale themes, structures, roles or motifs to convey universal and timeless concerns layered over more difficult or forbidden subject matter.

Fairy tales' tendency for a fixed understanding of polarities is explored, as Chapter 2 unpacks the ramifications of their 'simplicity,' tallied with the misconception that this implies shallowness. The fantastical, flexible realm of the fairytale world is capable of revealing and forming a dialogue with the complexities of human relationships and circumstances. Their seeming primal quality triggers a wealth of meanings and interpretations. Concepts of 'good' and 'evil' tend to remain as stable entities in the fairy tale, in contrast to the gothic, despite the journey or transformation powering many of the tales. Initiation tasks and discoveries propel the hero's voyage, and transitions between realms (such as childhood to adulthood) form a key part of the drive towards resolution. This chapter notes that the two-dimensionality and conventional trajectory of female roles in the classical fairy tale have come under close scrutiny and have been vehemently attacked by the application of second-wave feminist approaches that remain central to the considerations of this book. I also investigate the variety of approaches to specific versions of fairy tales at key historical moments, such as a recent queer reading of Hans Christian Andersen's work, which has helped to shed new light on the themes of borders and marginalization.

Aligning with the work of Rosemary Jackson (1991), I suggest that it is fairy tales' 'fantastic' capacity that allows for the boundaries of the imagination to be tested. Films are able to borrow from the open 'once upon a time' agelessness, and elastic settings associated with fairy tales, as a fast route to hopes, warnings, fears and horrors. This process enables insight into unspeakable or repressed scenarios of abuse within the home, associated with abandonment or even murder. Alternatively, films can uproot major, and often forgotten, tactics for finding our way through the dark woods, such as strategy and initiative. The 'civilizing' methods of transcribing and publishing fairy tales for children are also explored. However, the notion that fairy tales have evolved from a primal source is a myth. I am mindful when examining the films that there are multiple versions of fairy tales. Chapter 2 asserts the importance of focusing on the films themselves in the case study chapters. In addition, it creates a foundation for thinking about fairy tales and fairytale horror as both separate from—and merging with—gothic reflections and manifestations in film.

The bringing together of a number of fairy tales, as well as mixed fairytale versions and elements creates new meanings that the gothic contributes to and reacts against in enchanted ways. A key area of distinction between the fairy tale and gothic is confronted directly at the start of Chapter 3, with respect to the 'happily ever after' ending associated so strongly with the fairy tale. I suggest that while the haunting uncertainty at the heart of gothic casts a lasting shadow on any final resolution, there is nevertheless usually in some sense a reinstatement of order by the narrative's end. Having said this, the ambiguities and disturbances that gothic fictions upend project a shattering resonance, throwing expectations and norms into disarray long after the fiction's close. Examining the numerous trends over the centuries, the chapter unearths important traits and sentiments that help to lay firmer foundations for a sensibility of gothic that fuels the case study chapters that follow. In alignment with the approach taken by Fred Botting (1996), I place major emphasis on the gothic's propensity for transgression. I suggest that gothic is motivated by a continuous cycle of repression, which is triggered by an initial return of the repressed that in turn necessitates the return of repression. With respect to the 'return of the repressed,' my work remains indebted to Robin Wood (1986: 63–84), whose pioneering studies of the horror film helped me to think my way through chief parts of the case study chapters, and positively permeate the founding structures of Chapters 4 and 5. The cyclical impetus of gothic's relationship with repression means that the threat (of the return of the repressed) is not quite dampened; the razing of too many established norms and securities cannot fully be forgotten. Since gothic unrest is galvanized by repression, gothic fictions often express or imply some level of critique upon the repression itself, thus providing valuable insight into shifting cultural predispositions, restrictions and moral standards. Thus, gothic is able not only to repress but also to draw attention to unconscious drives and fears, bringing hidden, dangerous secrets out into the open, potentially making gothic texts a political *tour de force*.

The chapter explores the life–death quality of cinema, and moves on to consider the subtleties and complexities of style and tone that together help formulate a specifically 'cinematic gothic.' An investigation into the broader history of gothic enables the establishment of gothic's major (post-Enlightenment) struggles with the rational and irrational, passions and sense. Exploring features that infuse other art forms helps to unravel the vital and distinctive cinematic means that films draw on to convey boundaries and fusions between internal and external, conscious and unconscious, self and other. The doppelgänger and split self are examined in relation to peculiar editing, framing and camera devices that help ignite conceptual concerns, in addition to other gothic tendencies such as excess, fantasy/reality boundaries, or the persistence of the past within the present. The essay '*Das Heimlich*' / 'The Uncanny' by Sigmund Freud (2003: 123–162), originally published in 1919, is located as a seminal work that has become crucial for discerning the contradictions and dualities between public and private, or external and internal, that are central to gothic. The 'homely' becomes terrifying, as a familiar domain for the repressed, hidden and dangerous, stimulating the haunting return of something that should have remained private. By linking notions of the uncanny with the gothic, and in turn unpacking how the uncanny has generally been perceived as alien to classical fairy tales, it becomes clear that the uncanny (like the gothic) is not guaranteed by set items (rising corpses or animated toys for example) but rather needs to be conjured by a creator or consumer—attentive to style, tone and atmosphere. Moreover, it is possible to be alert to gothic tensions and uncanny situations beyond the protagonists' awareness, thus making the impact of the uncanny all the more horrific.

The transgressive possibilities of gothic are inherent in the prolonged reverberances of the past within the present or the notion that horror upsurges from within—devastating boundaries between the self and 'other' and preconceived concepts of 'home.' These deliberations concerning the ways gothic and the uncanny function, moment to moment as well as across and beyond a film, are explored further in Chapter 4, as gothic sensations collide with fairytale frameworks and references in particularly horrifying ways. Chapter 4 explores the labyrinthine assimilation of fairytale and gothic horror elements in *Rebecca*—a film that seemed to spawn a decade of 'Bluebeard' or 'persecuted wife' Hollywood movies. *Rebecca* opens with the young, unnamed heroine (Joan Fontaine) being whisked off her feet by her new husband, Maxim (Laurence Olivier), to take up residence at his beautiful, but dauntingly magnificent, ancestral home, Manderley. Haunted, through every room of the house, by the spectral return of Rebecca, Maxim's previous wife, the heroine is stunned by Maxim's sudden revelatory 'confession,' in the beach cottage, that he had (accidentally) caused Rebecca's death. The chapter suggests that while the core narrative thrust appears to align with the heroine's decision to stand by her husband, Maxim's aggressive response to what he refers to as Rebecca's infidelities also provides insight into the harsh brutality that is unleashed when there is a threat to the patriarchal bloodline.

I argue that the many hallmarks of a classical fairy tale that give structure to the film's opening are gradually challenged as gothic instabilities take hold. While the 'confession' of the revelation sequence triggers a closeness between Maxim and the heroine that realigns the narrative towards a fairytale ending, I read the heroine's sustained union with

Maxim as an added repression of her desires and dreams. I suggest that, read in this way, it is the repression itself, rather than the return of the repressed, that propagates the horror. A framework of fairytale signposts helps to universalize themes and create the sense that the heroine is rewarded by staying with Maxim, seemingly made whole by his return to find her escaping the flames that engulf Manderley at the film's close. However, Maxim's stifling control of their marriage is foregrounded in his manipulation of the home video images of their honeymoon, freezing the past to make it conform to his vision of his marriage (and wife). At the same time, he narcissistically mourns a past innocence that can never return. Applying his anger, he threatens the heroine into a maternal role bereft of her own dreams. The chapter explores the stylistic devices that generate gothic uncertainties, such as the near self-reflexive view on Maxim's 'confession' casting a shadow of doubt on the ostensible sympathy his monologue summons. *Rebecca* concerns the horror and levels of entrapment within the home, so ingrained in the familiar—the norms that surround us. Although the film works hard to conceal these secrets, uncertainties loiter long after the film ends. These uncertainties resonate throughout the 1940s cycle of harrowing Hollywood films that dwell on men who repeatedly kill—and repeatedly on men who kill their own wives. The chapter positions these films in relation to the fairy tale 'Bluebeard' and within a broader historical context, considering the many unexpressed tensions brought about by World War II. The uncanny moments of the revelation sequences are explored, contextualizing *Rebecca* in relation to significant films that followed, particularly *The Two Mrs Carrolls* (Peter Godfrey, 1947) and *Secret Beyond the Door* (Fritz Lang, 1947). I suggest that in *Rebecca*, the horror is not created by the threat of Rebeca's haunting return but by the heroine's repression and inability to question Maxim's narrative of events. The return of the past in the present, indicated by Rebecca's indelibility, suggests the (stifled) potential of living autonomously. Rebecca's haunting return speaks of the threat imposed upon generations of women who question the 'common sense' of patriarchal heritage.

Chapter 5 begins by exploring the werewolf, as an indeterminate creature, existing between the human and wolf realms. Motivating reflection on what makes us human, or animal, the werewolf expresses tensions between the conscious and unconscious self, the person and beast or the repressed and liberated. Predicated upon a dualistic understanding of self and other, or culture and nature, werewolf fictions are a reminder of the wild we come from or that is within us, pushing against the repressed to the point that societal repression itself comes under some scrutiny.

Exploring British werewolf films up to (and including) *The Company of Wolves*, Chapter 5 examines British and British–American movies, but also werewolf films that feature British locations and settings—looking at where the werewolf emanates from, where and when it bites, together with its movements and transformations, as the films mark out their territories in the construction of 'home' and the exotic or marginalized. Boundaries in British werewolf films made prior to *The Company of Wolves* have often contained stricter distinctions (between civilization and wilderness). Nevertheless, pushing against the overt reestablishment of order is a residing sense of the ambiguous. This chapter investigates the paradox of the werewolf; the wolf side tends to suggest nature and the human indicates culture, in a relationship that rotates around concepts of internal and external. However, the wolf bursts out of the human, shattering fixed boundaries and challenging any sense of a unified self, or a private, true self within.

'Little Red Riding Hood,' generally understood to originate in a werewolf story, inhabits the margins of all of the werewolf films looked at, and the multiple versions of the tale take centre stage in *The Company of Wolves*. I analyze the transition from the frames of the present-day middle class restrictions on the teenage heroine through to the elastic, fantastical setting of her dreams. Although werewolves tend to lurk in 'foreign' or imagined spaces in British films, American filmmaking has often looked to the UK as a likely haunt for werewolves, even if the beasts originate elsewhere. The Jekyll/Hyde dichotomies make London an apt setting. The rough end of London provides the backdrop for the nightly activities of Dr. Glendon (Henry Hull) in *Werewolf of London* (Stuart Walker, 1935), at the same time unleashing the dread and desire of being 'bitten' in the forbidden lands of Tibet. Similar compulsions are evident in the draw to the gypsy camp in *The Wolf Man* (George Waggner, 1941) and the complex tensions between father and son (repression and liberation). Transatlantic relationships are considered further in *An American Werewolf in London* (John Landis, 1981) with reference to the darker undercurrents of sudden brutality (fused with and defused by comical moments) that permeate European history; we witness the horror and terror of unexpected violence in an everyday setting.

Chapter 5 concludes with a return to the ending of *The Company of Wolves*—to the innovative inversion that sees the dream world flooding into the 'real,' as wolves jump through an ancestral portrait, bursting into rather than out of the home. The heroine's awakening scream, followed by the recital of the conservative caution not to stray, is a problematic finale that tugs against the film's emancipatory forces. Nevertheless, the film also gives voice to the dangers of over-repression, echoing the gothic stimulus to embrace the irrational within everyday life. For all the containment that infiltrates the films explored in the chapter, residues of the horror of societal repression remain.

The intricate interweaving of fantasy and 'real' worlds in *Pan's Labyrinth* is the focus of the sixth chapter. A rhetoric of hope and fear floods between realms. A world of elaborate monsters, gothic ambiguities and fairytale tasks is interlaced with scenes of brutality and horrors endured long after the Spanish Civil War. I suggest that while *Pan's Labyrinth* perpetuates some of the fears associated with the female role and body (rooted in fairytale and gothic horror conventions), it nevertheless questions the blind following of orders associated with all-consuming dictatorships, specifically referring to the pervasive violence of Francisco Franco's regime. The fantasy world, strongly connected to the young heroine, Ofelia (Ivana Baquero), and her vision, receives a similar amount of screen time to the 'real' world, although the two sometimes merge with each other, suggesting the breakdown of such boundaries. Vidal (Sergi López) has been posted to an isolated woodland hamlet in the north of Spain in 1944, five years after the end of the Spanish Civil War, in order to rid the area of the Resistance (the *maquis*). While the 'real' world he inhabits corresponds with a specific moment in history, the potentials of the two worlds become confused, due in part to the fluidity between worlds, but also due to an inversion of expectations. I argue that the simpler character types (more rigidly connoting good and evil) are reserved for the 'real' world, whose structures resemble a classical fairy tale while doubt and uncertainty resonate through the realm of fantasy, casting a shadow over its 'real' counterpart that makes us reconsider the immensity of events and decisions that take place. I suggest that fairytale structures, roles and narratives of the 'real' world help to universalize the historically specific, while the elasticity of the fantasy world enables unspeakable or taboo subject matter to be addressed. Although the fantasy world asks Ofelia to undertake fairytale-like trials and tasks, the results are ambiguous and perpetually perplexing.

I explore the function of doubling across the two worlds. The fantasy world's gothic elements function as allusions to the confusions that contributed to the rise of Francoist power. The woodland setting represents a liminal zone—a primal space—both for repression and freedom. It is a liberating location for outlaw Resistance, and a sphere for Vidal's fears regarding a loss of control and order. The wild wood also becomes a threat, leaving the Resistance starving and confined. The magical world is one that we are invited to share, enhanced by the framing of shots, and editing devices, such as the protracted dissolve that envisions words and images projected from Ofelia's imagination across her book, and the walls of the room. Ofelia plays a key role as writer, hero, reader and interpreter of meanings. Ofelia's decisions and tackling of the tasks indicate the necessity of disobedience. The more widespread complicity in violence, as the past continues to resonate in the present, comes under scrutiny. The chapter concludes by confronting the ambiguities and ambivalences that remain at the film's end. The hope of a longer term peace or resolution rests alongside the knowledge and existence of extreme pain, terror, horror and real-life atrocities that never finally perish.

On a personal note, the initial compulsion to write this book stems from the hunch that while as a term 'fairytale and gothic horror' might readily be conceived of as a sub-genre of horror, as a concept it also involves moments and modes of expression, and therefore it need not be restricted to a curbed existence within the horror genre. In his article on a fragment from *Caught* (Max Ophuls, 1948), V.F. Perkins (1990: 6) states that the "starting point" for his analysis was the urge to work out what it was about a particular moment that made him smile. The stimulus for this book was trying to unveil what it is about the films, and moments within them, that make me shudder—whether on first viewing, after repeated viewings, or long after seeing the film. The films selected for analysis have managed to trigger the latter, creating a lasting shudder that persists.

References

Botting, F. (1996). *Gothic* (London and New York: Routledge).
Freud, S. (2003). '"The Uncanny" (1919)', in *The Uncanny*, translated by D. McLintock (London: Penguin Classics), pp. 123–162.
Jackson, R. (1991, reprinted version). *Fantasy: The Literature of Subversion* (London and New York: Routledge).
Perkins, V.F. (Winter, 1990). 'Must We Say What They Mean?', *Movie*, 34/35, 1–6.

Short, S. (2015). *Fairy Tale and Film: Old Tales with a New Spin* (Basingstoke and New York: Palgrave Macmillan).

Tatar, M. (2003). *The Hard Facts of the Grimms' Fairy Tales* (Princeton and Oxford: Princeton University Press).

Wood, R. (revised edition, 1986). 'The American Nightmare: Horror in the 1970s', *Hollywood from Vietnam to Regan… And Beyond* (New York and Chichester, West Sussex: Columbia University Press), pp. 63–84.

CHAPTER 2

Fairytale Roots and Transformations

Fairy tales thrive today in a variety of shapes and forms. Children read, watch and listen to classical fairy tales like 'The Emperor's New Clothes,' 'The Frog Prince,' 'Jack and the Beanstalk' and 'Rapunzel' on screen, in the classroom and at home. Added to this is a wealth of revisionist and reflexive literature and media texts for children and adults alike, experimenting with form and archetypal roles. Many recent mainstream productions, such as the US computer-animated film franchise *Shrek*, also blend stories, elements and motifs from a wide range of different fairy tales, transforming plots and conceptions in complex ways.[1] Popular culture is rich with more literal adaptations that share the name of the fairy tale plus a multiplicity of subtle references, nostalgic homages and radical parodies. This chapter looks at some of the elaborate origins, versions, transitions and transformations of the fairy tale, exploring fairytale motifs, visual imagery, narrative or thematic elements that give insight and shape to the films (targeted primarily at adults) examined later in this book.[2]

---

[1] The franchise consists of four films: *Shrek* (Andrew Adamson, Vicky Jenson, 2001), *Shrek 2* (Andrew Adamson, Kelly Asbury, Conrad Vernon, 2004), *Shrek the Third* (Chris Miller, Raman Hui, 2007) and *Shrek Forever After* (Mike Mitchell, 2010). A fifth film is anticipated. Television series such as *Once Upon a Time* (created by Adam Horowitz and Edward Kitsis, ABC Studios, from 2011) and *Grimm* (created by Stephen Carpenter, David Greenwalt and Jim Kouf, GK Productions, Hazy Mills Productions, Universal Television, 2011–2017) also contain a blend of fairy tales.

[2] Some of the films examined in the case study chapters are equally targeted at teenagers, but none of the films are targeted specifically at children.

© The Author(s) 2018
L. Hubner, *Fairytale and Gothic Horror*,
https://doi.org/10.1057/978-1-137-39347-0_2

This helps to uncover not only what defines the fairy tale and what makes it distinct from the gothic, explored in the next chapter, but also to establish the links and syntheses that emerge between fairytale and gothic horror and new connections that are made possible when films draw on both. Part of this involves looking at the paradoxes of the fairy tale, as both fantastical form of escapism and as it articulates underlying horrors, giving expression to the difficulties and dangers of everyday life.

Fairy tales serve a variety of functions in contemporary society. Their malleability enables them to emerge in a wide range of forms, but they can also be used to anchor meaning, providing a short cut to shared understanding. Communal knowledge of the tales, together with catchphrases and visual motifs long associated with them, ensure that they attract attention quickly. This means that online, television and newspaper headlines are able to draw on myths propounded by fairy tales. News headlines about celebrities or political figures often use catchy captions that reinforce or sometimes critique myths of good and evil propagated in fairy tales. Popular media can hint at relationship issues or emotional motivations underlining a news story or fashion article; jealousy, vanity or greed can be alluded to with words (the mere mention of 'stepmother') and careful framing (positioning an older woman next to a younger one), for example. In the advertising world, the fairy tale is comparable to celebrity endorsement, functioning as a vehicle to convey meanings quickly, providing swift saliency for brand and product values, sometimes reinforcing established norms and expectations and often contributing something new.

At points in this book, I refer to 'classical fairy tales' as well as other forms and versions of fairy tales. As Jack Zipes (1988: 148) argues, "When we think of the fairy tale today, we primarily think of the classical fairy tale." By adopting the term 'classical', I allude to the tales that have become, as Zipes claims, "most popular in the Western world": 'Beauty and the Beast,' 'Cinderella,' 'Jack and the Beanstalk,' 'The Little Mermaid,' 'Little Red Riding Hood,' 'The Princess and the Pea' and 'Snow White' are among those he names as examples (1988: 148). Classical fairy tales tend to denote stories that have been written down, and published, and Zipes (2006a: 3) goes so far as to suggest they are the result of a civilizing process: "educated writers purposely appropriated the oral folktale and converted it into a type of literary discourse about mores, values, and manners so that children and adults would become civilized according to the social code of that time." On the whole, the classical fairy tale that has become popular in the Western world shirks ambiguity, in the sense that good and evil tend to remain firmly in place. Roles—such as the ogre, giant, beast, stepmother, stepsister, beauty, hero, princess, prince and witch—are clearly defined. Figures exist within the verisimilitude of the fairy tale world; it is rarely the case, for example, that a villain has ambiguous qualities, despite the openness for metaphoric significance that the villain itself conjures, and the notable ways 'the villain' can and perhaps should be interpreted. The moral base (often rendered visible by the tale's conclusion) tends to be communicated unequivocally. Themes address fundamental concerns, such as: curiosity; disguise and transformation; jealousy and cruelty; love and desire; nature and the wild; power and greed; pride and vanity. Thus, many films that adopt fairytale themes or roles to convey fundamental, universal or timeless concerns—even if these are layered over more complex, local or historically situated narratives—can draw in and engage audiences from a broader, more global reach.

Some fairy tales express the perils of curiosity ('Bluebeard,' 'Little Red Riding Hood') but the various versions of these tales place different emphasis upon these themes, often advocating alternative, or even completely opposite messages. As will be explored further in Chapter 5, there are hundreds of versions of 'Little Red Riding Hood,' but three major shifts stand out as the most documented. In their (1812) published version, the Grimm brothers, Jacob and Wilhelm, introduce the huntsman to rescue the girl, thus restoring a happy ending, but emphasising feminine dependence. They even add a second ending to reinforce the message, in which she goes again into the woods, and this time does not stray. Prior to this, Charles Perrault's version (first published in 1697) denies a happy ending, seeing both the girl and the grandmother swallowed by the wolf. To instil the message, Perrault adds the *verse moral* at the end, beginning with the lines: "Young children, as this tale will show, / And mainly pretty girls with charm, / Do wrong and often come to harm / In letting those they do not know / Stay talking to them when they meet'" (Perrault 2009: 103). Perrault implies that the fault lies with charming pretty girls, glossing over the predatory culpability of the stranger they encounter. However, as Catherine Orenstein (2002: 68) explains, there are accounts of an early oral folktale, in which the girl notably outwits the wolf by saying she needs to go outside to urinate and then undoes the rope from her leg and ties it to a tree so she can escape.

While numerous varieties of this version have been unveiled, the tales are united by their lack of harsh judgement or caution in relation to female sexual morality, deviation and dependency and by the remarkable factor that the girl survives, notably by using her own initiative. Curiosity is thus looked upon much more affirmatively as part of a necessary rite of passage than in the later published literary, or 'classical' versions.[3] Unpacking these layers is essential in Chapter 5 for examining the diverse ways in which werewolf films draw on the specific and varying concerns of 'Little Red Riding Hood.'

Disguise is a key feature of the fairy tale—for either the concealment or unveiling of the truth beneath. In the Grimm versions of 'Snow White,' for instance, we see the queen dressing as the crone to deceive Snow White; her duplicity is highlighted by her mask. While there is thus an exterior and an interior identity, these are centred on the notion of a fixed truth beneath, and within the bounds of the fairy tale, distinct notions of good and evil tend to remain at opposite poles. Although there are additional dimensions to this that will be unpacked further in the next chapter, it is worth emphasising here that characterization in the classical fairy tale tends to be thin and schematic, that the mask is a fitting motif to convey these features, and that de-masking generally functions to reveal the true self beneath, as distinct from more conflicted and opaque characterization in the gothic, where duality of the split-self is common. However, despite the general perception of the former's simplicity, projecting archetypal characters and linear narratives with explicit messages, the fairy tale often functions on a symbolic level that is far from 'simple.'[4] It is a misconception to infer that simplicity suggests

---

[3]As recounted by folklorist Paul Delarue in 1951, parts of this oral version had appeared in a journal adapted from a document owned by folklorist Achille Millien, who had in turn been told the tale by Louis and Francois Biffault in Nièvre, France around 1885, but it is generally accepted to be older, deriving from an oral folktale predating Perrault's version. Andrew Teverson (2013: 3) asserts that Delarue, Alan Dundees, Maria Tatar, Zipes, Robert Darnton and Orenstein accept the argument that the story is much older, suggesting that Perrault radically rewrote it, adding the red hood. Teverson (2013: 4) deduces, therefore, that there is no direct evidence, but it is "highly likely" that the oral folktale dates back to these earlier times.

[4]As discussed later, many of the stories from *Le Cabinet des fées* (1785–1789) emerging from the height of the French Court of Louis XIV are much more elaborate than this perception suggests. The *perception* is thus a contributory factor to the contemporary popular conception of a classical fairy tale.

shallowness; the vacuous cavern is an open vehicle for interpretation and layers of meaning. It is important that the complexities are addressed, both in relation to the fairy tale as informing subject and with respect to the diverse ways that films re-present and negotiate the fairy tale in specifically cinematic ways. While polarizations remain intact within the bounds of the fairy tale, the candidness afforded by this fantastical (or 'marvellous') realm allows the fairy tale to expose the complexities at stake in everyday life:

> With a stunning economy of means, they manage to create thunderous effects, taking up matters primal and pertinent – the paradoxes and contradictions on which culture itself is based and with which we wrestle on a daily basis. In 'Little Red Riding Hood,' we saw that it was innocence and seduction; in 'Beauty and the Beast,' monstrosity and compassion; in 'Hansel and Gretel,' hostility and hospitality... (Tatar 2012: xix)

Fairytale traditions contribute richly to film as spectacle, since visual imagery has always been crucial to the fairy tale. Story tellers bring to life the actions in a variety of ways—by listing the three tasks on each finger, for instance, or by pretending to be a wolf, gobbling up delighted listeners. Since the advent of print, illustrations have given visual expression and shape to the verbal descriptions. These illustrations, traditionally in monochrome, are often elaborately framed to provide the sense of going into another world. These images transfer easily onto film sets where an overgrown garden, a sleeping heroine or a waiting wolf quickly connote a transformation from the everyday to a magical world. But visual imagery blossoms in the language and description as well. Within the written text, the colour motif of red on white (blood on milk or snow, or red cheeks on white skin) is evident through a number of tales ('Snow White,' 'Sleeping Beauty' and 'The Juniper Tree'). This motif emphasizes the beauty and innocence (purity and essential 'goodness') of the child. However, it also symbolizes transitional phases, for example, of femininity and maturity: the menarche, menstruation and the first blood after sex (with the rupture of the hymen) and childbirth—a custom that colour film embraces. Similarly, iconic locations and settings are also essential and symbolic, acting not simply as a meaningless vessel for narrative events. For example, as investigated across Chapters 4, 5 and 6, woodland is an active symbol for connoting, amongst other things: a dangerous place for confronting matters of life and death;

a rite-of-passage or initiation space; a wilderness beyond the civilized world; or a portal to the unconscious, irrational and primal.

Transition and transformation are key components of the fairy tale, not only in relation to its different versions and incarnations across and within diverse communication and art forms, but also with respect to narrative elements and concerns. Change, and finally resolution, may be brought about by a magical transformation, good fortune, hard work, using initiative, intelligence, personal resolve, honesty, love and/or good faith. Rites of passage and processes of initiation are fundamental and, between them, fairy tales convey the journey of human life. Transformations from one stage of life to the next are given expression in the oppositional roles played out in the fairy tale (in encounters between a child and an adult, or between innocent and more experienced characters). For example, female transitions through life are often articulated in the fairy tale, through the roles associated with the conventional journeys from youth to adulthood, such as: (a) yearning for a child; (b) the birth of the child, the death of the mother, the Christening; (c) the innocence and truth-seeing capabilities of the child; (d) the prepubescent child; (e) the dangers presented to or by the teenager; (f) the cusp of womanhood, romance and burgeoning desire, that comes full circle again to the yearning for child; (g) the vanity or jealousy of the maturing female; and finally (h) the aged crone, often linked with the witch.[5] Because this book focuses mainly on rite-of-passage films, in which transformation is key, recognition of these conventions and trajectories helps to make sense of the effects produced by their specific and varied application.

Vladimir Propp's formal analysis of Russian fairy tales (first published in Russian in 1928) has been monumental in highlighting roles (or *dramatis personae*), narrative functions and formal patterns evident in tales, and has been hugely influential, enabling theorists to draw attention to similar formal qualities both within and outside fairytale traditions, across a range of literature, media and film texts and genres. Structuralist theorists have, by appropriating Propp's findings to explore

[5] Horror films that contain stages on this trajectory include: (a) *Otesánek/Little Otik* (Jan Svankmajer, 2000); (b) *Rosemary's Baby* (Roman Polanski, 1968), *The Omen* (Richard Donner, 1976), *The Hand that Rocks the Cradle* (Curtis Hanson, 1992); (c) *The Shining* (Stanley Kubrick, 1980); (d) *El laberinto del fauno/Pan's Labyrinth* (Guillermo del Toro, 2006); (e) *The Exorcist* (William Friedkin, 1973), *Carrie* (Brian de Palma, 1976).

film texts, carried out insightful analyses of specific case studies helping to draw parallels and distinctions in film and between films and other sources, as well as illuminating shared qualities, differences, and variances across and within film genres. Propp's work underlies much of today's knowledge and understanding of stories' formal capacities, and is present in the peripheries of this book rather than as a main framework for analyzing film. It is useful when considering, for instance, shifts in conceptions of 'the hero,' or the transition in the nature of narrative functions like the 'interdiction,' or the hero's 'departure' and final 'transfiguration' (Propp 1968: 150–154). However, I take a more qualitative and explorative approach, analyzing the films' thematic concerns, and the ideological, atmospheric and tonal features underlining the broad structures and formal qualities. The difficulties of identifying formal likenesses are compounded by the fact that fairytale elements, motifs and narrative strands are explored in this book as both distinct from and merging with the gothic imagination and many of the film texts looked at are expressions of the ambiguous, dreamlike and unreliable. As John L. Fell argues, "When one departs from the conventionalized generic idiom, the Proppian highway becomes narrower and steeper" (Fell 1977: 23). Nevertheless, the deviation itself can sometimes be helpful in pinpointing intricate kinds of in-depth tonal layering or levels of irony, for example, precisely because these cannot be discerned by applying a straightforward mapping method.

For all their simplicity, fairy tales are mutable and pliable, and interpretations of them are far from simple or unified. Fairy tales display, and flourish within, a boundless world of possibilities. The classical fairy tale is entirely unreal, fundamentally located in the imaginary zones of enchantment and magic, and yet vitally it is also seen as providing a basis for approaching real life. Complex human conundrums emanate from the root themes of jealousy, cruelty and greed that dominate, and the narrative twists that give them shape, so that difficult or taboo subject matter is suggested, including murder, brutality or abuse in the home ('Bluebeard,' 'Cinderella,' 'Rapunzel'), cannibalism ('Hansel and Gretel,' 'Little Red Riding Hood,' 'Sleeping Beauty') child abandonment ('Hansel and Gretel,' 'Snow White') and rape ('Sleeping Beauty'). Family rivalries also rest on boundaries of the 'natural,' including conceptions of true blood and birth rights ('The Princess and the Pea'), and themes coincide with moral judgements, concerning, for example: being true to yourself; internal and external qualities of beauty (and beast); and childhood innocence against corrupted experience.

Symbolism and meaning are thus vital to the fairy tale. Swiss literary scholar, Max Lüthi, has praised fairy tales' capacity to offer a form of initiation (sold to our unconscious minds dressed as entertainment) with the effect that the Grimm version of 'Cinderella,' for example, carries a universal message for humanity:

> Man is surrounded by hostile and helping forces; but he is not entirely at their mercy: through his own attitude – perseverance, humility, and trust – he can be supported through the help of nature and the enduring, strengthening love of the deceased mother and can thus be led to the light. (Lüthi 1976: 30)

Revisionist texts draw on this symbolism in creative ways. For example, Guillermo del Toro's *El laberinto del fauno/Pan's Labyrinth* (2006) relies on the fairy tale's universal message of perseverance and trust, with the support of nature and a deceased parent, while at the same time questioning this assurance by formulating a complex journey through and between two entwined worlds whose pathways are neither straightforward nor clear.

Psychoanalysis has played a major role in the interpretation of fairy tales. Bruno Bettelheim, in *The Uses of Enchantment* (originally published in 1976),[6] opened up discussions about the fairy tale's part in helping children to contemplate their inner conflicts and emotions, demonstrating its rich psychoanalytic potential: "The unrealistic nature of these tales (which narrow-minded rationalists object to) is an important device, because it makes obvious that fairy tales' concern is not useful information about the external world, but the inner processes taking place in an individual" (Bettelheim 1991: 25). To this end, the fairy tale may be seen to assist the child in becoming independent and enlightened. For Bettelheim, fairy tales can be extremely positive for the child's inner growth because they "represent in imaginative form what the process of healthy human development consists of," suggesting that: "This growth process begins with the resistance against the parents and fear of growing up, and ends when youth has truly found itself, achieved psychological

---

[6] He was awarded the Critics' Choice Prize for the best work of criticism published in the USA in 1976 and the National Book Award in 1977 (Bettelheim 1991: back cover).

independence and moral maturity, and no longer views the other sex as threatening or demonic, but is able to relate positively to it" (Bettelheim 1991: 12). While Bettelheim's work does not overtly drive this study, an understanding of the undercurrents of internal and external tensions in rite-of-passage narratives is indebted to ideas that have grown since his psychoanalytic approach. Fairy tales continue to generate elaborate interpretations that reach beyond the bounds of their overt simplicity. Indeed, the very sparseness of many of the narratives seems to encourage a need to interpret meaning in them.

Nevertheless, a reductive two-dimensionality can dominate representations of female roles in classical fairy tales, which have often not fared well with feminist approaches. For good reason, they have frequently come under attack for perpetuating the myth of female passivity and the need to be rescued, and revisionist writers have sought to redress the balance by rewriting tales, foregrounding female desire. Second-wave feminists have taken up arms against 'the great divide':

> Between Snow White and her heroic prince, our two great fictions, we never did have much of a chance. At some point the great divide took place: they (the boys) dreamed of mounting the great steed and buying Snow White from the dwarfs; we (the girls) aspired to become that object of every necrophiliac's lust, the innocent victimized Sleeping Beauty, beauteous lumps of ultimate sleeping good. (Dworkin 1974: 33)

An educational survey carried out by Pat O'Connor in 1989 continued with this route of inquiry, focusing on the motifs and images in fairy tales ordinarily available to children at the time of writing. Here, O'Connor moves on from some of the more generalized attacks to focus specifically on the *Ladybird Well-Loved Tales* "widely available in schools and supermarkets" (1989: 129). Based on evidence from these texts, she argues that the series "reflects and reinforces a patriarchal world view," identifying key features that do not provide a progressive picture of this popular series, including: "Adult female malevolence, especially to other females" with "Beauty, passivity and victimisation as defining characteristics of young females" (O'Connor 1989: 132). By contrast, the adult male is the courageous "rescuer," while merely the "saving power of domestic work" is available for women (O'Connor 1989: 132). While male figures such as "the ogre" are also clearly evil, she suggests that the distinction lies in the fact that there is no relationship with these malevolent figures and thus no expectation of kindness as there might be of the mother figures or other females (O'Connor 1989: 133). While O'Connor (1989: 143) points to examples of alternative, more progressive stories—such as those from a collection of international tales in *The Woman in the Moon and Other Tales of Forgotten Heroines* edited by James Riordan (1984) and (for younger readers) a collection of new feminist fairy tales, a mixture of revisionist reconstructions of classical fairy tales and entirely new tales, in *Don't Bet on the Prince* edited by Zipes (1986)—as "more humane and less stereotypical," it remains true that children's wide exposure to "patriarchal gender ideology" is likely to have a significant impact. Clear exceptions to this argument include the resourceful Gretel, who outwits the witch, and the multiple readings and interpretations of the tales as allegories. Largely, though, the more intricate and complex designs and functions of fairy tales are left out of open debates, revealing that a particular image of the fairy tale remains fairly prominent.[7] The fairy tale has many faces, which today decry reductive gender ideology, but some commercial industries continue to promote stereotypical norms of femininity in the modelling and marketing of classical fairytale merchandise emblazoned in pink. Classical fairy tales are often criticized for their fantastical settings and periods, for being out of touch and for selling impossible myths ('life is not a fairy tale').[8]

The paradox is that claims dismissing the fairy tale as removed from 'real life' bring us full circle to the opposite claims that have been made precisely on behalf of the fairy tale as fantastical mode—such as overcoming obstacles, and drawing on initiative. I examine this dilemma directly in Chapter 6 with respect to the complicated functioning of fairytale

---

[7]The successful 'Ever After High' franchise was recently followed by 'Fairy Tale High' dolls, accompanied by videos, ebooks and a semi-interactive web series, of teen fairytale characters (Snow White, Sleeping Beauty, Cinderella, Alice in Wonderland, The Little Mermaid, Belle, Tinkerbell and Rapunzel) attending a fine arts school.

[8]An advertising campaign 'Prepare for real life' (2013) for a female Catholic college (Mercy Academy) in Kentucky tells girls that if they attend the school they can be more than a princess, by learning "the art of critical thinking"; the "application of knowledge through real life situations" will make them "better equipped to overcome any obstacles the world sends their way": "Life's not a fairy tale"—it proclaims—"Don't wait for a prince... Be able to rescue yourself." For further details, see for example Anon (2013). While critiqued by traditionalists, the campaign was praised by many, including groups within and beyond feminist movements, for dispelling myths of female passivity (so often associated with the 'Some Day My Prince Will Come' yearnings of old-school Disney).

narratives, patterns, roles and themes in *Pan's Labyrinth*. Clearly, analysis of the functions of a fairy tale in cinema must crucially relate to the elements or versions of fairy tale that have been drawn upon and their specific use as contextualized within the film, in order to determine how far the film presents a formulaic, conventional, or more progressive, vision. Underlying this is the further complexity that the tales themselves are open to diverse and shifting interpretations. On the one hand, for instance, there have been harsh criticisms of the violence to women in Hans Christian Andersen's tales ('The Red Shoes' and 'The Little Mermaid'), which have been interpreted as cruel by P.L. Travers (Teverson 2013: 79) and more harmful to children than "soft-core porn" (Carter 1997a: 452). On the other hand, they have been read as a communication of Andersen's own suffering, as an outsider with working class origins and, as Teverson (2013: 81) summarizes, more recently as allegories of his bisexual feelings: "his complex response to his own feelings of ambiguity and uncertainty about sex and sexuality." Thus, interpretations of fairy tales can be as varied as the versions of them. It is important to remain mindful that meanings of a single tale can change shape, according to the specific times, interests and context of the interpreter.

One of the main aims of this book is to examine both cautionary, or 'civilizing,' and more destabilizing possibilities of film, looking at the darker undercurrents offered by the fairytale elements to create or inform expressions of fear, terror and horror, and to scrutinize what these elements contribute culturally, politically and ideologically. Examining female rites of passage in the horror film, Sue Short observes:

> Fairy tales and horror share a number of elements, including the possibilities and pleasures offered by a fictional domain in which many rules cease to apply – and the path to adulthood is often difficult to find. Far from viewing horror narratives, or the fairy tales that have preceded them, as being solely motivated by aims of conformity and containment, they also offer a vital opportunity to question what we know. (Short 2006: 22–23)

Short (2006: 29) also comments on the fairy tale's ability to critique domesticity and marriage as denouement, reminding us that while Snow White, Cinderella and Rapunzel find love with the prince, heroines of other tales "suggest more disturbing ramifications to marriage." Just as female self-sacrifice can be a fairytale ingredient for a truly fulfilled marriage, "it remains the case that fairy tales reveal contradictory feelings towards marriage, with tales of brutish husbands who are never redeemed and alliances that are equated with death" (Short 2006: 29). The fairy tale 'Bluebeard' contains probably the most grisly of newlywed scenarios, in which the young wife discovers the husband wants to kill her, in the same fashion that he has murdered all of his previous wives. But, regularly, the wife's essential qualities are blamed for her husband's lethal tendencies. By entering the forbidden chamber, in which Bluebeard's previous wives hang slaughtered and dripping with blood, the young wife may be seen as suffering (as the Biblical Eve did) the perils of curiosity. These versions detract from the perils brought about by domestic abuse at the hands of a violent husband. Sometimes Bluebeard's foreignness is accentuated in Western versions. Marina Warner (1989: 124) notes that it is usual, from first woodcuts through to later watercolours, to portray Bluebeard as "an Oriental":

> [A] Turk in pantaloons and turban, who grasps his wife by the hair when he prepares to behead her with his scimitar. In later tellings of the story, she is called Fatima; he is sometimes given a cod foreign name, like Abomélique, and the setting of his fabulous estate is sometimes specified: in Rackham, for instance, it is Baghdad.

While this tendency to exoticize the tale, and to present the villain as foreign threat, from a different time, the subject clearly pertains to matters within rather than outside the home, thus touching on more universal problems that have remained invisible or unmentionable even through quite radical and progressive periods of change.

The horror of an *internal* threat from a murderous husband is a central feature of the 1940s 'persecuted wife' Hollywood cycle. These 'Bluebeard' films, explored in Chapter 4, focus more directly on marital abuse, or at least the tensions arising from it, rather than simply couching their narratives within frames of prejudicial, exotic fantasy. Rose Lovell-Smith (2002: 208) underlines the transgressive foundations of 'Bluebeard':

> The degree of control a husband may properly exert over his wife, and how far that control may be enforced by violence or even murder, for example, is an area of social conflict regularly tested in and out of the

courts. The tale is not just about transgression, but is in itself transgressive, an underground or shocking tale.

While many of the illustrations in the various print publications of 'Bluebeard' have shied away from depicting the carnage, focusing rather on other moments such as Bluebeard handing over to his wife the key to the forbidden room, Georges Méliès' short (nine minute) film *Barbe-bleue/Bluebeard* (1901) shows the forbidden room with an almost unrivalled boldness. Like the blood that will not be removed from the key, the image of the bloody chamber with the hanging wives remains in the memory, hauntingly prominent and difficult to erase. It is a moment of shocking revelation and horror, as we realise—at the same time as the horrified and terrified wife—not only that her husband is a killer, but that having opened the door onto the scene she is fated to be the next victim. While generally conveyed in a less gruesome way than in Méliès' film, this performative revelation endures as a moment of chilling horror throughout the 1940s 'Bluebeard' cycle of films, whether it happens in the beach cottage when the heroine hears about the first wife's 'accident' (Alfred Hitchcock's *Rebecca*, 1940) or when the heroine discovers that the locked murder room is a replica of her own bedroom (Fritz Lang's *Secret beyond the Door*, 1947). The sudden realization unleashes the second blow—the threat to the heroine—after which the narrative takes a dramatic change of direction.

Exploring some of these areas helps to bring attention to the complex and specific use of fairy tales in cinema. Much of the uncanny tone of *The Shining* (Stanley Kubrick, 1980), for instance, is built upon accumulating fairytale references that help generate a sense of unease, as Jack Torrance (Jack Nicholson) takes over as caretaker at the remote Overlook Hotel, located in the forested Rocky Mountains of Colorado, bringing along his wife, Wendy (Shelley Duvall), and young son, Danny (Danny Lloyd). In the labyrinthine kitchen of the hotel, Wendy states that the place is such a maze they will have to leave a trail of breadcrumbs, a suggestion of the child abandonment and murder in 'Hansel and Gretel.'[9] The forbidden Room 237 recalls the Bluebeard room, fused with Jack's repressed unconscious. Each new fairytale reference adds a further layer, contributing new meanings, and the horror

---

[9] In 'Hansel and Gretel,' the birds eat the breadcrumbs, leaving the children lost in the woods, then becoming trapped in the lair of the cannibalistic witch.

culminates when Jack hacks his way through the bathroom door with an axe, exclaiming, "Then I'll huff and I'll puff and I'll blow your house down."[10] The crazed upbeat citation of the fairytale wolf's words to the three little pigs exaggerates the contrast between the fairy tale and this scene of extreme family collapse and unthinkable domestic ruthlessness. That the citation is more usually said in jest by a parent to a child when recounting 'The Three Little Pigs' as a bedtime story brings an added inhumanity to the horror. Rather than alluding to brutality via a symbolic wolf, as the fairy tale does, the reverse happens, and the wolf manifests in unadulterated husband/father guise. It is a double horror—the wolf as predatory outsider is a beast *within* the family. As the axe triggers Wendy's screams, the sexual threat is also indicated, evoking 'Little Red Riding Hood.' However, now the huntsman is the oppressor rather than the rescuer. The idea of a man seeking out and attempting to murder his wife and son is a horror of mythological proportions—a horror that the peculiar, repeated references to fairytale iconography and citation intensifies.

When the word 'fairy tale' is used in everyday English language it tends to register blissful, dreamlike or otherworldly wonder. Certainly, to have a 'fairytale wedding' connotes one that is not just extremely romantic, happy or fortunate, but one that seems enchanted to go right, providing a magical springboard for living 'Happily Ever After.' However, it is clear that this phrase registers just one side of the fairy tale and people are no strangers to the idea that fairy tales also venture into more complex terrain, confronting universal concerns, dangers and difficulties most ostensibly in the trials and tribulations faced and the power, magic or initiative needed to achieve dreams or to dispel nightmares and evils:

> Fairy tales address primal matters – survival, reproduction, and mortality – in ways that make direct hits. Eliminating inessential complications, they provide transparent models of cultural conflicts – stories that animate, energize, and enable us to talk about what otherwise might feel taboo. (Tatar 2012: xix)

---

[10] Geoffrey Cocks (2004: 38) observes that Jack's citation is from the Walt Disney version, *Three Little Pigs* (Burt Gillett, 1933), suggesting that this highlights the importance of the movies in the Torrances' lives, as is clearly evident at other points of the film as well.

2 FAIRYTALE ROOTS AND TRANSFORMATIONS   27

The framing of a (once upon a) time and space where anything is possible enables access to darker and sometimes forbidden subject matter. However, while it is tempting and common-place to suggest the fairy tale is Janus-faced, because of the tensions between its two polar—light and dark—characteristics, it is perhaps more beneficial to emphasize the fact that the fairy tale takes many shapes and forms, depending upon the emphasis placed by the author or 'teller' and by the multiple versions of the tales: at the same time, during different time periods and within different contexts. Thus, when core elements, parts or motifs of fairy tales are used or referenced in a film, there is always the haunting and often overt presence of fairy tales' other versions, alongside any sense of an 'essence' or 'original' form.

While the English-language term 'fairy tale' is not ideal for the tales explored in this book—with the exception of Chapter 6, fairies scarcely get a mention in them—the term has become the tales' most recognized name, and is therefore the most appropriate to use in this context. As Maria Tatar asserts, "magic remains in the form of gold and silver cascading down from trees, singing bones that indict murderers, tables that set themselves, cudgels that beat on command, or any number of other wonders, as well as horrors" (Tatar 2012: xv). Fairy tales provide a frame of wonder for anything to happen; a castle sleeps for a hundred years; gold is spun. The 'marvellous' quality resides in the boundless settings and sudden transformations that frame the narrative transitions: of human to animal and animal to human ('Beauty and the Beast', 'The Frog Prince'); of women reanimated ('Snow White') and awakened ('Sleeping Beauty'); of 'rags to riches' ('Cinderella,' 'Jack and the Beanstalk') and boy to bird to boy ('The Juniper Tree'). Wonder and horror also remains in the metamorphoses of creatures, and the transgression of boundaries between human and other entities, such as: werewolves, speaking animals and magical figures. The magical components, the indefinite time periods, the anonymous, elastic and faraway settings (such as woodlands or unnamed castles), the universalized or archetypal figures (princes, queens, witches, wolves, beasts) often provide a façade—or safe space—to suggest, and contemplate, fears, experiences and real-life horrors that are too sensitive to bear close up. Films that adopt core tropes and motifs from a fairy tale thus have the potential to adopt a similarly safe space to address traumatic actualities. For example, some of the 'Bluebeard' films of the mid-to late 1940s explored in Chapter 4 are able to allude to post-war psychosis, in conscious and sometimes less conscious ways. *An American Werewolf in London* (John Landis, 1981) and *Pan's Labyrinth* embrace fairytale iconography and horror to allude to unspeakable historical atrocities, as explored in Chapters 5 and 6. Such possibilities bring to mind Rosemary Jackson's suggestions concerning the radical and subversive potential of the fantastic and fantastic literature:

> [I]t opens up, for a brief moment, on to disorder, on to illegality, on to that which lies outside dominant value systems. The fantastic traces the unsaid and the unseen of culture: that which has been silenced, made invisible, covered up and made 'absent.' (Jackson 1991: 4)

This would suggest that it is the very fantastical, otherworldly and magical basis that (far from providing mere escapism in its shallowest sense) actually allows the difficult subject matter to be addressed.

Fairy tales possess a 'fantastic' quality as designated by Jackson (1991) in the sense that fears and unimaginable scenarios can be explored; boundaries of the imagination can be pushed—but often only so far. The 'brief moment' of inversion and 'disorder' tends to resolve safely, culminating in the restoration of order at the tale's conclusion. Having said this, new versions of a fairy tale that emerge in different time periods and contexts generate diverse meanings and messages, suggesting that there is no fixed understanding of a single tale. Thus, the degree to which a fairy tale may be seen to shake up or restore order depends on the specific *version* of the fairy tale examined and the intricate variations of its use and reception. Films draw on the 'once upon a time' quality in diverse ways, as a short cut to hopes, warnings and fears. Here, there are clear parallels with horror movies, as Short (2006: 35) argues: "Horror may equally be seen to tap into subconscious fears and fantasies, as well as provide an outlet for criticism, and, like stories of abandoned and abused children in the fairy tale, the genre may therefore admit to realities that are otherwise ignored and repressed." Horror often provides a predictable format for licensing expressions of desire and anxieties; the extent to which these expressions take on a radical or more reactionary form in the films analyzed in this book is part of the puzzle that later chapters need to unravel.

Shared knowledge of fairy tales can make it seem like they have always been here, not only because many of them have a long history, but also because they are usually first encountered during infancy or early childhood, making it difficult to remember when we first heard them. Whether we know one version of a tale or many, we may nevertheless find ourselves still thinking about one version as in some way more traditional than another, depending on whether it is the first version we knew, the earliest version we are aware of, or the most classical or popular version. For instance, some might debate whether or not Little Red Riding Hood is saved by a huntsman (she is in the Grimm version, but not in others), or whether Cinderella is visited by a fairy godmother, as this does not occur in the Grimm version.[11]

The study of films that use or evoke fairy tales often entails an investigation into the fairy tale's 'origins,' or versions. Many of the tales that remain popular in the Western tradition originate in the context of an oral storytelling tradition, initiated and propagated primarily by adults, often in the company of other adults by the fireside or while working. While male names (Grimm, Andersen, or even Perrault) might be more widely known in the Western world today, by all accounts 'original' oral storytellers prior to print were likely to be women. However, trying to locate a beginning or 'source' can be problematic, and often the earlier we trace back, the more general and open the associations. It demands us to be open as well, since the root of fairy tales lies in stories, and as J.R.R. Tolkien (2001: 17) argues: "To ask what is the origin of stories (however qualified) is to ask what is the origin of language and of the mind."[12] Distinguishing fairy tales specifically from mere storytelling traditions thus involves separating out those tales with the 'fairy' element (the 'wonder' or marvellous element). Zipes tracks the gradual transition from millennia-old "tales with fantastic creatures, magical transformation, and wondrous events" told amongst tribes and communities, evidenced in cave paintings or found on pottery and scrolls through to "the rise of early European civilization in Latin and vernacular languages

---

[11] Relating this to film, in *Rebecca* Mrs. Danvers (as witch figure) ostensibly reverses the 'Cinderella' story by encouraging the heroine to wear a costume that shockingly reminds her husband of Rebecca. However, an interpretation based on the film's more gothic qualities suggests that, in the long run, Mrs. Danvers may also function as female helper (fairy godmother) for seeming to raise Rebecca from the dead, thus bringing about the 'confession.' These positions are unpacked further in Chapter 4.

[12] 'On Fairy-Stories' (Tolkien 2001: 1–81) was originally delivered as a lecture in shorter form at the University of St Andrews in 1938, and first published with slight enlargement in 1947. Only very minor alterations were made in the current reproduced version (Tolkien 2001: vi).

and in many cases written down mainly by male scribes, many of them religious" (Zipes 2006b: 13). Over the years, tales have mixed together in alchemical ways to create new versions, as shared motifs, characters and plots have filtered through society via ceremonies, the work place, in taverns and homes.[13] Zipes observes that although oral tales were very likely written down thousands of years ago in India and Egypt, it has taken certain developments from 1450 to 1700 for the literary fairy tale to become established in Europe and then America, such as "the standardization and categorization of the vernacular languages that gradually became official nation-state languages; the invention of the printing press; the growth of reading publics throughout Europe that began to develop a taste for their reading pleasure; the conception of new literary genres in the vernacular and their acceptance by the educated élite classes'" (Zipes 2000: xx). Due to these developments, the Western tradition of fairy tales can be traced to relatively recent times, though the sources remain open, and the journey between tales somewhat fluid. The Grimm brothers continue to be amongst the most renowned authors. Their monumental publications of *Die Kinder- und Hausmärchen* (*Children and Household Tales*), through the years 1812–1857, stem from an aspiration to revive German identity with a collection of 'authentic' German tales.[14] Andersen's first fairy tales *Eventyr, fortalte for børn* (*Tales, Told for Children*), published in 1835, consisted of two slim volumes, with the first containing four stories, including 'The Tinderbox' and 'The Princess and the Pea,' adapted from folk tales Andersen had reportedly heard as a child in the spinning room where his grandmother worked in Odense (Teverson 2013: 74).[15] He produced new collections in 1837 ('The Little Mermaid,' 'The Emperor's New Clothes'), 1838 and 1839. From around 1843, and with the publication in 1844 of *Nye Eventyr* (*New Fairy Tales*), the subtitle 'Told for Children' was dropped, which Teverson (2013: 77) suggests

---

[13] Tatar (2012: xvii) points out the blurring between myths and fairy tales (for example, tracing links between Greek myths about Zeus and Europa and fairy tales 'Little Red Riding Hood' and 'Beauty and the Beast').

[14] The 'Fairy Tale Route' in Germany is an example of a contemporary practice that celebrates the history and mythology of 'original' fairy tales, or 'true' stories, by marketing 'authentic' locations for tourists to journey to and interact with.

[15] However, Andersen is said to have made up 'Little Ida's Flowers' (Teverson 2013: 74–75), which is about the poet's ability to kindle the child's imagination.

signifies a new craft of writing for both adults and children at the same time, a skill that we see in many fairytale creative works today.

The rise of the literary fairy tale across Europe can be traced back to the fashionable court culture of eighteenth-century France, and the heyday of French fairy tales. This 100-year custom culminated with the publication of the 41 volume *Le cabinet des fées* in 1785–1789, targeted to a generally but not exclusively adult audience. Beyond this, the backward journey continues through to Italy with Giambattista Basile's *Lo cunto de li cunti* (*The Tale of Tales*), also known as the *Pentemerone* published posthumously in 1634–1636 and, further back still, to the publication in 1550 and 1553 of the 75 stories in two volumes, *Le piacevoli notti*, by Giovan Francesco Straparola (published in English as *The Nights of Straparola* or *The Facetious Nights of Straparola*). Many identify the even earlier influence of literature activity in fourteenth-century Florence, and the inspirational work of Boccaccio's *Decamerone* with its 100 tales and 'frame story.' In contrast to some of the more tailored later French and German publications, the fairy tales of Straparola and Basile have a certain sparky, rugged edge.[16] As Zipes asserts, "Though all their fairy tales have moral or didactic points, they have very little to do with official Christian doctrine. On the contrary their tales are often bawdy, irreverent, erotic, cruel, tragic; many are hilarious" (Zipes 2000: xxi). Thus, while Carter's stories, such as those in *The Bloody Chamber* first published in 1979, are clearly innovative and revisionist, it is also possible

---

[16] Drawing on tales from oral traditions, one of the most striking elements of Straparola's work is his rich use of language, using succinct Tuscan or standard Italian, at a time when print was dominated by Latin (Zipes 2006b: 13). Basile's *Pentmerone*, consisting of 50 fairy tales containing stunning metaphors and idioms, is also remarkable for its Neapolitan dialect and vulgar expressions alongside a unique elevated Baroque style. While intriguingly little is known about Straparola, whose name might even be made up, the suggestion that he spent time in Venice makes a fascinating bridge with Basile's later journey (in 1608) from Naples to Venice. It is easy to imagine that Venice itself, the fairytale port city, trade centre between East and West, has played a key role in adding spice to the fairy tale's mixed heritage. Straparola's stories tell of adventurous heroes, taking off from Italy across oceans and through forestlands to seek fortune and undertake grand missions in other countries and realms (Zipes 2006: 15). See also Ruth B. Bottigheimer (1750/2002). *Fairy Godfather: Straparola, Venice, and the Fairy Tale Tradition* (Philadelphia: University of Pennsylvania Press). These cross-pollinations help to shed light on other parallels, and might explain why 'Bluebeard' bears some similarities with the frame tale of *One Thousand and One Nights* (*Arabian Nights*), a collection in Arabic of Middle Eastern folk tales compiled over many centuries.

to trace earlier published works that resonate with her own 'bawdy,' 'irreverent' and humorous approach.[17]

A major influence on classical Western fairy tales is Charles Perrault's *Histoires ou contes du temps passé* or *Contes de ma Mère l'Oye* (1697), "the collection which inaugurated the fairy tale as a literary form for children" (Warner 1994: XII). Published in Paris, it contains many recognizable tales such as: 'The Sleeping Beauty,' 'Red Riding Hood,' 'Bluebeard,' 'Puss in Boots,' 'Cinderella, or the Little Glass Slipper' and 'Tom Thumb'. While Perrault's work is among the authors in *Le Cabinet des fées*, the female presence in this collection is also notable, as Warner (1994: XII) highlights: of its 20 authors, over half were women. As well as Perrault, the enormous volume contained work by authors as varied as Marie-Catherine Le Jumel de Barnville, Baroness d'Aulnoy, Jeanne-Marie Leprince Madame de Beaumont and Jean-Jaques Rousseau ('La Reine Fantasque').[18] Soon after its publication, the aristocratic court culture in which this grandiose fairy tale era flourished was brought to an end by the French Revolution, crystallizing this epic volume into a "monument and mausoleum for the French fairy tale" (Teverson 2013: 61). Modelled on the Italian tales, and drawing on oral tales, the vogue for lengthy fairy tales reached a peak at the court of Louis XIV.

Specialists in the field of fairy tale have detected a 'civilizing' process in the art of transcribing the fairy tale from oral traditions. Earlier versions of tales can sometimes be surprising, enlightening and crude, and thus can also help to reveal specific and intricate 'civilizing' processes involved with the development of print and the targeting of fairy tales to children. Nevertheless some of the best known fairy tales of the Western tradition—written by authors such as Perrault, the Grimm brothers, or Andersen—seem to speak out to us from another time, not just the authors' own time, but much earlier than this, appearing to shed light onto a primal, bygone tradition of cautionary, moral and magical tales passed down over the centuries. However, the art of transcribing tales inevitably bears the marks of the process itself, as authors necessarily select, emphasize, insert and discard key elements. The tales find

---

[17]Carter's lively, crude and witty style is evident across all her writing (from dramatic works to articles) and is reported in anecdotes of real-life interactions with her, as indicated in the title of her selection of works: *Expletives Deleted* (1993).

[18]Madame Leprince de Beaumont's *Le Magasin des enfants*, which included 'Beauty and the Beast,' was published in 1743. Her fairy tales contain a governess discussing morals.

new shapes and forms, as authors rework them and reinterpret them stylistically, structurally and ideologically to address specific audiences, tastes and expectations.

In addition to the multiple versions of the same tale through a variety of authors, there is also evidence of different versions of a tale by the same author. Tatar writes of the colossal editing and rewriting carried out over many years in a number of publications by the Grimm brothers, partly: "to turn the 'poetry of the people'—their banter, gossip, and chat—into literary fare suitable for children" (Tatar 2003: xiv). What also becomes apparent through these revisions is the reshaping of figures into more appropriate or acceptable models for young children, such as the splitting of the mother figure in two, as good (natural) mother and stepmother, thus ridding the natural mother of any evil-doing. Often, the father's brutality was tamed and he became ineffectual at worst ('Hansel and Gretel,' 'Snow White,' 'The Juniper Tree').[19] The first volume of *Die Kinder- und Hausmärchen* first went to press in December 1812, and Wilhelm was still working on the eighth edition when he died in 1859. The successive adaptations of 'Hansel and Gretel' before it finally settled serve as an example of some of the civilizing processes at the heart of discussions. Amendments in the 1812 edition included: the addition of Christian elements (the children plea to God), the embellishment of the witch's wickedness, and the removal of the father's complicity. In 1819, the mother becomes the wicked stepmother, and by 1857 the story is nearly twice the original length (Teverson 2013: 68).

In previous work, Zipes (1988: 148) has slated the "classical fairy tale" as a particular demon in disguise, arguing that while it might seem that these tales have always been there, "as if they were part of our nature," or in some essential way universal, they are actually culturally produced: "The fairy tale is myth. That is, the classical fairy tale has undergone a process of mythicization." Zipes uses the word "myth" in this instance to connote a specific meaning, and to promote an important political point. Acknowledging the work of Roland Barthes, specifically *Mythologies* and *Image—Music—Text*, Zipes refers to the notion of "myth" as "a collective representation that is socially determined and

---

[19] Chapter 6 looks at the double function of Captain Vidal in *Pan's Labyrinth*. On the one hand, deeds and behaviours of previous generations working for Francisco Franco can be addressed directly, in the sense that Vidal functions as a father figure, but on the other hand this is kept within the bounds of a safe zone, because he is coded as evil stepfather.

then inverted so as not to appear as a cultural artefact" (Zipes 1988: 148). In other words, there is the sense that the classical fairy tale that has come to seem natural in a perhaps unspoiled, primal sense is actually a cultural artefact. The carefully cultivated art form of the classical fairy tale is thus reliant on the ideologies and belief systems of its time and place of transcription. The problem for Zipes lies not in this reliance per se but rather in the misconception—society's belief that these cultural artefacts are natural—that Zipes sees as stemming from an active inversion, or deception, in the Barthesian sense:

> [M]yth consists in overturning culture into nature or, at least, the social, the cultural, the ideological, the historical into the 'natural'. What is nothing but a product of class division and its moral, cultural and aesthetic consequences is presented (stated) as being a 'matter of course'; under the effect of mythical inversion, the quite contingent foundations of the utterance become Common Sense, Right Reason, the Norm, General Opinion, in short the *doxa* (which is the secular figure of the Origin).[20] (Barthes 1977: 165)

While there is always, inevitably, a complex interrelationship between all stories in all their incarnations and their wider social contexts, it is the seeming dishonesty that stimulates Zipes' main criticisms of the classical fairy tale, where overt innovative retelling is seen as more honest than passing off cultivated stories as 'original' or unspoilt.[21] Another major concern Zipes has is that, relative to the animated, mobile oral tales of the past, the "mythified classical fairy tale," together with many of the "frozen" illustrations that accompany it in its classical forms, has become "petrified" (1988: 150)[22]:

---

[20] It is worth noting Antonio Gramsci's political critique of "common sense" as: "the traditional popular conception of the world" (Gramsci in Quintin Hoare and Geoffrey Nowell Smith 1971: 99). Gramsci posits that while the term is often taken to imply something understood (as without doubt a universal given), on the contrary, "common sense" pertains to perceptions of the world "common" to a specific cultural context, at a given time, and is thus subject to change.

[21] In a similar way, as explored in Chapter 4, the more self-reflexive devices used in *Rebecca*, for example in the beach cottage when the camera seems to foreground its devices, shattering cultural myths of patriarchal control, might be seen as more honest than the unquestioned matching of Danvers with witch at other points of the film.

[22] Zipes (1988: 150) goes on to discuss 'Sleeping Beauty': "Take Sleeping Beauty. Her story is frozen. It appears to have always been there, and with each rising sun, she, too, will

What belonged to pagan tribes and communities was passed down by word of mouth as a good only to be hardened into script, Christian and patriarchal. It has undergone and undergoes a motivated process of revision, recording, and refinement. All the tools of modern industrial society (the printing press, the radio, the camera, the film, the record, the videocassette) have made their mark on the fairy tale to make it classical ultimately in the name of the bourgeoisie which refuses to be named, denies involvement – for the fairy tale must appear harmless, natural, eternal, ahistorical, therapeutic. We are led to believe that this air has not been contaminated and polluted by a social class that will not name itself, wants us to continue believing that all air is fresh and free, all fairy tales spring from thin air. (Zipes 1988: 150)

The published written word has an undeniable permanence; relative to this, spoken language can seem much more vibrant, fluid and flexible, fluctuating from one storyteller to the next. In the cinema, voices, sounds and images are fixed permanently—recording or embalming the time from which they were produced. Here, Zipes cites the "tools of modern industrial society" as playing a key role in the refinement of tales. He gives the crucial warning that popular, classical fairy tales are culturally and ideologically oriented.

Such a warning should be extended to every single incarnation of the fairy tale, however fresh, crude or untainted by 'civilization' earlier versions might appear. As Teverson (2013: 4) argues, "First of all: fairy tales do not have single, stable originals that we can depend upon as source texts; they proliferate as narratives, and it is often unclear which version, if any, should have priority over others." To propose a primitive, primal or pagan purity in early oral versions is to invest them with cultural significance. The fairy tale's history is an elaborate web, and the concept of an evolutionary, or chronological, process is something of a myth in itself. It is not only a myth but also an engaging story. Oral traditions and versions continue to be represented in literature, poetry, film, theatre and on the internet as the holy grail, as offering a less tamed, more primal or 'truer' insight into humanity, thus making the myth indispensable and worthy of investigation. As explored in Chapter 5, such a myth is

always be there, flat on her back, with a prince hovering over her, kissing her or about to kiss her."

confronted directly in *The Company of Wolves* (Neil Jordan, 1984), which refers playfully and indiscriminately to a variety of 'sources' for its multiple tales, while allowing the heroine's unconscious to reimagine 'original' strengths, including the use of initiative and strategy.

Tracking the source of a fairy tale can be like embarking on a long quest narrative, with the added hunch that however many doors are unlocked an abiding mystery is likely to remain. As Warner highlights, the limitations of attempting to compose a history of the fairy tale or position fairy tales on a timeline is the lack of "firm chronology or origin":

> The nature of the genre is promiscuous and omnivorous and anarchically heterogeneous, absorbing high and low elements, tragic and comic tones into its simple, rondo-like structure of narrative. Motifs and plotlines are nomadic, travelling the world and the millennia, turning up on parchment in medieval Persia, in an oral form in the Pyrenees, in a ballad sung in the Highlands, in a fairy story in the Caribbean. (Warner 1994: XVII)

The closer we look at the tales, the more evident it becomes that variation itself is one of the most prominent factors. While elements can be tracked from one version to another and basic story and essence can be seen to remain intact, I would suggest that at times even these can be at variance with each other. The *essence* is sometimes fundamentally lost, transformed or just plainly different. Rather, the essence or story should be looked at specifically within the context of the film explored, as well as in relation to the intertextual references to specific fairytale versions. If the message in one version is not to stray from the path, but in another is to use initiative when faced with dangers, then these are essentially different versions with profoundly different stories to tell. Folklorists and cultural historians have found that investigating the origins of any fairy tale can be a painstaking and sometimes impossible task, though rarely a fruitless one. Nevertheless, regardless of whether a specific 'origin' is located, the varieties and strands emerging through time help to highlight the malleability of the tales as they shift and develop at specific moments in history. The commonalities and distinctions become a key point of fascination, providing insight into a culture's shifting belief systems, fears and dreams.

In whatever shape or form a fairy tale emerges in film, we may struggle to locate a single "source text," as Zipes expounds in his scholarly and comprehensive book, *The Enchanted Screen: The Unknown History of Fairy-tale Films*: "the term adaptation in its strict sense does not fully capture how filmmakers have used and re-created fairy tales and folk tales for the cinema" (2011: 7). While my focus is not determined specifically by *adaptations* of fairy tales, but rather by the ways in which films adopt and make use of fairytale narratives, roles and themes in the production of horror, it is important to register that even a clearly defined adaptation of a fairy tale, with the title of the tale preserved in the title of the film, does not often stem from a precise source. Thus, adaptation is always different and unique with respect to the fairy tale:

> Despite numerous adaptations of source fairy-tale texts, the majority of filmmakers have not relied upon a single text as hypotext to adapt a fairy tale. The hypotext is generally considered the pre-existing text upon which a film or hypotext is based. (Zipes 2011: 8)

This is not only due to the multiple incarnations and versions of most fairy tales, but also due to less tangible considerations, such as how the memory or imagination of the filmmaker plays a part in the final production. Beyond this, the various artists working on the film contribute their interpretations or recollections.

With the making of a feature-length movie, there is also the inevitable padding out to feature-film length, which clearly brings with it a new and unique set of ideological values, not to mention a nuance of motifs, tones and thematic concerns, together with a unique set of romances or motivations. A film may contain any combination from multiple references to multiple fairy tales, and versions, through to just one prevailing reference to one specific version. The multiple 'versions' a film may potentially draw upon do not just include oral traditions and literary versions, but also radio, television or stage productions, other films, internet sources, video games, 'true' stories, myths or historical accounts and cultural practices. It is always enlightening to trace and explore these, while remaining mindful of the haunting of previous versions or other tales. There is thus an echoing, intertextual reverberation even in the most overt or seemingly straightforward applications of fairy tale in film. The rich tapestry of fairy tales paid homage to in *The Company of Wolves* illustrates the complexities at stake. Allusions to 'Little Red Riding Hood' include, for example: werewolf mythology; accounts of the fairy tale's oral versions; Perrault's and Grimm's versions;

Carter's stories, such as 'The Werewolf' (Carter 2007: 126–128) and 'The Company of Wolves' (Carter 2007: 139) originally published in *The Bloody Chamber* (1979) and the various screenplay versions written by Carter and Jordan.[23] This is before we even consider the impact of production design, costume, music, setting or other elements of mise-en-scène. Because of the intricacies involved, the complex strands are explored through the films in the case study chapters. The films are the main focus. This emphasis is inspired by fairytale specialists who have paved the way in their approaches to fairytale films: "Our question is not how successfully a film translates the tale into a new medium but, instead, what new and old meanings and uses the filmed version brings to audiences and sociocultural contexts" (Greenhill and Matrix 2010: 3). This means that fairytale characters, themes, motifs and narrative elements are contextualized within the film that gives meaning to them. In turn, these elements are examined with respect to what they contribute and the meanings they generate, emanating outwards to focus on the broader social and historical contexts.

The fairy tale, as an elastic vehicle for fantastical worlds, is able to tread very closely to societal fears and taboo subject matter. The reimagining of fairytale structures, themes and elements within film sometimes entails a reliance on fear, purifying and refining long-established boundaries and pathways, but it can also subvert as much as revert, challenging existing codes and practices, giving voice to alternative or marginalized ways of thinking. This study establishes a framework for considering broader cultural, ideological and political concerns, tensions, complexities and contradictions. As Tolkien (2001: 20) advises, it helps to look at the "soup" (the story as it is served up) not the "bones" (the sources and material the story is made up of):

> For with the picture in the tapestry a new element has come in: the picture is greater than, and not explained by, the sum of the component threads. Therein lies the inherent weakness in the analytic (or 'scientific') method: it finds out much about things which occur in stories, but little or nothing about their effect in any given story. (Tolkien 2001: 21, footnote 1)

---

[23] The radio play 'The Company of Wolves' is reprinted in Carter (1997b: 61–83) and the screenplay of the same name is reprinted in the same volume (185–244).

As Tolkien suggests, while we might have discovered common elements, or ancient beliefs, "there remains still a point too often forgotten: that is the effect produced *now* by these old things in the stories as they are" (Tolkien 2001: 31). My approach to the films examined in this book relates to this, because my central concern is the films as they are, looking at the semiotic, intertextual and contextual effects produced. Establishing this focus is crucial for developing a foundation for thinking about fairy tales and fairytale horror as both distinct from, and merging with, gothic concerns and manifestations in film. Fairytale simplicity can enable the sense of a universal quality that seems primal while at the same time provides access to difficult subject matter, generating a wealth of interpretation, specifically related to fundamental and sometimes marginalized concerns. Everyday horrors and real life atrocities can be alluded to on a symbolic or metaphoric level, opening up a dialogue with repressed and sometimes taboo subject matter. The bringing together of different fairy tales and fairytale versions creates new meanings that the fusion with gothic adds to in complex and magical ways.

REFERENCES

Anon. (13 November 2013). "'You Are Not a Princess" Ads From Mercy Academy Tell Girls They Can Be So Much More', *Huffington Post*. https://www.huffingtonpost.com/2013/11/13/you-are-not-a-princess-mercy-academy_n_4268020.html [last accessed 3 November 2017].

Barthes, R. (1977). *Image—Music—Text* (London: Fontana Press).

Bettelheim, B. (1991). *The Uses of Enchantment: The Meanings and Importance of Fairy Tales* (London: Penguin).

Bottigheimer, R. (2002). *Fairy Godfather: Straparola, Venice, and the Fairy Tale Tradition* (Philadelphia: University of Pennsylvania Press).

Carter, A. (1993). *Expletives Deleted* (London: Vintage).

Carter, A. (1997a). *Shaking a Leg: Collected Journalism and Writings*, ed. Jenny Uglow (London: Chatto and Windus).

Carter, A. (1997b). *The Curious Room: Plays, Film Scripts and an Opera* (London: Vintage).

Carter, A. (2007). *The Bloody Chamber* (London: Vintage).

Cocks, G. (2004). *The Wolf at the Door: Stanley Kubrick, History, and the Holocaust* (New York: Peter Lang Publishing, Inc.).

Dworkin, A. (1974). *Woman Hating* (London: Dutton Paperback).

Fell, J.L. (Spring 1977). *Film Quarterly*, 30: 3, 19–28.

Greenhill, P., and Matrix, S.E. (2010). 'Introduction: Envisioning Ambiguity', in P. Greenhill and S.E. Matrix (eds.), *Fairy Tale Films: Visions of Ambiguity* (Logan, Utah: Utah State University Press), pp. 1–22.
Hoare, Q., and Nowell Smith, G., eds., (1971). *Selections from the Prison Notebooks of Antonio Gramsci*, translated by Q. Hoare and G. Nowell Smith (New York: International Publishers).
Jackson, R. (1991, reprinted version). *Fantasy: The Literature of Subversion* (London and New York: Routledge).
Lovell-Smith, R. (October 2002). 'Anti-Housewives and Ogres' Housekeepers: The Roles of Bluebeard's Female Helper', *Folklore*, 113: 2, 197–214.
Lüthi, M. (1976). *Once Upon a Time: On the Nature of Fairy Tales* (Bloomington: Indiana University Press).
O'Connor, P. (1989). 'Images and Motifs in Children's Fairy Tales', *Educational Studies*, 15: 2, 129–144.
Orenstein, C. (2002). *Little Red Riding Hood Uncloaked: Sex, Morality, and the Evolution of a Fairy Tale* (New York: Basic Books).
Perrault, C. (2009). 'Little Red Riding-Hood' (1697) in C. Perrault (2009) *The Complete Fairy Tales*, translated by C. Betts, with illustrations by G. Doré (Oxford and New York: Oxford University Press) pp. 99–103.
Propp, V. (1968, second edition). *Morphology of the Folktale* (Austin: University of Texas Press).
Short, S. (2006). *Misfit Sisters: Screen Horror as Female Rites of Passage* (Basingstoke and New York: Palgrave Macmillan).
Tatar, M. (2003, expanded second edition). *The Hard Facts of the Grimms' Fairy Tales* (Princeton and Oxford: Princeton University Press).
Tatar, M. (2012). 'Preface', in J. Grimm and W. Grimm, *The Annotated Brothers Grimm: The Bicentennial Edition*, edited and translated by M. Tatar, with an introduction by A.S. Byatt (London and New York: W.W. Norton), pp. xv–xxi.
Teverson, A. (2013). *Fairy Tale: The New Critical Idiom* (London and New York: Routledge).
Tolkien, J.R.R. (2001). *Tree and Leaf* (London: HarperCollins).
Warner, M. (Autumn, 1989). 'Bluebeard's Brides: The Dream of the Blue Chamber', *Grand Street*, 9: 1, 121–130.
Warner, M. (1994). *From the Beast to the Blonde: On Fairy Tales and Their Tellers* (London: Chatto and Windus).
Zipes, J. (1986). *Don't Bet on the Prince: Contemporary Feminist Fairy Tales in North America and England* (New York: Methuen).
Zipes, J. (1988). *The Brothers Grimm: From Enchanted Forests to the Modern World* (London and New York: Routledge).
Zipes, J., ed. (2000). 'Introduction', *The Oxford Companion to Fairy Tales* (Oxford: Oxford University Press), pp. xv–xxxi.

Zipes, J. (2006a). *Fairy Tales and the Art of Subversion* (New York and Abingdon, and Oxon: Routledge).

Zipes, J. (2006b). *Why Fairy Tales Stick: The Evolution and Relevance of a Genre* (New York and London: Routledge).

Zipes, J. (2011). *The Enchanted Screen: The Unknown History of Fairy-tale Films* (New York and London: Routledge).

CHAPTER 3

Gothic Transgression, Horror and Film

Gothic is pervasive, but not easy to define. While there are movements of gothic, it cannot be pinned down as a genre. It has been applied to arts, subjects and cultural practices as diverse as architecture, landscape design, literature, music, clothing, jewellery, lifestyle and identity. With such a slippery creature it is difficult to estimate its size and durability at any given time, and particularly difficult—until afterwards—to know when it is at its peak. Nevertheless it seems reasonable to suggest that the contemporary age is at least rich in the gothic, if not completely saturated by it, with gothic film festivals, seasons and television series infiltrating screens across the globe. Before embarking on an investigation into the gothic, it is worth contemplating—as a major point of distinction from the previous chapter—the 'happy ending' that has become one of the key determining factors of the fairy tale for so many, despite notable exceptions to the rule, and leaving aside revisionist versions and re-workings. As Rosemary Jackson (1991: 154) argues, "Theorists of fairy tales all stress this consolatory function of the marvellous"; the fairy tale, if it is to satisfy any generic code of practice at all, is expected to close with a sense of security, fulfilment and gratification. The ambivalence and uneasiness associated with gothic fiction suggests a major departure from this final framing sanctuary, but not a complete abandonment of it. While gothic villains, and the evil associated with them, are likely to be quashed by the end of the fiction, or at least quietened as a sense of order (even if only temporarily) is restored, it might be said that the questions opened up by the fabric of gothic uncertainty, and the

© The Author(s) 2018
L. Hubner, *Fairytale and Gothic Horror*,
https://doi.org/10.1057/978-1-137-39347-0_3

obscurities and demons unlocked and explored through the course of a gothic text remain forever, forming a shadow that is alien to fairy tale; this is an area that is explored through the course of this book, as various and diverse film texts are unravelled.

Gothic is an ever-evolving, decaying monster, dying or long dead, and reviving often when at its most corpselike. Gothic has transmuted and faded a number of times. It was pronounced dead by Fred Botting in 1996, following the release of a single film—Francis Ford Coppola's *Bram Stoker's Dracula* (1992):

> With Coppola's *Dracula*, then, Gothic dies, divested of its excesses, of its transgressions, horrors and diabolical laughter, of its brilliant gloom and rich darkness, of its artificial and suggestive forms. Dying, of course, might just be the prelude to other spectral returns. (Botting 1996: 180)

Botting (1996: 177) suggests that despite the film's "artificial claims to authenticity", emphasized by the title's assertions to be "Bram Stoker's," its premise rests more on the humane endurance of love, "tolerance and understanding" corresponding to the "caring 1990s", and it is more akin to Emily Brontë's "tale of excessive individual passions" *Wuthering Heights* than traditional vampiric horror (1996: 179). Botting argues that the new frame story of tragic love "turns Gothic horror into a sentimental romance" (178). He also suggests that the replacement of Dracula's demonic qualities with those of suffering, creating a "less libertine and more sentimental hero," is a further nail in gothic's coffin (178).

This pronouncement demands a particularly strict (but I would not say restrictive) understanding of what constitutes gothic, and is an extreme claim to make for a film that seems to draw heavily on certain elements of 'gothic,' not to mention the implicit judgements made about *Wuthering Heights*. But sometimes it is necessary to be strict, and the argument that too much 'sentimentalism' or 'romance' can obscure gothic to the point of killing it raises the very important (and often ignored) question concerning the role that gothic plays, or should play, in projecting ideology and tone. This is helpful here, particularly as a major focus of this book is gothic *horror*, and the underlying roots of fear and terror. Clearly transgression is also a key consideration for Botting, and one that I return to later in this chapter, and throughout the course of this book. My interest lays not so much in establishing rigid confines around gothic—it necessarily bleeds and transforms—but rather in looking into how gothic is conjured in cinema, what gothic contributes to cinema, what makes a horror film a *gothic* horror film, or what makes the gothic in a horror film *horrific*. Like Botting, I sense that transgression is gothic's lifeline. Repression is a major instigator of gothic uprising, and a key to its political clout. Gothic is often propelled by a perpetual cycle of repression, triggering a return of the repressed, followed by repression's return. While the return of the repressed causes chaos, as explored in the case study chapters, frequently the repression itself is also questioned to some degree, providing insight into society's prejudices, restrictions and norms at a given time.

Botting's pronouncement of gothic's demise in the 1990s is all the more fascinating in light of what appears to be the current gothic revival. As Catherine Spooner (2010: ix) asserts, "The dominant mode of the twenty-first century, it increasingly seems, is Gothic." She asks whether this is just a hangover from the twentieth century or whether it represents a new zeitgeist, heightened by the post 9/11 condition, suggesting that "arguably twenty-first century Gothic has its roots decades earlier, back in the 1970s when the novelist Angela Carter declared that we are living in 'Gothic times'" (Spooner 2010: x). It is fitting (considering the focus of this book) that Spooner should make reference to Carter, whose writing was inspired by fairy tales' darker undercurrents, bringing attention not only to gothic's repetitious rising and falling but also to the potential spaces that 'fairy tale' and 'gothic' seep into. While I want to avoid imposing a rigid ideological framework onto the films explored in the case study chapters, central to the book's thesis is positioning cinematic renditions of fairytale and gothic horror in relation to underlying cultural fears and tensions. Monstrosity has often been seen to refer to fears of otherness, whether this be in relation to differences of race, ethnicity, gender, sexuality, mind or body. Furthermore, excess is a key feature of gothic aesthetically and stylistically, but also in relation to passion and sensitivity, cued by venturing dangerously into imaginary, disorderly and irrational territories. In this chapter, I explore cinema as a medium for channeling the gothic, and contextualize this within a broader historical and critical evaluation of gothic. A central aim is to locate a 'cinematic gothic,' as both reliant upon and distinct from a literary gothic, for example, looking at how gothic concerns with uncertainty, duality and 'the uncanny' are manifested in cinema.

Since its inception, cinema, as a medium giving life and spirit to dead forms, has consumed from literary works of gothic horror with a voracious appetite, using its distinct magical charms, however primitively or seamlessly, to adapt, rediscover or reimagine literary works, as is evident in the copious *Frankenstein* and *Dracula* movies, for example. Whether drawing loosely on 'source' material, or presenting more overt 'adaptations,' filmmakers have continued to find inspiration both from earlier gothic horror writers, such as Mary Shelley, Edgar Allen Poe and Robert Louis Stevenson through to more recent contemporary writers as diverse as Robert Block, Daphne du Maurier, Clive Barker and Stephen King. In many respects, cinema appears naturally inclined towards bringing horror to life, having the facility to visualize beasts and ghosts, to bring movement and sound to gothic illustrations and verbal descriptions, to cast new light and deep shadows onto gothic landscapes, figures and architectures—projected in new extremes of close up or long shot on the large screen.

But cinema also moves away from literary gothic sources, bringing with it a bag of new gothic tricks, and stunning visual spectacles, such as the capacity to make images suddenly disappear, or to transform humans into beasts and ghosts. Louis Lumière's dancing skeleton in *Le squelette joyeux* (1898) springs to mind, as its bones repeatedly detach and dance autonomously before re-forming to dance again. Clearly indebted to the theatre, the magic thrills of early cinema also drew inspiration from the traditions of other shows and exhibitions that had formed an integral part of nineteenth-century culture. Essentially, cinema is an illusory medium, seeming to bring to life—temporarily and repeatedly—objects and 'beings' that lack life. These uncanny and interstitial qualities position cinema somewhere between fantasy and reality. For in both the illusion of images that are not there and the illusion of movement projected onto a flat, static screen lies the promise of unfulfilled dreams—the projection of terrors and desires. While it is no marvel that early cinema experimented with horror films, and that horror has been a key staple since its birth, it is also worth noting influences that go back much further:

> Horror movies predate the machinery of Edison and Lumière by at least a century. Indeed cinema might well be described as a temporary phase in the supernatural tradition which started as long ago as the seventeenth century and looks set to continue into the future with computer controlled 'virtual reality'. (Christie 1994: 111)

Christie elucidates on the experimentations with sound techniques, shadows, sudden movements, illusions and atmospheres to conjure terror and intrigue in audiences, and we might think of the long traditions of immersive magic tricks and the circus in presenting illusions of the supernatural.[1] As Christie observes, specific parallels with cinema can be seen in the magic lantern, which tended to have "a somewhat macabre reputation" (Christie 1994: 111). The "Phantasmagoria", popular in Paris during the late 1790s, used a mobile lantern with a shutter projecting from behind the screen, displaying skeletons, ghosts and transmutations to the live sounds simulating thunder and lightning.

However, beyond this (and related to it) is the life–death quality of cinema itself. Here I am referring to the gothic horror of life, phantasm and death that are inherent in cinema (often traditionally perceived as a medium originating from photography) aside from the gothic horror films it frequently projects. As James Walters (2011: 36) argues, "The fusing together of artistic representation with a desire to capture life in near-resistance to the universal fact of death reveals the twin satisfactions that cinema might provide its audience." The satisfaction is tallied with frustration. It is indeed a "near-resistance" because the life-quality it seems to promise points only backwards to a time that is already frozen. Roger Luckhurst (2013: 36), developing Roland Barthes' ideas, emphasizes the "complete contradiction" inherent in the art of photography:

> It captures the living instant, the here and now, and magically makes what is momentary live forever. Yet the same shutter also freezes and fixes the moment, taking it out of time, making every image deathly and every portrait a *memento mori*. The delight at what is captured and preserved by the black box of the camera is haunted by the monument to loss that every photograph becomes. (Luckhurst 2013: 36)

In *Camera Lucida*, Roland Barthes contemplates death springing out from its seeming opposite in the photographic image:

---

[1] For example, direct links can be traced from nineteenth-century magic and conjuring tricks through to the early transformations of filmmaker–magician George Méliès, where film projections often formed part of a larger immersive stage set.

For the photograph's immobility is somehow the result of a perverse confusion between two concepts: the Real and the Live: by attesting that the object has been real, the photograph surreptitiously induces belief that it is alive, because of that delusion which makes us attribute the Reality an absolutely superior, somehow eternal value; but by shifting this reality to the past ('this has been'), the photograph suggests that it is already dead. (1982: 79)

Barthes (1982: 91) draws parallels with 'Sleeping Beauty,' when a specific moment in time is captured in a photograph bringing about "Time's immobilization" or an "*arrest*" in time. These musings written not long before the sudden incident that brought about Barthes' own death, recall the work of French film critic André Bazin, who in his seminal essay 'The Ontology of the Photographic Image,' taking cinema as essentially rooted in the same mechanical methods as photography, theorizes about the "embalming" quality of the photograph. He suggests that in psychoanalytic terms the origin of painting and sculpture lies in a "mummy complex," which might be traced back to the Egyptian religious practice of embalming the dead (Bazin 1960: 4). He proposes that the preserved body served to resist time, and that the terra cotta statuettes near the sarcophagus acted "as substitute mummies which might replace the bodies if these were destroyed," concluding that therein lies the core function of statuary: "the preservation of life by a representation of life" (Bazin 1960: 5). For Bazin, photography as a medium brought about by "an impassive mechanical process" (by the mechanical process of light on celluloid and the spectral emergence of the image from the indexical original) had the effect of producing a phantom quality to family albums, halting and mummifying time: "for photography does not create eternity, as art does, it embalms time, rescuing it simply from its proper corruption" (Bazin 1960: 8). The irrevocability of death remains the one impasse of being alive. Cinema might seem to conquer or reverse the process of death with its recording of time or 'change' (instead of a single instant) as well as image. However, like photography, cinema is similarly mummified. Bazin argues that cinema is "objectivity in time"; it captures movement—rendering it lifeless—"Now, for the first time, the image of things is likewise the image of their duration, change mummified as it were" (Bazin 1960: 8). Thus, we begin to find some intriguing parallels between gothic and cinema itself.

In his analysis of early cinema's fascination with accidents, James Leo Cahill paints a vivid picture of the delight caused by the "death-defying effects" of the kinetoscope, phonoscope and cinematograph. He also observes the immortalization of momentary incidents in early cinema, the beauty and the grand significance of the everyday or accidental— kissing, eating, sneezing, dancing (Cahill 2008: 290). He cites Théo Hannon, writing as 'Hannonyme' in the 13 November 1895 issue of Brussels-based *La Chronique* on the capacity for both the dead to relive for us, and for the living to relive their own actions and words:

> Beings we have known and loved, who, according to the routine civil state, are no longer of this world never-the-less act, look at us, talk to us and by a miracle, an authentic one, relive a short instant of their past... [T]he genius of man will do what the vital force was impotent to do: we will relive the entirety of our acts, our words. And even stranger, we will appear to ourselves. (cited in Cahill 2008: 290)

Thus, Hannonyme's words anticipate the double fascination of seeing others who have deceased looking back at us, talking to us, but from the past, again, strangely immobilized in time, and of seeing ourselves "appear to ourselves." He sees the latter as particularly "strange," presumably because seeing the self as a double belies and reimagines 'self' or 'other' distinctions that normally reinforce notions of the individual as a finite unit.

Intriguingly, the first public screening of films to a paying audience (by the brothers Auguste and Louis Lumière on 28 December, 1895, at the Salon Indien du Grand Café in Paris) caused critics to wonder at cinema's gift to seemingly overthrow the finality of death. In this case, it was the recording of the everyday, mundane movements of a family as they interacted with each other, or workers going about their daily lives, that generated such extreme reactions, as is evident in a review published two days after the Paris screening in *Le Radical*: "We already can collect and reproduce words; now we can collect and reproduce life. We might even, for instance, see our friends or family as if living again long after they will have disappeared." (reprinted in Richard Abel and Rick R. Altman 2001: 8) These testimonies foresee the emergence of accessible home video equipment. The single phrase "as if living again" (rather than simply "living again") acknowledges the simulation rather than the actuality of life. Christopher Frayling (2013: 5) relates the condition of watching Hollywood movies on the television today to a similar affirmation of the living dead in cinema:

> It is said that all photographs – by turning a moment into a memory – are like spirit photographs; by extension, all motion pictures become ghost stories, especially in retrospect. Late night Hollywood movies on television have a cast of dead people, something that was inconceivable before the 20th century. No wonder then that only with the advent of cinema did 'the Gothic' come into its own.

The paradox is that while cinema might be seen as continuing the long sought after urge to halt death, these moving images lack life; materially, cinema is as lifeless and as dead as any art.[2]

The united fascination that the apparatus of cinema has summoned draws attention to its potential as a vehicle for the uncanny. The strangeness of seeing ourselves, and others, appearing to ourselves is potentially unsettling, as is cinema's capacity to seemingly repeat—to invoke another, to duplicate (or reproduce) an 'other' self. There is the potential for the rising doppelgänger, inherent in the machinery from which cinema is born, lurking in the everyday—in representations of incidental or mundane happenings—as much as in the spectacular. Cinema can be uncanny, as Walters (2011: 35) observes, with respect to the concurrence of fantasy and cinema: "Here is a world like ours, but different; a world familiar yet strange." Gothic is a facility that cinema can exploit. Cinema conjures gothic effects in its framing, editing and sounds, as they impact on the narrative, as well as drawing on other arts. While certain subject matter is deemed to be gothic, I suggest that gothic is determined by cinema's relation to the illusions it conjures, radically affected by style and tone. Cinema thus has a capacity for gothic, but gothic is not a given. Capacity alone does not ensure effect.

Cinema's seeming duplication (or reinvention) of lives and selves has evolved and expanded as new technologies emerge. Spooner (2010: xi) observes the "new lightness" in much of the twenty-first century gothic, and we might also note a relatively recent trend for hybridizing gothic texts, or using gothic as a gloss for representing (masking) more conventional teen romance. Part of this book's premise is to disentangle these elements from what might be seen as purer instances of 'gothic,' while at the same time suggesting that alternative visions of hope or tonal variances (such as humour) need not always drown out gothic tendencies. Significantly, Xavier

---

[2] This feature was picked up by Maxim Gorky, describing the Lumière brothers' show as "the Kingdom of Shadows" conveying "not life but its shadow, not motion but its soundless spectre" (cited in Luckhurst 2013: 36).

Aldana Reyes, in his article about gothic horror cinema from 1960 onwards, provides a helpful rationale for the selection of texts he analyzes, stating that "the supernatural romance of a number of films that have derived from the paradigm-shifting *Twilight* (Hardwicke, 2008) should be neatly separated from the more visceral forms of horror covered" (2014: 388). Obviously, any work on gothic texts is necessarily selective, but Reyes stresses that the focus of his chapter is "gothic horror" specifically. While the *Twilight* franchise is not explored in this book, for reasons similar to Reyes', addressing certain distinctions does help to contextualize gothic, providing further insight into the margins and confluences at stake with respect to gothic and fairytale horror.[3] I am not content to allow that key features such as gloomy imagery, monstrosity, eerie environments or moving corpses necessarily entitle an invite to the gothic party. They frequently get in anyway. But additional credentials are needed to be properly invited.

A gothic sheen is cast over many aspects of contemporary life, sometimes lightly and sometimes overbearingly, and there is a gothicization of products and services, from gothic monster dolls for teenagers to a number of gothic social networking sites and conventions. Gothic subcultures emerge, with a faint nod to a goth lifestyle and music scene born in the 1980s, having resurfaced in a transformed state to reach new peaks in the present age with the advent of digital display and distribution. A range of products from black nail varnish to basques can be bought from an array of online fashion companies selling an 'alternative' lifestyle, offering a flicker of the past rekindled and ignited by the new, a means to stepping into a fantasy free from current-day, run-of-the-mill restraints.

As much as gothic has always haunted the shadows, it also lurks in the everyday. Gothic in plain sight is perhaps more likely to create a shudder than an item that has all the known ingredients—the mask of gothic, but none of the essence. Present-day practices and technologies, such as plastic surgery and the digital uncanny, reek of gothic potential.[4]

---

[3] *The Twilight Saga* consists of five films: *Twilight* (Catherine Hardwicke, 2008), *The Twilight Saga: New Moon* (Chris Weitz, 2009), *The Twilight Saga: Eclipse* (David Slade, 2010), *The Twilight Saga: Breaking Dawn—Part 1* (Bill Condon, 2011), *The Twilight Saga: Breaking Dawn—Part 2* (Bill Condon, 2012).

[4] For an insightful analysis of the split between the 'self' and 'other' in plastic surgery—the urge to replicate and the sense of a before and after in becoming something 'other,' as fantasy becomes reality but only so far, see Virginia Blum (2005) 'Becoming the Other Woman: The Psychic Drama of Cosmetic Surgery,' *Frontiers: A Journal of Women Studies*, 26: 2, 104–131.

And it is not just the 'alternative' social networks, but also the mainstream; 'Facebook' sees its members forging an ongoing investment in exhibiting, representing and archiving the self, an 'other' temporally paralleling 'real' life, charting a lifetime, petrifying life, and fixing the temporary, a museum of a life intersecting with other lives and—in the longer term—a mausoleum for exhibiting identity, enforcing a dual existence (between the real and the fantasy). Although these practices are not gothic in themselves, they have the potential to be as chilling as any gothic horror if represented, or perceived, in this way. They are made of the same fabric that—if ignited with an excessive drive, or an individual's compulsion—echoes classic gothic literature like Shelley's *Frankenstein; or, The Modern Prometheus* (first published anonymously in 1818), Oscar Wilde's *The Picture of Dorian Gray* (1890) and R.L. Stevenson's *The Strange Case of Dr Jekyll and Mr Hyde* (1896). However, in themselves, plastic surgery and social networking are cultural practices that are vacant until rendered gothic by a creator, or consumer, just as the adaptation of a film from a gothic literary text will not necessarily be gothic at all, nor will it be gothic in the same ways as the 'source' material.

The opening of *Rebecca*—in book and film form—is a useful point of reference for illustrating both the perils of assuming that gothic is a portable phenomenon that naturally survives the adaptation process and that literature and cinema draw on separate strengths and devices in the creation of gothic. Gothic undercurrents permeate the first chapter of Daphne du Maurier's novel, *Rebecca*, first published in 1938. The language filtered through the first person narrator, the unnamed heroine who at moments veers close to becoming (unreliably) merged with Rebecca herself, Maxim's first wife, and the heroine's revered and feared predecessor, conveys the tensions brought about by the encroachment of untamed nature (with its "long tenacious fingers") on the civilized (but now decaying) structures of Manderley (du Maurier 1975: 5). The narrator seems to look nostalgically upon colonial prejudices, raging excessively against the immigration of new foreign species of plants, ranting against "some half-breed from the woods" (6–7). At the same time, a haunting suggestion of unease breaks the surface. Nature is personified with verbose language—excessive adjectives and commas—that mirrors the unwieldy cross-breeding wilderness as it consumes Manderley in the heroine's dream. The arrival at Manderley is given a sexualized energy:

3 GOTHIC TRANSGRESSION, HORROR AND FILM   53

[T]his path led but to a labyrinth, some choked wilderness, and not to the house at all. I came upon it suddenly; the approach masked by the unnatural growth of a vast shrub that spread in all directions, and I stood, my heart thumping in my breast, the strange prick of tears behind my eyes. (du Maurier 1975: 6)

Manderley, conveyed through the narrator's eyes, represents the "perfect symmetry" of life restored to an impossibly ordered level. It is akin to the heroine's repressed self. Conflicting with this, untamed nature takes possession of the house and grounds, destroying order with a monstrous appetite. Colonial fears are spelt out through this excessive voice; the house is "inviolate," "untouched," but the garden has obeyed the "jungle" law, gone feral and become susceptible to foreign, illegitimate breeds:

The rhododendrons stood fifty feet high, twisted and entwined with bracken, and they had entered into alien marriage with a host of nameless shrubs, poor, bastard things that clung about their roots as though conscious of their spurious origin. (du Maurier 1975: 6)

The imagery of the wilderness relates to the fears of, or threat brought about by, Rebecca, who in her infidelity seemed to endanger the traditional family bloodline. The extent to which du Maurier shares this reactionary fear remains ambiguous, but it is a fear that is challenged by the couple's present day ennui that creeps in at the end of the first chapter, as the nightmare fades to the dawning of a second hell within their current exile on the continent.

These gothic themes of the tensions between the wild and the tamed, the past in the present, plus the death–life quality as the rooms of Manderley seem to come to life in the heroine's imagination, are largely lost in the opening of Alfred Hitchcock's *Rebecca* (1940). The seamless passage through the gate to the wooded driveway is a powerful gothic image of crossing barriers. However, despite the direct citation of a few lines from the book ("Last night I dreamt I went to Manderley again..."), accompanied by literal, complementing visuals, the strains, ambiguities and uncertainties underlying the words simply cannot find expression in images and sounds. The fast track through the woods to Manderley, clearly a lit up model, is ill-equipped to adapt the underlying colonial fears (enhanced by the gothic, excessive style of language) in cinematic form—even if the filmmaker should wish to do so. Cast in this light, apart from the haunting resonances of the book, and du Maurier's few words delivered in voice-over by the unmistakably precise accenting of the heroine (Joan Fontaine), the opening of Hitchcock's film is ostensibly lacking. As George Bluestone (1957: 1), one of the seminal writers on key distinctions between novels and films, argues: "between the percept of the visual image and the concept of the verbal image lies the root difference of the media." Thinking through and beyond this cyclical sticking point—that we imagine (conceive imagery in the mind) when we read, whereas we perceive the imagery and sounds presented to us when we view a film—leads to a necessary contemplation on cinema's diverse and distinctive applications of gothic ambiguity, uncertainty and tone. As I argue in Chapter 4, gothic elements and drives (repression, repetition, 'the uncanny,' excess) manifest in Hitchcock's *Rebecca* in complex and specifically cinematic ways, necessitating the move away from an adaptation study, while at the same time acknowledging where applicable the haunting presence of the book, especially in relation to the limits of what could be shown at the time of the film's release.

In 1926, Virginia Woolf (1972: 89), remarking on the relatively new art of cinema, writes in despair about cinema's dire condensation of literature, and denounces film as a poor and primitive "parasite" preying on a literary work as its "victim."[5] However, Woolf also had the vision to see film's autonomous potential, arguing that it is only when we abandon trying to compare cinema with the book that it is possible to imagine "what the cinema might do if it were left to its own devices" (Woolf 1972: 89). She writes about recently seeing *Das Cabinet des Dr. Caligari /The Cabinet of Dr. Caligari* (Robert Wiener, 1920) when a tadpole-shaped shadow (she presumes to be unintended) emerged on one corner of the screen:

> It swelled to an immense size, quivered, bulged, and sank back again into nonentity. For a moment it seemed to embody some monstrous, diseased imagination of the lunatic's brain. For a moment, it seemed as if thought could be conveyed by shape more effectively than by words. The monstrous, quivering tadpole seemed to be fear itself, and not the statement 'I am afraid'. (Woolf 1972: 89)

---

[5]Woolf's essay, 'The Movies and Reality,' was originally published in *The New Republic* (4 August, 1926) 308–310.

Woolf's wonder at cinema's potential to express emotion ("fear itself"), even before cinema's full embrace of synchronized sound and colour, is a powerful motivator from beyond the grave that helps give shape and focus to this study. Woolf fantasized about seeing "thought in its wildness" (1972: 90). Her visions are as profoundly gothic as they are prophetic:

> The most fantastic contrasts could be flashed before us with a speed which the writer can only toil in vain; the dream architecture of arches and battlements, of cascades falling and fountains rising, which sometimes visits us in sleep or shapes itself in half-darkened rooms, could be awakened before our eyes. No fantasy could be too farfetched or insubstantial. (Woolf 1972: 91)

The distinct and varied ways that films invigorate gothic potential in all its forms are examined through the course of this book. While certain items, topics or concepts—such as animated objects, spectral visions or immortal creatures—seem to be more predisposed towards representation in gothic fictions, gothic is also about more intricate, visual and intangible features, related to tone, mood and atmosphere as well as style, subject matter and aesthetics.

It is wise to tread carefully. Although my aim is not to be overly prescriptive or reductive about determining what gothic is or should be in more general terms, I nevertheless need to lay some foundations for the gothic terrains that are traversed in this book. A brief overview of gothic's vibrant history aids this process. Over the centuries, 'gothic' has been used as both a celebratory and derogatory term. The Goths were seen as one of the Germanic tribes who aided the disintegration of the Roman Empire in the fourth century. They came to be seen retrospectively as encompassing all Germans, including the Anglo-Saxons, setting up a mythological identity, as David Stevens (2012: 8) explains: "From this position, subsequent historians and propagandists were able to proclaim a 'native' freedom-loving gothic tradition within British culture, in opposition to 'foreign' imperialism as epitomised by the Norman invasion of 1066 and the authoritarian rule it ushered in." 'Gothic' as a term is relatively recent. As Nick Groom advises (2012: 13), while we might look to the grand architecture of the twelfth to fifteenth centuries as 'gothic,' this would not have been a term used at the time. During the Renaissance period, the disproportionate, heavy piles of gothic architecture were looked down upon as the crude product of the Middle Ages, the 'dark period' "following the fall of Rome and prior to the beginning of the modern period" (Groom 2012: 13) in fierce opposition to the order of the classical period, so admired by Italian Renaissance humanist scholars at this time. In 1550, Giorgio Vasari famously wrote a scathing attack (in *Lives of the Artists*) on architecture "invented by the Goths," during which he called upon God to protect every country from what he saw as a travesty of style:

> We come at last to another sort of work called German, which both in ornament and in proportion is very different from the ancient and the modern. Nor is it adopted by the best architects, but is avoided by them as monstrous and barbarous, and lacking anything that can be called order. Now, it should rather be called confusion and disorder... (cited in Robson-Scott 1965: 5)

Little more than two centuries later, there was to be a shift in taste, evident in the growing cultural and aesthetic interest in medievalism in England that has come to be known as 'The Gothic Revival': "In different ways, the Gothic gradually permeated every aspect of cultural and social life: from gardening to graveyard poetry, from fashionable architectural statements to the editing of old literature" (Groom 2012: 65). However, this shift was a gradual process, and can be seen to rise with, out of and as a critique of the progress associated with the Age of Enlightenment (or Age of Reason) spanning from the last decade of the seventeenth century through to the first decade of the nineteenth, although the term did not come into the English language until the middle of the eighteenth century (Pagden 2013: vii). The wider context to this was the dislocation of religion by Enlightenment rationalist thinking, which grew to dominate European politics, philosophy, science and communications, perceived as a mode of explaining and ultimately governing civilization. The Enlightenment, inspired by the classical cultures of Ancient Rome and Greece, saw beauty in order, symmetry and equal proportion and sought to move on from a Middle Ages darkness, "which conjured up ideas of barbarous customs and practices, of superstition, ignorance, extravagant fancies and natural wildness" (Botting 1996: 22). This emergent mode of discerning the world, which has had such a widespread impact on current thinking, caused writers and historians to focus on science and reasoning, moving away from faith, belief, superstition or a 'divine plan.' The prioritization of the rational made perfect sense. Alongside this emerged the rising gothic understanding that too much repression by symmetry and order invites uprising. Human emotions cannot always be rationalized, and there is always the residing possibility that the 'other' side to humanity, governed by passions, unexplainable urges and rages, will rise. However, the gothic reaction to the Enlightenment was not so much one of rebellion or rejection but one of curiosity, and once this investigatory process had taken place, there was likely to be a restoration of order. However, to some degree, order had still been destabilized if not overthrown, as Andrew Smith and William Hughes argue:

> One of the defining ambivalences of the Gothic is that its labelling of otherness is often employed in the service of supporting, rather than questioning, the status quo. This is perhaps the central complexity of the form because it debates the existence of otherness and alterity, often in order to demonize such otherness. However, any restoration of Enlightenment certainly tends to be compromised by the presence of a debate within the Gothic concerning the relationship between rationality and irrationality. (2003: 3)

Thus, retrospectively, it is clear that the emergence of gothic writers at this time in history is complexly reliant upon the Enlightenment. As well as being wary of a complete saturation of order and rational thinking, the gothic is also amenable to the dualities it opens up, revelling in the 'debate' or brawl between one and the other. As Jonathan Dent (2016: 14) notes, the gothic is able to give attention to the gaps in Enlightenment thinking—to what it "ignores," overlooks, or represses:

> The Age of Reason is haunted by the spectre of the Gothic. One of the reasons the Gothic endured throughout the eighteenth century (and well beyond) is because it continually questions what it is to be human and preys on primeval anxieties and fears. (2016: 15)

The abiding force of gothic, then, is the capacity for it to consider our relationship to the turbulences of the past, and to allow for the notion that these turbulences resonate in the present, that they are relevant now, and the human story cannot always be ordered chronologically within the frame of immaculate progress. As explored in the case study chapters that follow, and specifically in relation to *El laberinto del fauno /Pan's Labyrinth* (Guillermo del Toro, 2006) in Chapter 6, a history of unreasoning brutality cannot always be consigned to the past but needs to be confronted with respect to its continuous haunting of the present.

Towards the end of the eighteenth century, readers with quickening heartbeats were captivated by novels displaying the full terrors of decaying buildings, wild settings, mysteries and shady or frightening characters. While popular, and probably in part due to their popularity, these novels were often dismissed by critics of the literary establishment as frivolous, or even morally ambivalent. However, over time, the characteristics that had served to put 'gothic' out of favour, such as its associations with nature, instinct, mood, imagination and human emotion, started to become its most valued assets.[6] As Anna M. Wittmann (1990: 60) writes, "The condemnation of Gothic taste, never total, is gradually undone in late eighteenth-century England. Just as in landscape gardening, the qualities of variety, natural wildness, and asymmetry are now favored and propagated, so the irregularity and seeming disorder of Gothic architecture and ornamentation gain in approval." Despite the very different contexts and applications required for studying gothic architecture and landscape design, it is clear that certain concepts might also be seen to recur in gothic literature, such as 'disorder' and 'confusion,' emphasized by those writing about these disciplines (whether favourably or not). In addition, we might add to these a sense of excess, boundlessness, asymmetry or irregularity. Establishing these shared tropes and emphases is particularly important when taking this study forward to consider the specificities of gothic horror cinema. Literary gothic qualities of excessive style and interiority might also be seen to have a specific (and varied) incarnation within cinema.[7]

---

[6]And as Botting (1996: 46) points out, these shifts also formed part of wider social, industrial and political changes, such as increasing access to books brought about by more economical printing practices and new libraries. There was also a significant increase in the number of women emerging on the scene as both keen writers and consumers (Botting 1996: 47). Perceived traditionally, and paradoxically, as both frivolous and corruptive, there are associations with the female gender through gothic's unsteady history that can be compared with key aspects of fairy tale's oral tradition. Marina Warner (1994: XIII) has written about the reductive and stereotypical labelling of fairy tales, recalling the feelings she had that her own childhood interests in reading them were implicitly perceived as "girly," revealing "a lack of intellectual—and possibly moral—fibre."

[7]As explored in the next chapter, for example, an excess of style is evident in Hitchcock's *Rebecca*: in the filming and décor of Rebecca's bedroom in the West Wing; in the performance style of Maxim de Winter (Laurence Olivier), and particularly Maxim's monologue in the beach cottage sequence; and in the camera's near self-reflexive stylization during this monologue.

Horace Walpole's *Anecdotes of Painting in England* (first published 1762), which mourns the loss of gothic buildings in the Reformation and Civil Wars, directly contrasts gothic with the classical school of architecture, fuelling the distinction of gothic as something other or opposed to Augustan order: "One must have taste to be sensible of the beauties of Grecian architecture; one only wants passions to feel Gothic" (Walpole 1762: 107–108). Here words like "sensible" arise (rather than sensibility) connoting order and reason, contrasting with terms like "passions" and "feeling," taken to represent the alternative, opposing side of culture, civilization and the rational.

Walpole himself lived at Strawberry Hill (first conceived in 1749/1750), his own grand tribute to the gothic revival, and he published *The Castle of Otranto: A Gothic Story* in December 1764, which has since been taken to be the founding gothic literary text. Spooner and Emma McEvoy (2007: 1) summarize that, traditionally "it was taken for granted that the gothic novel flourished from the publication of Horace Walpole's *The Castle of Otranto* in 1764 to Charles Maturin's *Melmoth, The Wanderer* in 1820." However, as they go on to explain, the confines have become looser, moving from the established tropes of "imperilled heroines, dastardly villains, ineffectual heroes, supernatural events, dilapidated buildings and atmospheric weather" (2007: 1) that have been found to be insufficient to address the full conception of 'the gothic,' which continues to evolve and flourish to this day.

As Groom (2012: xiv) argues, some "introductions to the Gothic distort the word, stretching it into an umbrella term for transgression, marginality, and 'otherness,'" to the point where it "now risks being emptied or nullified as a meaningful term" (2012: xv). The alternative risk is for the term's meaning to be too narrowly defined, overlooking the enduring capacity for growth and evolution of the term itself. Glennis Byron and Dale Townshend celebrate this capacity:

> Forever extending its remit, and continuously enlarging the realms of its critical purchase and applicability, the term 'Gothic' has become as culturally ubiquitous as that which it is used to describe. Though once exclusively the preserve of a select group of seventeenth- and eighteenth-century British politicians, historians and antiquaries, the term has substantially extended its semantic field so as to become one of the most important terms of aesthetic identification, classification and distinction in western cultural production of the nineteenth, twentieth and twenty-first centuries. (2013: xxxvii)

Often captivated by medievalism and a fever for the past, gothic fiction is paradoxically rife with the technologies of the new; it is often fabricated out of them. Gothic literature often riles against new orders of modernity, but these also form the architectural bones that galvanize it, and give it renewed force. Gothic is the ghost in the machine that will not be made silent; technology grinds at the heart of Shelley's *Frankenstein* and surging engines fuel Bram Stoker's *Dracula* (first published in 1897). It is a haunting return of the past into the present. For all its diverse guises, the unifying features of gothic are its aptitude for articulating the irrational and its endeavour to find expression for desires, urges, feelings and susceptibilities that cannot always be explained rationally. As Clive Bloom (2007: 291) asserts, "Gothic horror is about that which should *not* be, whose comprehension is the end of sanity and the opening of the abyss, in which cursed state of knowledge the forbidden becomes manifest, the veil is withdrawn and the fabric of the material universe falls to dust." While two-dimensional characterization or texts that favour superficial gothic iconicity over traditional gothic sensibility may dampen any transgressive potential, this is not to say that sentimentalism, romance or comedy, so often hybridized with gothic, always threaten to renounce these tendencies for the 'abyss' and 'the forbidden' or that a fusion of these elements cannot have the potential to actually enhance the horror.[8] Gothic is excess, seeping from the arcane crevices we like to hide away, and hide away from. Seeping in from outside, it is already within us. These contradictory riddles touch on a duality that is at the heart of the gothic, providing a way to understand it, or gain some kind of access to it. In line with this duality, I suggest it is more precisely the pull between the rational and the irrational that designates gothic, forging an unsteady balance between the two, rather than the absolute loss of the rational. These claims about the gothic mean that it is a tall order to be in its full presence. Having said this, it is important to stress that the text does need to dare to enter into the irrational, not just to stare darkness and uncertainty in the face but to trespass in the more difficult areas, in ways that the solace found in the entirety or culmination of the text cannot entirely eradicate.

---

[8] Indeed, this is a complex area; not only do gothic and romantic fiction have shared roots but the former can also be seen to draw on the 'romances' that preceded it (see Botting 1996: 44–47).

Often, gothic fiction elicits a quick shudder coupled with a long drawn out sense of discomfort brought about by an excessive probe or slippage into an area that feels like it should have been left alone. There is the sensation of being driven out of one's natural self by forces located within the self, though never those you would willingly show in daylight. I suggest there is often something about gothic that makes you blush, because it is difficult to talk about in public or the cold light of day. Gothic horror has the capacity to fill the heart or mind with terror, and to make the body physically recoil. It is often the case that the height of this terror will subside and then be killed by the end of the text. Nevertheless, the terror tends to linger, as the memory of it or the threat of its return remains. Jackson examines gothic fiction from (approximately) *Frankenstein* (1818) to *Dracula* (1897). She suggests that, while early gothic romances veer more towards the supernatural or "marvellous," changes can be seen emerging from the end of the eighteenth century through the nineteenth century: "As Gothic undergoes transformations through the work of Ann Radcliffe, M.G. Lewis, Mary Shelley and Charles Maturin, it develops into a literary form capable of more radical interrogation of social contradictions" (Jackson 1991: 97). Significantly, she observes an increasing movement towards psychological concerns and uncertainty, a movement from an external to an internal 'other' (the 'other' within the self): "The subject is no longer confident about appropriating or perceiving a material world. Gothic narrates this epistemological confusion: it expresses and examines personal disorder, opposing fiction's classical unities (of time, space, unified character) with an apprehension of partiality and relativity of meaning" (Jackson 1991: 97). Jackson notes the duality evident as early as William Godwin's *The Adventures of Caleb Williams* (1794), in which the first person narrator 'I' (Caleb) is fascinated by his ideal Falkland, who it transpires is a murderer. Their identities become inextricably linked:

> From the moment when Caleb becomes attached to this ideal, there is no possibility of returning to an unknowing self. His link with his reflection gives rise to a complex knot of repression and guilt which he then spends the rest of his life attempting (unsuccessfully) to un-do. (Jackson 1991: 98)

Caleb ends up cursing not only his identity and the guilt raised by the drives of his repressed ideal, but also the entire human race and the repressive elements of society, order and justice.⁹ These tensions between repression and an interior drive, linked also to bounds of morality and feelings of guilt, clearly anticipate the influx of psychoanalytic theory, analysis and practice that would infiltrate Western perceptions of the psyche.¹⁰

Cinema is a rich forum for developing innovative representations of the double, or split self, which over the years has been conveyed via a wealth of camera, sound, framing and editing techniques, in addition to more literal motifs—such as mirrors, shadows, echoes and repeated mannerisms. For instance, *Strangers on a Train* (Alfred Hitchcock, 1951) sets up the doubling of the two protagonists, Guy (Farley Granger) and Bruno (Robert Walker), from the opening scenes by cross-cutting between their separate arrivals at the station. The tracking shots are positioned close to the floor to display their different shoes. Bruno's flamboyant, pied brogues (accented by a rambunctious musical flourish on the soundtrack when he steps out of the cab) contrast with Guy's dull, very ordinary shoes. They are about to run into each other on the train, and Bruno will transform Guy's life into chaos by suggesting he partake in an exchange of murders, dismissed by Guy as ludicrous from the outset. Even so, the shots of Bruno's shoes lead each time, and he sits down on the train before Guy, meaning that Guy chooses to sit with him. As Robin Wood (2009: 172) observes, it is made clear that Bruno "has not engineered" their encounter: "it is Guy's foot that knocks his accidentally, under the table, leading directly to their getting into conversation." Thus, while Bruno—this dandy, macabre figure—seems to be the last being in the world Guy wishes ever to meet, the cinematic devices playfully acknowledge the unexpressed similarities between the two of them. The fleeting close-up on the inadvertent knock of a foot foregrounds the summoning of a hidden, repressed Freudian 'id' fully prepared, and irrepressibly so, to know and carry out the taboo deeds that Guy could only wish unconsciously to undertake. A knowing wink is given to this moment near the beginning of *Harry, un ami qui vous veut*

---

⁹Jackson (1991: 99) argues that Godwin's daughter, Shelley, presents an even more extreme view than her father in her novels *Frankenstein* and *The Last Man* (1826), losing complete faith, or proffering revolutionary utopianism: "They intensify the pessimism of *Caleb Williams*, by presenting the impossibility of resolving internal conflicts generated by cultural institutions. Both *Frankenstein* and *The Last Man* are fantasies of absolute negation or dissolution of cultural order."

¹⁰We might also consider Edgar Allen Poe's short story 'William Wilson,' first published in 1839, in which William Wilson's doppelgänger, also called William Wilson, repeatedly returns as the protagonist's shadowy conscience.

du bien / *Harry, He's Here to Help* (UK) / *With a Friend Like Harry…* (US) (Dominik Moll, 2000). When Michel (Laurent Lucas) first meets his doppelgänger, Harry (Sergi López), in the service station toilet, attention is drawn to their similarity as the other people exit, leaving the two of them reflected in the large mirror, both wearing grey. As they wash their hands, it becomes apparent in a successive run of overt shot / reverse shots that Harry is staring at Michel, and that he slowly begins to smile. As discussed in Chapter 5, the doppelgänger is elaborately conveyed in *Werewolf of London* (Stuart Walker, 1935), whereupon the forbidden werewolf encounter gives meaningful expression to the fear and pleasure of being 'bitten' by the exotic Dr. Yogami (Warner Oland).

The relationship between ventriloquist Charles 'Corky' Withers or Corky (Anthony Hopkins) and his dummy Fats in *Magic* (Richard Attenborough, 1978) reaches a new dimension when it is revealed to the audience, in one trembling moment, that he is speaking to (and for) Fats when nobody else is there. It thus ceases to be a performance, and registers that he is losing his mind. The gothic tension is conveyed visually through the utilization of space, as we see through the open door from the bedroom to Fats sat before another open door—to the outside world (see Fig. 3.1). A light comes on in the building opposite.

Fig. 3.1 The boundary is crossed; Corky slips out of control—*Magic* (Richard Attenborough, 1978)

Fig. 3.2 The camera comments on the horror of Fats taking over—*Magic* (Richard Attenborough, 1978)

Fats sits on the border to the public, civilized world of order, and tension is built by the knowledge and fear that Corky's insanity is going to be discovered, when all that has been repressed is about to surface uncontrollably, as it does when Ben Greene (Burgess Meredith), the powerful television agent on the verge of signing him up, walks in and witnesses everything. The gothic split self is articulated through spatial relationships that draw attention to the exterior and interior (public and private) while at the same time witnessing their collapse.[11] When Ben demands that Corky functions without Fats for five minutes, testing his levels of sanity, Corky eventually crumbles, as Fats takes over. Corky's moment of breakdown, as he folds into the 'other,' is underscored by the camera's panning action that eventually realigns Fats' face directly in front of Corky's. Initially Corky's face is in focus (see Fig. 3.2).

But as the camera reaches the end of its pan, Fats' face comes into full focus, eclipsing Corky's entirely. Through Fats, Corky has been able to give a voice to his internal untamed, irrational and taboo thoughts, fears, dreads and desires. Fats swears, talks about sex and makes dirty jokes

---

[11] Other notable horror films during this period that incorporate diverse notions of a split self or double include: *The Exorcist* (William Friedkin, 1973) and *Legend of the Werewolf* (Freddie Francis, 1975). The latter film is explored in Chapter 5.

and, when confronted by the threat of being outed as insane, Corky uses him as a killing implement thrashing Ben to a pulp in the bushes.

It is important to stress that Sigmund Freud's essay '*Das Unheimlich*' / 'The Uncanny' (first published in 1919) has become vital in establishing an understanding of the competing tensions and dualities (between external and internal forces) intrinsic to 'gothic.'[12] Setting up a foundation for analyzing 'The Uncanny' in a variety of texts and examples, and in particular E.T.A. Hoffman's story 'The Sandman,' Freud (2003: 126–134) investigates the German root of 'uncanny' /'*unheimlich*' (unhomely, unfamiliar) all the way to its opposite '*heimlich*.' The crucial point materializes when Freud traces the numerous and convoluted definitions of '*heimlich*' until '*unheimlich*' surprisingly resurfaces:

> [A]mong the various shades of meaning that are recorded for the word *heimlich* there is one in which it merges with its formal antonym, *unheimlich*, so that what is called *heimlich* becomes *unheimlich*... This reminds us that this word *heimlich* is not unambiguous, but belongs to two sets of ideas, which are not mutually contradictory, but very different from each other – the one relating to what is familiar and comfortable, the other to what is concealed and kept hidden. (2003: 132)

As Freud deduces, the convergence between the two (formally designated) antonyms "says something quite new—something we certainly did not expect—about the meaning of *unheimlich*, namely, that the term 'uncanny' (*unhemilich*) applies to everything that was intended to remain secret, hidden away, and has come out into the open" (Freud 2003: 132). Within the realm of the homely, there is something locked away, "hidden and dangerous," so that "*heimlich* acquires the sense that otherwise belongs to *unheimlich*":

> *Heimlich* thus becomes increasingly ambivalent, until it finally merges with its antonym *unheimlich*. The uncanny (*das Unheimliche*, 'the unhomely') is in some way a species of the familiar (*das Heimliche*, 'the homely'). (Freud 2003: 134)

---

[12] It is worth noting contemporaneous works contemplating the familiarly strange incarnation of the doppelgänger: the film *Der Student von Prag* / *The Student of Prague* (Paul Wegener, Stellan Rye [co-director] 1913) and Otto Rank's (1925) psychoanalytic study, *Der Doppelgänger: Eine psychoanalystische Studie* (Leipzig: Internationaler Psychoanalysticher Verlag), pp. 68–69. Rank, a close associate of Freud's, wrote *Der Doppelgänger* in 1914, although it was not published until 1925.

Freud locates the peculiarly frightening element of the uncanny as that which leads back to what is already long known or familiar, but has been repressed, or hidden; the uncanny conveys the haunting or return of something that should have remained private or unseen. As explored in some depth in Chapters 4 and 5, gothic fictions are driven by this dual relationship of the familiar and the strange, and it is this very duality that produces, or exposes, the fear. Linked to the struggles between the rational and irrational, the conscious and the unconscious, or the civilized and the wild, duality also emerges in the gothic text as doubling—the split self and the doppelgänger. As Freud (2003: 142) articulates with respect to 'The Uncanny': "a person may identify with another and so become unsure of his true self; or he may substitute the other's self for his own. The self may thus be duplicated, divided and interchanged." In works of fiction and film, the double can be used to articulate notions of the split self. Two characters who might initially appear to be opposites are incarnations of the duality of 'self.' The 'other' and the 'self' fuse to denote consciousness, by which "a special authority takes shape within the ego" (Freud 2003: 142). This gives expression to the ways that humans observe themselves, the ways that humans censor behaviour "and so becomes what we know as the 'conscience'" (Freud 2003: 142). The uncanny returns and renewals of multiple female identities in the narrative and stylistic devices of Hitchcock's *Rebecca* are examined in Chapter 4 with regard to what they reveal about the layering of gothic horror and the various conflicting interpretations of meanings. At key points in the film, the sense of the uncanny reaches beyond the text, towards a sensation of the uncanny that is not shared by the characters on screen, thus making the moment all the more horrific. This relates to what Freud (2003: 158) terms the "privileges that fiction enjoys in arousing and inhibiting a sense of the uncanny." Further to this, beyond the bounds of authorial control, are the subsequent and varied *readings* of a text, reliant upon specific and shifting cultural and political contexts, that add new layers to the sensation or *reception* of 'the uncanny.'

Dread and desire are often rooted in the same or merging drives. It is intrinsically gothic to desire that which is most dreaded. At this level, gothic can be seen as potentially radical and subversive within specific historical contexts, in the sense that it is suggestive of unreason and terror in the light of a rational or ordered society. As Botting argues, "Not only a way of producing excessive emotion, a celebration of transgression for its own sake, gothic terrors activate a sense of the unknown and project an uncontrollable and overwhelming power which threatens not only the loss of sanity, honour, property or social standing but the very order which supports and is regulated by the coherence of those terms" (Botting 1996: 7). However, this revolutionary quality tends to reach only so far; by presenting these horrors in the most extreme, terrifying or menacing ways, gothic fictions often function as a means to restoring boundaries of order, or reinforcing societal values and norms, rather than, ultimately, transgressing them.

It is the strain or precarious balance between disorder and order that keeps gothic vibrant. By identifying with central protagonists, overthrowing or confronting demons and returning to the safety of rational order and morality, we are licensed to face the darker terrors that linger beyond these civilized confines. It is thus the tension or wavering balance between disorder and order that stimulates gothic. As Botting suggests, the gothic resides in the interplay between reason and passion (1996: 8), which depend on each other, and there is "ambivalence" at play that "both restores and contests boundaries": "The play means that Gothic is an inscription neither of darkness nor of light, a delineation neither of reason and morality nor of superstition and corruption, neither good nor evil, but both at the same time" (1996: 9). A blending of light and dark, together with an 'ambivalent' establishment and dissolution of boundaries, is expressed visually in Swedish film *Låt den rätte komma in* /*Let the Right One In* (Tomas Alfredson, 2008), which opens at a slow, considered pace—initially in silence—and with a rising emotional, orchestral score. The initial silence is accompanied by a black screen, with the slow interjection of small white credits on the left side. After about one and a half minutes, white snowflakes softly fall, on two thirds of the right side of the frame. The first long take is the static shot of the surrounding flats in the estate of this Stockholm suburb set in the 1980s.[13] The specific setting is likely to be familiar to Swedes, but less so to audiences outside Sweden. In addition, the openness of the location and period (at this point of the film) suggests this might be any European suburban housing estate, provoking the unsettling quality of both the familiar and the unfamiliar, merging together to create unease. The young protagonist, Oskar (Kåre Hedebrant), gazes through the window from the flat where

---

[13] It is reportedly filmed in Blackeberg, a suburb of Stockholm, and set in the 1980s. In contrast to the remake, *Let Me In* (Matt Reeves, 2010), there are no overt signposts at this point in the film to the precise time and place.

he lives, looking out towards the surrounding estate. The long takes of the boy, juxtaposed with the shots of the arrival of the newcomers—a man, Håkan (Per Ragnar), and a child, Eli (Lina Leandersson)—foreground a connection between them that is yet to unfold. The haunting, cyclical parallels between Håkan, who takes care of Eli, a vampire, by spilling blood for her, and Oskar, who will later make the decision to leave with Eli, moving on as new-comers to another place, do not fully resonate until the end of the film. Oskar's image slowly appears in the window's reflection; we are sharing his view, and the link between internal and external worlds is made, as Oskar's bare-chested ghostlike body is projected onto the cold snowy landscape. The importance of the close links between the central figures is evident in the cut to the extreme close up of the man and child, allowing attention to fine details—the lines on the man's face, and the smile that emerges when he turns to look at Eli. As his smile slowly fades to a pained expression, he turns his head back to face the front of the vehicle and the music begins. The next shot shows Oskar by the window again; he places his palm on the window, drawing attention to the barriers between himself and the outside.[14]

Through the opening shots, the divide between inside and outside continues, with Oskar naked apart from his pants, in contrast to the frosty clouds of snow outside. The shots of Oskar are framed either side of the intimately filmed arrival of the newcomers. Already, there is a connection between the characters. The glow of the shot, on Oskar's white blonde hair, suggests his innocence (see Fig. 3.3). However, there is also a sincere seriousness to his expression, and the uplighting creates a more sinister effect just prior to the moment when he seizes the knife, saying, "Squeal like a pig!" He is alone as he performs these words—a repetition of the first words of the film, whispered on the soundtrack over the silent, falling snow.

---

[14] The shot also bears an uncanny resemblance to two moments in films by Swedish filmmaker Ingmar Bergman. Firstly, it is reminiscent of the boy's palm on the train window near the start of *Tystnaden / The Silence* (1963), as he tries to make sense of the violent world beyond. The second moment occurs in the opening of *Persona* (1966)—when the boy puts his hand flat on the glass, especially at the point when it seems to touch the projected face of Elisabet/Alma (Liv Ullmann / Bibi Andersson), and when the reverse shot looks back at the boy from the other side of the glass. The lack of contact is emphasized. That the image Oskar contacts is his own reflection emphasizes a similar breakdown of contact represented by glass screens, as well as the breakdown of 'self' and 'other.'

Fig. 3.3 Innocence fuses with the sinister—*Let the Right One In* (Tomas Alfredson, 2008)

Extreme moral oppositions seem to be rife in the gothic tale. However, these are not stable like they are in fairy tales. As Lisa Hopkins argues:

> In the first place, Gothic tends to create polarities: extreme good is opposed to extreme evil, extreme innocence to extreme power, and very often extreme youth to extreme age… And yet at the same time, there is an uncanny sense that the polarizations so beloved of the Gothic are not in fact as absolute as they seem – that things which appear to be opposite can actually be frighteningly, uncannily similar. (2005: xii)

Thus, the innocent embodies traces of the evil associated with its opposite, and vice versa, and often there is a blurring or a sense of ambiguity between the two. A chief emphasis in the opening of *Let the Right One In* is kinship, an openness to the shifting of rigid polarities, as well as the sense of Oskar's summoning of the chaos that ensues. Furthermore, there is also the sense of the intrusion of the external upon the internal, and vice versa, and the shattering of illusions. What might initially appear to be a bright leafy tree from outside reflecting in Oskar's bedroom turns out to be a poster on the wall behind Oskar's bed. The confusion is just enough to cause a shudder.

The next sequence begins with a cut to the next morning. But this brings only the lingering twilight, in monochrome, with the fluorescent light (over the entrance to the school) working overtime. Our first view of this next day is from the submerged darkness of the underpass—a fusion or collision between night and day, the wild (and untamed) rubbing shoulders with the civilized and institutional. This is gothic horror exhibited visually, framed by the camera, recalling Botting's perspective: "Relations between real and fantastic, sacred and profane, supernatural and natural, past and present, civilised and barbaric, rational and fanciful, remain crucial to the Gothic dynamic of limit and transgression" (1996: 9). As Charlene Bunnell (1996: 80) stresses, the result of gothic writers' interest in both "reason" and "sensibility" is "a balance" that is itself a key feature of the duality embedded in gothic, or as Bunnell (1996: 81) terms it, "the symbolic dual worlds"—a "diurnal world and a nocturnal one." It is not the case that the diurnal world simply represents 'good' and the latter 'evil':

> One world is the external one – cultural and institutional; it is 'light' because it is familiar and common. The other world is the internal one – primitive and intuitive; it is dark, not because it necessarily signifies evil (although it may), but because it is unfamiliar and unknown. (Bunnell 1996: 81)

In cinematic representations, then, dual external and internal worlds find expression in a variety of forms beyond and linking to narrative concerns, including: doubling; the split body; split settings and set designs; monstrosity; editing; lighting; framing; dialogue; words; sound; music; colour; and lens focus. Bunnell's reference to the terms 'familiar' and 'unfamiliar' clearly links back to 'the Uncanny,' demonstrating how fundamental it is in appreciating gothic tone and atmosphere.

Indeed, the uncanny itself is a slippery concept, so inextricably linked to tone that care needs to be taken to avoid making definitive statements about it. Having said this, paradoxically, definitive statements can be extremely helpful for locating the uncanny, and in turn returning to the gothic. Freud (2003: 152–153) argues that fairy tales are not uncanny, even though they seem to have the key happenings and themes (of objects and dead figures coming to life, for example). Freud (2003: 153) even claims that he cannot cite a single fairy tale in which anything uncanny occurs:

> In the world of the fairy tale, feelings of fear, and therefore of the uncanny, are totally ruled out. We understand this and therefore ignore whatever occasion they afford for such a possibility. (Freud 2003: 158)

Freud is clearly wrong to rule out feelings of fear from our experiences of fairy tales, but in so doing he touches on an important principle—that the capacity for the uncanny does not guarantee the uncanny. As discussed in the previous chapter, different effects are created depending upon the specific version, narration and interpretation of a fairy tale. Like the gothic, the uncanny needs to be conjured by an author or audience. Indeed, having moved away briefly from the fairy tale, Freud (2003: 157) himself articulates the importance of authorial licence in fiction for "arousing and inhibiting a sense of the uncanny," suggesting that the moods the writer induces "can direct our feelings away from one consequence and towards another" (2003: 158). This extends to who we identify with, and the consequences of the audience knowing more than the character, for example. These considerations of the ways the uncanny functions, on many levels, are unpacked further in the next chapter, particularly with regard to how horror is intensified during vital moments in Hitchcock's *Rebecca* as our awareness extends beyond the heroine's.

It is clear that 'gothic' as a concept continues to evolve, just as it rises and falls at given historical moments. However, key features remain, and the transgressive potential of gothic resides in the lingering of the past in the present and the understanding that horror rises from within—the home, or the self—and thus shatters boundaries between the 'self' and 'other,' reality and fantasy, the conscious and the unconscious. The return of the repressed creates disruption, but often the repression itself comes under some scrutiny, revealing hidden restrictions and prejudices, and challenging norms and societal expectations. While the irrational passion and disorder released by gothic fictions tend to be lulled as a sense of order is at least temporarily reinstated at a narrative's close, the queries and uncertainties unleashed by the gothic linger on, overwhelmingly forming a shadow—a persistent doubt that should not be evaded.

References

Abel, R., and Altman, R., eds. (2001). *The Sounds of Early Cinema* (Bloomington and Indianapolis: Indiana University Press).

Barthes, R. (1982). *Camera Lucida: Reflections on Photography*, translated by R. Howard (New York: Hill and Wang).

Bazin, A. (Summer 1960). 'The Ontology of the Photographic Image', translated by H. Gray, *Film Quarterly*, 13: 4, 4–9.

Bloom, C. (2007, 1998). *Gothic Horror: A Guide for Students and Readers* (Basingstoke and New York: Palgrave Macmillan).
Bluestone, G. (1957). *Novels into Film* (Baltimore: The Johns Hopkins University Press).
Blum, V. (2005). 'Becoming the Other Woman: The Psychic Drama of Cosmetic Surgery', *Frontiers: A Journal of Women Studies*, 26: 2, 104–131.
Botting, F. (1996). *Gothic* (London and New York: Routledge).
Bunnell, C. (1984, 1996). 'The Gothic: A Literary Genre's Transition to Film', in B.K. Grant (ed.), *Planks of Reason: Essays on the Horror Film* (Metuchen, New Jersey and London: Scarecrow Press), pp. 79–100.
Byron, G., and D. Townshend. (2013). 'Introduction', in G. Byron, D. Townshend (eds.), *The Gothic World* (London and New York: Routledge), pp. xxiv–xlv.
Cahill, J.L. (Fall, 2008). 'How It Feels to Be Run Over: Early Film Accidents', *Discourse* (Wayne State University Press) 30: 3, 289–316.
Christie, I. (1994). *The Last Machine: Early Cinema and the Birth of the Modern World* (London: BFI).
Dent, J. (2016). *Sinister Histories: Gothic Novels and Representations of the Past, from Horace Walpole to Mary Wollstonecraft* (Manchester: Manchester University Press).
Du Maurier, D. (1975). *Rebecca* (London: Pan Books Ltd).
Frayling, C. (2013). 'Foreword', in J. Bell (ed.), *Gothic: The Dark Heart of Film* (London: BFI), pp. 5–7.
Freud, S. (2003). 'The Uncanny' (1919), in *The Uncanny*, translated by D. McLintock (London: Penguin Classics), pp. 123–162.
Groom, N. (2012). *The Gothic: A Very Short Introduction* (Oxford: Oxford University Press).
Hopkins, L. (2005). *Screening the Gothic* (Austin: University of Texas Press).
Jackson, R. (1991, reprinted version). *Fantasy: The Literature of Subversion* (London and New York: Routledge).
Luckhurst, R. (2013). 'The Living Dead', in J. Bell (ed.), *Gothic: The Dark Heart of Film* (London: BFI), pp. 36–42.
Pagden, A. (2013). *The Enlightenment: And Why It Still Matters* (Oxford: Oxford University Press).
Rank, O. (1925). *Der Doppelgänger: Eine psychoanalystische Studie* (Lepzig: Internationaler Psychoanalysticher Verlag), pp. 68–69.
Reyes, X.A. (2014). 'Gothic Horror Film, 1960—Present', in G. Byron, D. Townshend (eds.), *The Gothic World* (London and New York: Routledge), pp. 388–398.
Robson-Scott, W.D. (1965). *The Literary Background of the Gothic Revival in Germany* (Oxford: Clarendon Press).

Smith, A., and Hughes, W. (2003). *Empire and the Gothic: The Politics of Genre* (Basingstoke and New York: Palgrave Macmillan).
Spooner, C. (2010). 'Preface', in B. Cherry, P. Howell and C. Ruddell (eds.), *Twenty-First-Century Gothic* (Newcastle upon Tyne: Cambridge Scholars Publishing), pp. ix–xii.
Spooner, C., and McEvoy, E., eds. (2007). *The Routledge Companion to Gothic* (Abingdon, Oxon and New York: Routledge).
Stevens, D. (2012). *The Gothic Tradition* (Cambridge and Mexico City: Cambridge University Press).
Walpole, H. (1762). *Anecdotes of Painting in England; with some Account of the principal Artists; and incidental Notes on other Arts; Collected by the late Mr. George Vertue; And now digested and published from his original MSS. By Mr. Horace Walpole* (Twickenham: Strawberry Hill).
Walters, J. (2011). *Fantasy Film: A Critical Introduction* (Oxford and New York: Berg Publishers).
Warner, M. (1994). *From the Beast to the Blonde: On Fairy Tales and Their Tellers* (London: Chatto and Windus).
Wittmann, A.M. (1990). 'Gothic *Trivialliteratur*: From Popular Gothicism to Romanticism', in G. Hoffmeister (ed.), *European Romanticism: Literary Cross-Currents, Modes, and Models* (Michigan: Wayne State University Press), pp. 59–75.
Wood, R. (2009, second edition). '*Strangers on a Train*', in M. Deutelbaum and L. Poague, (eds.), *A Hitchcock Reader* (Malden, Massachusetts, Oxford and Chichester, West Sussex: Wiley-Blackwell), pp. 172–182.
Woolf, V. (1972). 'The Movies and Reality', in H.M. Geduld (ed.), *Authors on Film* (Bloomington and London: Indiana University Press).

CHAPTER 4

Rebecca Returns: Death and Renewal Beyond the Door

Alfred Hitchcock's *Rebecca* (1940) is a richly complex film, incorporating an intricate web of fairytale and gothic horror elements. It is known primarily as an adaptation of Daphne du Maurier's novel of the same title, first published in 1938, and as Hitchcock's first Hollywood picture, guided by the visions of producer David O. Selznick, who held a keen interest in maintaining fidelity to the original source. The film has been variously classified as 'female gothic,' 'gothic romance,' 'thriller' and an initiator of the 'Bluebeard' or 'persecuted wife' 1940s Hollywood cycle.[1] It has also more recently been reinvestigated with respect to the notable 'horror' credentials that fascinated reporters on its first release.[2]

[1] There is no consensus on a definitive term for the cycle, but Andrew Britton's (1986) term "persecuted wife melodrama" pinpoints a predominant narrative component. Other examples include: "Freudian feminist melodrama" (Thomas Elsaesser 1972) and the "paranoid woman's film" (Mary Ann Doane 1988). Contemporaneous reviews spot 'Bluebeard' associations; Frank S. Nugent (1940: 25) notes "the Bluebeard room" in *Rebecca*. (I am grateful to Mark Jancovich for helping me to track down Nugent's article). More recently, Maria Tatar uses the term 'Bluebeard films.'

[2] Jancovich's recent investigation of the 1940s cycle of "female gothic films" (including, and triggered largely by, *Rebecca*) demonstrates that "at the time of their initial release these films were understood as women's horror films" (Jancovich 2013: 20). He argues that examples of the gothic (or paranoid) woman's film "were usually explicitly identified as horror films within the period" despite the fact that they have tended to be excluded from accounts of the horror film since the 1960s, noting that the "exclusion is often based on a tendency to privilege 'masculine' traditions of horror over 'feminine' traditions" and that "a similar set of oppositions can also be identified in feminist criticism" (Jancovich 2013: 21). Prior to this, Ed Gallafent (1988: 84–103) also notes *Rebecca*'s and, more generally, melodrama's connections with horror.

© The Author(s) 2018
L. Hubner, *Fairytale and Gothic Horror*,
https://doi.org/10.1057/978-1-137-39347-0_4

Rebecca concerns a young heroine (Joan Fontaine) finding her way in a new marriage to the wealthy and mysterious Maxim de Winter (Laurence Olivier) who is several years her senior. Initially full of awe, the heroine—who significantly remains unnamed throughout the film—becomes plagued by social insecurities, and by Rebecca, Maxim's beautiful, late wife, whose spectral presence seems to haunt her new married life. Beyond this, *Rebecca* navigates other difficult subject matter, when towards the end of the film in the beach cottage Maxim reveals privately to the heroine that he was the cause of Rebecca's death, saying that he must have lost control when she intimated she was pregnant with another man's child. The main narrative drive that follows the revelation seems to identify with the heroine's support of Maxim's response to what he presents as the unspeakable horrors of Rebecca's infidelity. However, Maxim's violent reaction to Rebecca's taunt also bears witness to the brutality that can be aggravated when the patriarchal bloodline is threatened.

The initial story that unfolds at the start of *Rebecca*, as a flashback following the opening dream sequence, comprises many of the hallmarks of a classical fairy tale, but such assurances are steadily undercut as gothic turbulences take a resilient hold. The orphaned, vulnerable 'Cinderella' heroine meets Maxim, the intriguing and recently widowed British aristocrat, while she is working in Monte Carlo as paid companion to the wealthy, domineering dowager Mrs. Van Hopper. The girl is devastated when she is told they will be moving on early from this holiday resort until, on hearing this, Maxim out of the blue proposes to her, thus rescuing her from the clutches of her current employer. But as the young wife nervously takes up residence as the new mistress of Manderley, Maxim's beloved ancestral estate in England, she encounters new demons, as she struggles to master the etiquettes of her new role, and it becomes clear that the memory of Rebecca cannot be so easily erased. Rebecca's identity seems to cast an indelible shadow over everything in the house—with her initial 'R' still confidently, and elaborately, adorning napkins, handkerchiefs and stationery. The second Mrs. de Winter fears that she cannot in any way match her predecessor, shuddering under the impression that Rebecca was adored by all who encountered her, including the severe, loyal housekeeper, Mrs. Danvers (Judith Anderson), who torments her with stories about Maxim's devoted and undying grief. The cyclical return of the past within the present, so central to the gothic, runs through the core of the film, as Michael Walker articulates: "And, although we never see Rebecca's body, it is central to the film's plot: in a spectacular example of the return of the repressed, it resurfaces from its grave on the seabed to confront Maxim with his crime, forcing him into a confession" (Walker 2005: 130). I suggest that beyond this, the heroine herself is subject to, carefully coded, repressions of her own. Although the 'confession' elicits a closeness between the couple, progressing outwardly to a more classical fairytale ending, the heroine's continued alliance with Maxim can also be read as a further repression—of her freedom, autonomy, dreams and desires—that the film scarcely manages to contain.³ Read in this light, it is the uncanny return, and cyclical renewal, of the repression itself, rather than that which has been repressed, that perpetuates the horror.

The fairytale markers that coat the subtleties and uncertainties explored through the film help to universalize the themes, drawing us into the narrative. In this respect, the young wife—having remained loyal to her husband—is seemingly rewarded at the end of the film, rescued by Maxim a second time, when he returns to find her escaping from the fire started at Manderley by Mrs. Danvers. This is markedly different from du Maurier's book, in which Maxim returns *with* his wife[4] to see the orange glow on the horizon, and (since Mrs. Danvers has previously left) there are no concrete explanations as to the cause of the fire. In the film, however, Maxim drives back with Frank, and they arrive to see the skeletal remains of the house ablaze with fire. The heroine emerges safely with the dog, Jasper, and her call to Maxim is scripted with a romantic flourish: "Thank heavens you've come back to me."[5] She tells him Mrs. Danvers has gone mad, saying that she would rather destroy Manderley than see them happy there—thus casting Mrs. Danvers in the role of

---

[3] Janet Harbord's analysis of du Maurier's *Rebecca* also resonates with this cycle of repetition: "The past returns to haunt, to ghost the present and disturb the familiarity of 'home' … the appeal of returning and repetition offers a form of pleasure that is never fully contained" (1996: 95).

[4] Furthermore, in du Maurier's *Rebecca*, on the return to Manderley the heroine dreams she is looking in the mirror having become Rebecca, laughing back at her, and that Maxim, brushing her hair, smiling, coils it around his neck (du Maurier 1975: 396).

[5] Jasper was Rebecca's dog: he leads the heroine to the beach cottage, inciting Maxim's anger and he greets Jack Favell, alerting us to Favell's affair with Rebecca. But he seems to save the heroine at the end. Alert to Danvers' movements with the candle, he is with the heroine when she appears outside, conforming to the ostensible 'happy ending' that the heroine replaces Rebecca.

jealous and hysterical female.⁶ These notable choices in the film certainly reduce the levels of ambiguity and resistance to romance upheld at the end of the novel. It is also telling that the novel's second chapter, which casts a shadow across the entire narrative, conveying the ennui of the de Winters' day-to-day lives, drifting from hotel to hotel in a state of limbo far from British shores, is a glimpse of the present that we do not see in the film. Alternatively, the opening dream sequence voice-over transitions straight back to their first meeting in Monte Carlo. The film draws to a close with a shot of the couple embracing, and there is then a cut to the unforgettable image of Mrs. Danvers becoming engulfed by flames, mirroring the conflagration of 'the witch' at the end of a number of fairy tales. As Mary Ann Doane (1988: 171) notes, the heroine's "full appropriation" of Rebecca's position allows for "the reunification and harmony of the couple which closes the film."⁷ However, uncertainties remain about this harmony at the film's close, not least due to the loss of Manderley that taints the temporary image of the couple, borne out in Maxim's look of deep concern and the heroine's worried glance towards the blaze (see Fig. 4.1).

It is a moment of togetherness, but also an uncanny reminder of the image of the couple's brief embrace after Maxim's revelation in the beach cottage, when the telephone rings, alerting them to the fact that the police have realized that the body they have found is Rebecca's (see Fig. 4.2).

Likewise, the film's final shot of the burning house penetrates Rebecca's bedroom, capturing the moment when the elaborate 'R' embroidered on the case of her nightgown fights through the flames, suggesting that certain memories cannot be entirely eradicated.

The temporariness of the couple's happiness is conveyed earlier in the film when Maxim and the heroine watch their honeymoon on the home movie reels that have just arrived at Manderley. Significantly, the honeymoon is only viewed as something already in the past. Moreover, the screening is interrupted twice. The first occasion is when the film breaks

---

⁶Note the similarity with the first wife Bertha Mason who sets fire to Jane's old bed and burns Thornfield down in Charlotte Brontë's *Jane Eyre*, first published in 1847 under the pen name Currer Bell, a nod to which is suggested in the subsequent casting of Fontaine to play Jane in Orson Welles' 1943 film version.

⁷Alison Light (1984: 11) investigates similar structures in du Maurier's *Rebecca*: "What the girl has to attempt, and what she must compulsively repeat in the telling of the tale, is a kind of self-murder. It is a violent denial of those other versions of female sexuality which Rebecca has come to represent."

Fig. 4.1 The ending, just before the west wing goes up in flames—*Rebecca* (Alfred Hitchcock, 1940)

up after the heroine says she wishes their honeymoon could have lasted forever, indicating not simply the damaging effects of marriage on romance, but also more specifically, "Maxim's unconscious hostility to the sexual intimations of the heroine's wish" (Walker 2005: 33). The second interruption occurs when Maxim physically obstructs the home movie image by standing in front of the projector and then switches the machine off, enraged by his wife's comment that he only married her because there would be no gossip about her.[8] She has unintentionally unveiled the taboo topic of Rebecca. At the end of the sequence of them watching the home movie, a close-up image of the happy couple fills the screen, but it is overwhelmed by a complexity of tensions evident in their present marriage. The image is introduced by Maxim when he tells the heroine that this is

---

[8] See Doane's chapter, 'Female Spectatorship and Machines of Projection' (1988: 155–175), for a detailed analysis of the home movie sequence as a "process of projection constituted as an assault on the diegetic female spectator" (Doane 1988: 163).

Fig. 4.2 In the beach cottage, when the telephone rings—*Rebecca* (Alfred Hitchcock, 1940)

the moment when he "left the camera running on the tripod—remember?" A long shot of them picnicking cheerily in front of their car appears on the screen they are watching. The camera of the main film tracks forwards to the screen within the scene to fill the frame. This is followed by a cut (within the home movie) to a closer shot of the couple, and then a further tracking shot orchestrated by the camera of the main film, until the shot of the couple fills the frame. The cut seems to defy Maxim's comment about leaving the camera running, creating a slight uneasiness, which we might overlook as the more forceful operation of the main film takes over, fusing with the home movie, as if to hide its mechanisms.[9]

---

[9] That Robin Wood originally suggests the objective tripod set-up was impossible because of the track forward, but then (Wood 2002: 231, endnote 6) returns to correct himself when he revisits the film years later is telling of the very easy slippage between these shots from the home movie to the image becoming framed and immersed in the larger story world they inhabit. It suggests that without the technology to accommodate multiple viewings, the fissure between the home movie and the viewpoint of the on-set camera is less apparent.

Maxim's words and the combined cinematography of the home movie and main film draw us into this fixed image of a happy past, just at the point when awareness of its present demise is most pronounced.

The image of the honeymoon couple is framed in the past, captured and embalmed by Maxim for posterity.[10] Prior to the sequence, the heroine had visited Frank, which further triggers her desire to become like Rebecca. Having asked Frank what Rebecca was really like, his response—"I suppose she was the most beautiful creature I ever saw"— seems to prompt a refrain of Rebecca's theme music and a dissolve to the cover of a magazine entitled, "BEAUTY: THE MAGAZINE FOR SMART WOMEN." A hand turns the page to an image, encased in a picture frame, of an elegant woman wearing a long black evening gown adorned with a diagonal strip of white flowers, and the words in elaborate typestyle (incidentally not dissimilar to Rebecca's handwriting)[11]: "For the Gala Evening." The dissolve to the heroine wearing the same dress clearly connotes her attempt at replicating Rebecca's beauty and allure so as to capture her husband's attention. But the matching of the heroine's image with the ideal of feminine beauty that she desires to be is hampered by her childlike awkwardness and then crushed by Maxim's response to this transformation: "What on earth have you done to yourself," he says laughing, "Do you think that sort of thing's right for you?" On realizing her attempts to impress him, he laughs, "very nice… for a change." Maxim's approval, on the other hand, of the image of his wife in the home movie ("Oh won't our grandchildren be delighted when they see how lovely you were")—as she appears in a plain cardigan and skirt, shying away from the geese she is feeding and holding her hands up gleefully at the camera—negates the heroine's fantasy to be a confident and sexually mature woman, like Rebecca.

We might recall that, when courting, Maxim had stopped the car forbidding the heroine her wish to be "a woman of 36 dressed in black satin with a string of pearls." In dressing this way in this sequence, the heroine has transgressed Maxim's order. As Ed Gallafent (1988: 95)

---

[10]This is another example of the past being exhibited within the present—a constant theme within the film—but also central to 'Bluebeard', as Stephen Benson (2000: 244) observes, "The past hangs heavy in Charles Perrault's 'La Barbe Bleue' ('Bluebeard,' 1697), both literally, in the shape of the suspended bodies of the eponymous villain's former wives, and metaphorically, as a pervasive air of unknowing."

[11]It is also similar to the handwriting of Favell—Rebecca's "favourite cousin" (lover).

argues, "Not only is Fontaine's begowned image hugely less satisfactory to Maxim than her image in the home movie, but his inability to control the image, to make Fontaine into mother rather than sophisticate, is articulated in the breakdown of the projector, and Maxim's assumption that this is his fault: 'threaded it up wrong, as usual.'" When Frith arrives during the first interruption of the film, wanting to speak to Maxim about a china cupid that Mrs. Danvers blames the servant Robert for stealing, the heroine confesses that she had accidentally smashed it to pieces and then hidden it in the back drawer. The scene serves to emphasize the heroine's fundamental differences from Rebecca, who knew how to deal with the servants. Maxim's comment, "You behave more like an upstairs maid or something, not the mistress of the house," draws attention to issues brought about by the heroine's lower social status as well as her inexperience. But these are also distinct attributes that Maxim seeks to maintain. As Walker notes, the crushed, hidden cupid functions as a "metaphorical comment on the infertility of the marriage" (Walker 2005: 33), suggesting that despite Maxim's demands that the heroine take a more active role, he is in actuality impotent when faced with a knowing "figure of real domestic authority and power" (Gallafent 1988: 95). The tension sits between Maxim's desire for an inexperienced young bride and the heroine's fantasy of a fulfilling marriage.

Maxim's urge to fix and control the heroine's fantasies is maintained through to the moments that follow the end of the sequence. The final image of the happy couple is preceded by a close-up of the heroine's face, her tearful eyes lit in the darkened space. The projecting film flickers on her face and she looks down as Maxim tells her that happiness is something he knows nothing about. As the camera tracks into the final image of this sequence, the honeymooners kiss and chatter away on the silent screen of the home movie—a dead, lifeless image of transitory lightness lost in the present day. The shot fades to black, and then to a stark formal letter signed simply "Maxim," with no adornments of style, stating that he has gone up to London to carry out some business and will return before evening: "this brief holiday from me should be welcome." Thus, the home movie sequence is bookended by scenes that convey both the repression of the heroine's desires by Maxim's denial or rescripting of the narrative: the sequence is preceded by the heroine's fantasy of becoming "beautiful" and "smart" and is followed by Maxim's abrupt departure. There is a petulant, narcissistic edge to Maxim's Romantic notion of himself as a long sufferer from past injuries—one that threatens to cajole the heroine into the role of mother, into focusing her attentions on him, starved of her own desires, lest she incite his anger.

The Oedipal trajectories of the film are governed by the progression from an alignment with the second wife towards, ostensibly, an allegiance with Maxim (through her decision to support him). We might also note the influx of all-male scenarios in the final sequences following Maxim's revelation—from the identification of Rebecca's body, and the visit to the doctor who discloses that Rebecca was not pregnant but had a terminal illness, thus giving substance to the 'suicide' verdict, through to Maxim and Frank's return to Manderley to retrieve the young wife. As John Fletcher (1995: 354) argues, "The film is of course complicit with Maxim's rewriting of the fantasy of Rebecca, completing his punitive erasure of the sexually transgressive woman by producing the medical certification of her cancer, and clearing a space for Fontaine's final accession to full wifely status while denying her the position of Mistress of Manderley." Added to this is the sense that the older female figures in the film resemble fairytale (step)mothers: Mrs. Van Hopper (Cinderella's stepmother); Rebecca (the Evil Queen of 'Snow White') and Mrs. Danvers (the witch, often synonymous with the stepmother, in 'Hansel and Gretel'). While the narrative might be read as fulfilling an Oedipal desire of the heroine's to be rid of the three mother figures that control her, the cyclical return of the film towards regeneration of the marriage suggests that, within this fantasy, the heroine scarcely progresses at all. However, despite this powerful narrative pull, through the spectral images of Rebecca, the film affords access to some of the most engrained and unspeakable taboos in exposing the threat that might be posed by a female who disobeys the rules, who by threatening to break the bloodline threatens the foundations of the ancestral home—prising open a deep-rooted sense of uncertainty about the future.

Rebecca coincided with the tensions brought on by rapidly changing times. In 1928, the Equal Franchise Act had been passed in the UK giving women aged over 21 years the right to vote, thus attaining equal voting rights with men, and some of the increased social freedoms and autonomy for women through the 1920s onwards can be seen embodied in allusions to Rebecca's less inhibited lifestyle and active sporting prowess, including her ability (and preference) to sail singlehandedly. However, women's rights were still very limited within marriage, and *Rebecca* exposes the importance of family heritage and respectability.

While changing times mean that Maxim is threatened to some degree by fear of social gossip, and he confesses to the heroine that Rebecca knew that he could not face a divorce because of what the newspapers might report, he remains supported by an 'old boys' network (potentially getting together for a game of golf with Colonel Julian, Chief Constable of the County, once the case against him is over). Moreover, his friend Frank needs no further explanation concerning what drove Maxim to strike Rebecca other than "she stood there laughing." *Rebecca* sheds light on the horror that lies within rather than outside the home and on the realization that certain forms of entrapment are so entrenched in the familiar—in cultural expectations of ownership and marriage masquerading as 'natural'—that they are (almost) hidden in plain sight. While the film goes some way in restoring the cracks that reveal these secrets, uncertainties linger long after the film's ending.

Such uncertainties resonate throughout the 1940s in the cycle of harrowing Hollywood films, following *Rebecca*, in which the thrill of marrying a virtual stranger transforms into terror upon the discovery that the husband could be a murderer.[12] When the victim proves to be the previous wife, the threat of repetition lurks close beneath the surface,[13] a repetition that is directly referred to in the title of one of the films from the cycle, *The Two Mrs. Carrolls* (Peter Godfrey, 1947). The context of World War II can be seen as a significant backdrop for this cycle of 'Bluebeard films.'[14] As Andrea S. Walsh (1984: 73–74) observes, newspapers portrayed stories of violent war veterans, at a time when there were widespread fears of infidelity, abandonment, and soldiers deserting families. Gender roles were shaken through the 1940s, which saw both the increase of female independence at home and work and the abrupt

---

[12] The 1940s 'persecuted wife' cycle maintains its own uncanny compulsion to repeat, noticed by newspaper critics. In *The New York Times* Bosley Crowther (15 April 1946: 35) criticized the predictability of *Dragonwyck*'s "elemental features of the familiar old tale" with its forbidden tower amounting to a "repetition of the Bluebeard story." *Rebecca*, a reworking of du Maurier's book, itself to some degree a reworking of Brontë's *Jane Eyre* and 'Bluebeard,' would prove to be an inspiration through the 1940s, and beyond.

[13] In some of the films, the husband makes his wife think she is going mad, such as *Gaslight* (George Cukor, 1944) and the British original *Gaslight* (Thorold Dickinson, 1940).

[14] A few days before shooting had begun on *Rebecca*, England declared war on Germany, and although World War II would not come to the US for over two years, it took its toll on the making of the film, casting a shadow over the lives of Hitchcock, and many of the British actors.

end to this brought about by the return of the male breadwinners, which forced women "back to the home after the Armistice" (Diane Waldman 1984: 30).[15] In addition, there were the long-term psychological effects of the violence of war on male veterans to which Elizabeth Bronfen attributes the paranoia and claustrophobia underlying the 1940s cycle of films: "While representations of the threat of domestic violence may have seemed less disturbing to Hollywood than those of the lasting effects of war neurosis, the implications are perhaps more insidious, for they place the danger at the very heart and hearth of the home for which wars are fought" (Bronfen 2009: 137–138). In short, a number of factors, such as hurried pre-war marriages, wartime separation, post-war trauma and the high divorce rate of 1946 (Waldman 1984: 40), created a setting for uncertainty and distrust.

The 'Bluebeard' features bubbling under the surface in *Rebecca*—a film that is prophetic of many of the fears that would drive the decade—are brought to the fore in the 1940s 'persecuted wife' films. Retrospectively, watching the films in succession is a dizzying experience and the narrative becomes uncannily familiar; repetitions appear as direct homages, as if the films converse with each other. As Maria Tatar argues:

> The Bluebeard story, with its heroine who lives with a sinister stranger in a remote castle, provided the perfect plot apparatus for working through the marital crises experienced by men and women whose lives had been unsettled by the war experience. (Tatar 2004: 90)

'Bluebeard' is one of the most horrific but captivating fairy tales ever recounted, with one of the most grisly moments of revelation. Unlike most classical fairy tales, in which marriage is a part of, or even an affirmation of, the 'happily ever after' that denotes the tale's ending, 'Bluebeard' notably begins rather than ends with marriage, morbidly tracing the fate of the young female who marries a rich stranger only to discover her husband's dark secret. In Charles Perrault's version of the fairy tale (first published in 1697), Bluebeard allows his new wife the freedom to go anywhere in his elaborate palace but prohibits her from using the small key to the 'private room' at the end of the

---

[15] Andrea Walsh (1984: 76) notes that with 11 million war veterans returning in the first six months after the war, the unemployment figure rose to 2.7 million, with a significant proportion of job loss being experienced by women.

long gallery in his apartment downstairs, declaring, "I forbid it to you so absolutely that, if you did happen to go into it, there is no knowing what I might do, so angry would I be" (Perrault 2009: 106). While he is away, Bluebeard's new wife unlocks the forbidden door trembling. Initially the closed shutters obscure her view, but gradually she sees clotted blood across the floor, and in it reflected the hanging dead bodies of Bluebeard's previous wives, "whose throats he had cut one after the other" (Perrault 2009: 108). Paralyzed by fear, the young wife drops the key, and it falls in the blood, which she is unable to remove, and it is the sight of this blood that gives away her disobedience to Bluebeard. While female strategy and initiative play a key role in this version, as the new wife plays for time while her sister keeps lookout in the tower for their brothers to come and save her, Perrault ignores this, injecting an authorial voice that emphasizes instead her "temptation" (2009: 108). In the first 'moral' after the tale, formatted in verse form, the narrator addresses female readers on the perils of their curiosity, stating: "the pleasure" is lost once "taken": "And the knowledge you looked for is not worth the cost"[16] (Perrault 2009: 113). In the second 'moral,' he again plays down the husband's brutality, saying that this all happened long ago, and that husbands no longer expect their wives to undertake a task that she cannot do, implying that husbands tend to be more subservient (Perrault 2009: 113). Thus, clearly the way the story is controlled by careful framing has a strong bearing on the precise emphasis and meanings conveyed within the narrative.

In *Rebecca*, the shifting levels of control over the way the story is envisioned are pivotal to the conversation that takes place in the beach cottage, sometimes referred to as the confession sequence, or the revelation scene, in which Maxim chillingly tells his second wife that he was responsible for Rebecca's death. This 'confession' is triggered by the discovery of Rebecca's boat,[17] which contains Rebecca's body, thus highlighting the fact that previously Maxim had incorrectly identified as his wife an unknown drowned woman whose body had washed up on the shore. Storytelling has an uncanny hold in this sequence; cinematic point of view and the framing of shots work together with the dialogue suggesting specific shifts of identification. Although initially shocked, the second

---

[16] Perrault also insinuates that women are essentially nosy.
[17] Rebecca's boat is called 'Je Reviens' in du Maurier's novel.

Mrs. de Winter opts to stand by Maxim to fight the situation together. Gaining confidence, with survival instincts akin to an accomplice, she begins to think through ways of explaining the discovered body. The sequence thus plays an important part in shaping and reshaping who audiences identify with, and the extent to which we (continue to) see Rebecca, ever present in her absence, as a haunting 'other' whose corporal return poses an external threat (to the happiness of the couple).

While it might seem that the heroine gains some power through the sequence, this strength is enabled only through her allegiance with her husband, whose staging of the scenario plays a part in its reception. When the second Mrs. de Winter first opens the door to the cottage, and walks past the shipping tackle to stand in the entrance of the internal door, our identification with her remains intact, and is even intensified, as we share her viewpoint of Maxim sat across the far end of the main room saying "Hello" in a soft voice, looking directly at her (and the camera). At this point, Maxim's control over the situation is not foregrounded—the emphasis being rather (more sympathetically) upon his loss of hope. But a remarkable moment occurs approximately half way (five minutes) through the beach cottage sequence when, in a dramatic monologue, Maxim tells his story of what led to Rebecca's death, and the camera tracks the movements of the absent Rebecca, matching Maxim's account impeccably, but with such staggering blatancy that the cinematography borders on becoming self-reflexive.

Prior to this, the camera and editing techniques are more conventional, conveying the sequence with less obvious intervention. When Maxim tells his wife that he knows the body they have found is Rebecca's, because he put it there, there is a dramatic musical accompaniment (a variation of Rebecca's theme tune), and the heroine stands up and walks away towards the doorframe. She pauses there, holding the door. At this key moment, the heroine's body is in focus, whereas Maxim's head (turned to face her leaving) is at the front left of the frame, but out of focus (see Fig. 4.3).

The camera tilts and pans round to Maxim, and with a subtle lens adjustment, the heroine goes out of focus as Maxim comes into sharp focus, remaining framed in medium close-up, but more centrally positioned, as he turns his head away from her. Maintaining the camera's gaze now, Maxim says, "You see… " and, getting up, "I was right. It's too late…". The camera pans to his movements, keeping him in focus, as he steers further from his wife. There is a cut to a shot of her at

Fig. 4.3 The heroine is at the door, about to leave—*Rebecca* (Alfred Hitchcock, 1940)

the open doorway, about to leave. His words make her turn. Notably, before the heroine rushes back to Maxim, she is stood by the doorway—the threshold to a future away from Maxim. On return viewings of this sequence, we might also note (with a shudder) that she is standing in the precise location, cited by Maxim later in this sequence, of Rebecca's death. The melodramatic force of the love story means that such a key moment—in which the wife almost escapes—is virtually steamrollered by the romanticism of her return. Clasping the edges of his coat, the heroine pleads with her husband that it is not too late: "You're not to say that—I love you more than anything in the world." The heroine looks small, clutching onto Maxim, but he is also childlike—turned away, like a domineering boy. By falling victim to the traditional expectations of a romantic love story, the heroine is positioned as supplicant female, begging, "Please Maxim kiss me please...". Notably, no mention has yet been made of how he caused Rebecca's death, or whether he actively murdered Rebecca; this is withheld until his monologue of events later in this sequence. While this no doubt adds suspense, it also makes it clear that Maxim receives unwavering support from a loyal wife no matter what he has done. In the subtle refocusing of attention onto Maxim's concerns, little overt consideration is given to the fact that the heroine is coaxed back to attend to her husband rather than to take stock of her own shock at the news. At this point, Maxim's manipulation of his wife is neither hidden nor palpably critiqued.

While initially the young wife's response is shock, this is soon substituted by her support of her husband and even her extreme delight when he professes aggressively that he never loved Rebecca. While one ghost is partly laid to rest when Maxim declares that he did not love Rebecca, another haunting terror is released, if only scarcely glimpsed, hinting at the extremely limited choices available for the new wife. Were she to stray from the path, her own life might be at risk—an inkling that would position Rebecca not as a threat but alternatively as an enduring figure of warning of the violence that the husband might be capable of should a wife not behave entirely as he wishes. We might also reflect on the survival mechanisms open to a wife when faced with such knowledge. There are different ways of reading the extreme joy on the heroine's face when Maxim says he did not love Rebecca. There is scope to either embrace the romantic influence and share her joy, or, by the conspicuousness of the cut to the shot of her wide-eyed face breaking into a smile, to be alert to its peculiarity under the circumstances, noting her blindness to the atrocities of the revelation.

Meanwhile, by completely inverting the heroine's impression of Rebecca, from adored beauty to abhorred adulteress, Maxim refocuses attention away from the ruthlessness of his own actions onto the inhumanity of his late wife—presenting her cruel conduct as the root cause of his current predicament. The seediness of the image he presents is enhanced by the setting of his tale. As Fletcher observes, "It is now the dust-laden and cobwebbed beach cottage that is revealed as the site of Rebecca's liaisons, to which Maxim's narrative is relocated from the library (where it takes place in the novel) thus allowing its current state of dilapidation as the scene of narration to contaminate retrospectively the narrated scene" (Fletcher 1995: 352–353). More broadly speaking, beach/boat houses tend to be aligned in 1940s Hollywood with criminal activity and the sexually illicit, as the beach cottage is here.[18] In this instance, the beach cottage represents a gothic duality. As a place set apart from the main house, sunken into the rocks next to the thrashing wild ocean, and hidden from view, it represents the rough and untamed side of Manderley.

The relocation also seems to enable an authentication of Maxim's narrative, by helping to visualize what happened. Leonard J. Leff outlines the great deal of care that went into working out how to film Maxim's explanation of Rebecca's death. Hitchcock reportedly questioned whether conveying it just through Maxim's words would be "sufficient" to maintain audience interest, "or must it be done pictorially, in order to make absolutely sure that we do not lose any sympathy for him?" (Leff 1987: 43). The quandary here, as Leff sees it, is that the audience "might need to see Rebecca in order to comprehend what a heinous woman she was," but it was also important to maintain the novel's ability to "*feel* rather than *see*" Rebecca (43). Added to this is the further layer that Rebecca's absence not only keeps open the terror of her as unseen 'other,' but also contributes to the very uncertainty that challenges such a fixed notion of "heinous woman" that Maxim's narrative visualizes.

Horrified by the idea of a traditional flashback, Hitchcock initially planned to portray "not the incident itself but a refraction of it in time and space," by superimposing with special lighting and other effects a shifting background depicting Maxim's previous physical movements while he continues speaking in close up (Leff 1987: 45). However, bound also to Selznick's desire for a film that would remain faithful to the book "without tricks" (Leff 1987: 53), there was the sense of trying to find a solution, of bringing the confession sequence to life through

---

[18] I am grateful to Leighton Grist, and his conversation with Michael Walker, who drew my attention to this tendency for beach houses to be aligned with the sexually illicit and /or the criminal in 1940s Hollywood, for example: *Mildred Pierce* (Michael Curtiz, 1945), *Murder, My Sweet* (Edward Dmytryk, 1944), *Humoresque* (Jean Negulesco, 1946) and *Daisy Kenyon* (Otto Preminger, 1947). The boat house in *The Reckless Moment* (Max Ophüls, 1949) functions similarly. The building in Hitchcock's *Rebecca* bridges the beach and boat house—described as "a cottage by the sea," with a boat alongside. Such a representation of the boat /beach house seems to be a specifically 1940s phenomenon. It does continue into the 1950s (e.g., *Kiss Me Deadly*, Robert Aldrich, 1955) but with modified narrative connotations. The stables in *Undercurrent* (Vincente Minnelli, 1946), one of the 1940s 'persecuted' wife films, also functions in a structurally similar fashion to the beach cottage in *Rebecca*.

simple visualization of Maxim's words whilst overcoming the issue of what might end up becoming a lifeless monologue. Robert E. Sherwood was employed less than two weeks before production, and came up with the solution of moving the setting to the beach cottage (Leff 1987: 53). This meant that that the camera could give a sense of the events, as they are recounted to have happened, in the same location, drawing attention to the items associated with Rebecca's final moment and the cause of her death, helping to provide a virtual re-enactment or *staging* of the scene.

However, it is also possible to read against the grain of interpreting the scene as authenticating Maxim's words. While unreliable flashbacks are not unknown to the cinema, or even to Hitchcock's work,[19] a flashback, framed by Maxim's accompanying voice-over, would have certainly given more credence to his story. As Helen Hanson (2007, 101) stresses: "In not giving over to flashback, the cottage sequence does not accord Maxim as narrator the power to call up images to illustrate his memories," thus it "prevents a close relationship between spectator and character." Beyond this, it is also possible to view this sequence as a *performance*—with the repeated setting, Maxim's (or Olivier's) acting style and the near self-reflexive camerawork that is used to convey his account functioning as a commentary on story-telling itself. Throughout Maxim's monologue, we are poised between (almost) witnessing what happened, in an uncanny sense, and being aware of the process of this being filmed, and performed. I would suggest that the devices used in this monologue help to maintain a prolonged distancing effect during which it is possible to stand outside the narrative, to see briefly beyond it, revealing a further layer of uncertainty beyond simply absorbing the narrative being recounted. Following this moment, this revelatory process seems to be brought to an end, as the thriller genre takes a firm hold—more directly aligned with the fusing together of the romantic couple trying to escape the hauntings of a powerful first wife.

As Maxim speaks, the camera tracks—in an extended take—the movements of Rebecca on the night of the killing, matching Maxim's staging of events. Maxim begins his report with the story-telling opener, "One night…," which has the effect, as Hanson (2007: 99) observes, of dividing the scene off from the rest of the sequence, with a "discrete narrative" to itself. Maxim tells how he came down intending to have it

---

[19] For example, *Stage Fright* (Hitchcock, 1950) uses an unreliable narrator and flashback. But, the flashback's fictitiousness is revealed later in the film.

out with both Rebecca and her lover, Jack Favell, but finding the former alone, he says—his eyes darting around—"She was lying on the divan." There is a cut to his second wife, who turns her head to look in the direction of the divan, followed by a cut to the divan with a full ashtray centre frame just as Maxim says "A large ashtray of cigarette stubs beside her," as if to authenticate or give substance to his story. Other items seemingly add layers to the story (and the sense of this being Rebecca's haunt)—such as the women's magazine, the spread of cushions on the divan and the silver tea set in the foreground, laid out for receiving visitors. The camera then continues to present Maxim's description of Rebecca's movement, a quick if rather heavy movement up ("suddenly she got up") followed by a taut, slow movement to the left, tracking the windows of the beach cottage, and as he says, "Started to walk toward me," taking a stiff panning action around the corner catching the array of Rebecca's possessions—a large sea shell, two Art Deco vases and a picture of the sea—completing a full turn to encounter Maxim face-to-face. Thus, the camera, triggered by Maxim's words, which initiate the heroine's look, seems to follow Rebecca's actions, shifting seamlessly from matching the eyeline of the heroine's gaze upon the divan to an absent Rebecca. Then, in following Rebecca's actions, the camera moves to a viewpoint that can no longer be the heroine's literal point of view as it takes the semi-circular action to face Maxim. Thus, while it might feel like the camera takes on the role or being of Rebecca, it is determinedly not acting *as* Rebecca, but is rather placed in the position of *viewing* her, as it would have been if it were actually filming events when she was originally present, thus emphasizing her absence.

Indeed, Rebecca's absence is very much pronounced. Tania Modleski (1988: 52) argues that significantly Rebecca is "never sutured in as object of the look"; her absence is "stressed," and also that "the camera pointedly dynamizes Rebecca's absence" (53): "For those under the sway of Mulvey's analysis of narrative cinema, *Rebecca* may be seen as a spoof of the system, an elaborate sort of castration joke, with its flaunting of absence and lack" (53). I would suggest that such a reading is given further justification by the idiosyncratic camerawork, which, in its obviousness and slow clunky style, has a degree of self-reflexivity to it, pushing against the film's naturalism. Initially, the scene is triggered by the second Mrs. de Winter looking to the divan, listening to and imagining Maxim's words. By the end of Maxim's story, the camera is positioned as if it were over her (absent) shoulder in a shot/reverse shot set up with Maxim. Thus, it is clearly not a panning shot from the second Mrs. de Winter's viewpoint. The final cut back to her from the image of the floor (where Rebecca reportedly fell) does allow us her reaction—and we witness the shock on her face as she looks to the floor taking in the revelation—but it also flags up the fact that the camera had no longer been positioned from her viewpoint, but had taken its own journey, jolted into action to mirror Maxim's narration, leaving the heroine's fixed position. The camera's heavy overtness makes this a near self-reflexive moment, provoking awareness not only of Rebecca's absence but also of the camera's presence. This momentary distancing effect helps to draw attention to the manipulative forces of Maxim's narrative, at the point when the heroine's own fears and dreams become subsumed in solving her husband's problems.

Coupled with the distinctive camerawork is Maxim's recount of Rebecca's words (beginning, "I'll do a bargain with you Max… "), which he presents as direct speech, using the first person "I," as if his own, rather than in third person. There are many layers to the effects of this direct speech. Mary Ann Doane (1988: 174)[20] argues that "Just as the tracking subjective shot guarantees that the story of the woman literally culminates as the image of the man, the construction of the dialogue allows Maxim to appropriate Rebecca's 'I.'" Hanson, on the other hand, interprets this scene as Rebecca gaining a presence through her words being performed directly in this way, "Although Rebecca may be spectacularly absent, she asserts an insistent auricular presence" (Hanson 2007: 99). While seemingly contradictory, Doane's and Hanson's readings are both tenable. As Hanson suggests, "The way that Maxim/Laurence Olivier distinctly produces Rebecca's voice as different to his own frustrates a clear and canny tie up of masculine voice and male body: Rebecca's voice occupies, invades and talks *through* Maxim" (106–107) with this "ventriloquism of Maxim by Rebecca" (108).[21] As Hanson goes on to unveil, Maxim's (or Olivier's) voice—in its vulnerably confessional style in this scene—"is much closer to what is considered an appropriate *feminine* style" (111) while Rebecca's voice and speech conveys a more stereotypically masculine aligned control of range and lack

[20] A revised version of this chapter, '*Caught* and *Rebecca*: The Inscription of Femininity as Absence,' was published in Constance Penley (ed.) (1988) *Feminism and Film Theory* (New York and London: Routledge and BFI publishing), pp. 196–215.

[21] Fletcher (1995) and Tatar (2004) also use the word 'ventriloquism' in this context.

of emotion, with the effect of a "haunting possession" that takes place "across gender" (112). She suggests that the "paradoxical" element of this is that Maxim is much more feminized when he presents his own words than when he produces Rebecca's (112). I would suggest that in addition to this inversion or "haunting possession" across genders, the process of ventriloquism itself might also be seen to work both ways. If, as Hanson suggests, Rebecca's words speak through Maxim, then there is the sense that he becomes her puppet, under her control. However, in the sense that it remains Maxim's voice, exaggerating or scripting Rebecca's words, he instruments the framing of the story, thus "appropriating" as Doane suggests, and possibly *shaping*, the representation of Rebecca. Blurring roles further, Maxim (Olivier) stands and gestures exactly as he says Rebecca did (hand in pocket smoking a cigarette), effecting a strange affinity between Rebecca and Maxim. Maxim has shared experiences with Rebecca, is of a similar class, and knows something of the London scene (he is still going to London for business) that he tries so hard to keep separate from Manderley. Indeed, he reveals that it was not such a problem when Rebecca kept her liaisons in London (where perhaps times were progressively changing) but on home territory he must have the semblances of tradition maintained. This doubling effect of Maxim's direct echoing and mirroring of Rebecca also helps to foreground the fact that Rebecca transgressed norms of acceptability because they were similar, and she tried to behave autonomously on (his) home territory. Maxim's citation of her phrase, "What a leg pull Max," suggests she saw herself as able to jest like a man.

In its level of excess, the theatricality of Olivier's performance also has a self-reflexive edge to it. Maxim's monologue culminates with his recital of Rebecca's final provocation, "Well Max. *What* are you going to do about it? Aren't you going to kill me?" He is mechanical in his delivery, and is not facing the heroine. His body becomes quite limp, and "his eyes flit upwards, as if he is going to swoon" (Hanson 2007: 112) as he says:

> I suppose I went mad for a moment [*he looks slightly downwards*]. I must have [*he looks right down and across the floor*] struck her [*he says briskly*].[22]

---

[22] The words in italics indicate my own description of Maxim's actions.

Olivier's delivery and performance of these lines is particularly striking.[23] His swift but sweeping look across the floor of the room they are in provides both the sense that he is trying to see something he could mention to add weight to the description and that he is confused about what exactly happened. As he recounts the fact that Rebecca started towards him again "smiling," he leans, gently edging the door backwards, and says, "suddenly she stumbled and fell." At the same time, he pushes back the door abruptly, which makes a noise to match with the sound that Rebecca's falling body would have made, and the camera pans down to reveal the ship's tackle on the floor that had been hidden behind the door (followed by the cut back to the heroine looking on aghast). He tells the heroine that it was then that he realized Rebecca had struck her head on a piece of ship's tackle; he had wondered why she was still smiling, but then realized she was dead. The heroine quickly deduces that her husband did not kill Rebecca, announcing, "It was an accident!" This summation of the act as an accident was a move to appease Hollywood's Motion Picture Production Code (published 31 March 1930), which would not allow a murderer to get away with their crime unpunished, and thus represents another key departure from du Maurier's novel, in which Maxim confesses to shooting Rebecca (du Maurier 1975: 293). However, I would suggest that the combined effects of Maxim's/ Olivier's excessive, theatrical performance style and the conspicuously laborious camerawork during the monologue help to question or negate this summation. As Leff (1987: 54) asserts, the length of the monologue "sustains tension by counterpointing the agitato of de Winter's narrative and the legato of the camera's languorous movement." However, this counterpointing device can also have a distancing effect, laying bare cinema's storytelling mechanisms, making us reassess the authenticity of the narrative at the same time that it is unremittingly professed and enforced.

Although the sequence seals the couple's union, more sinister qualities can be inferred from this moment when Maxim supposes he went mad. Tatar (2004: 84) points out that Maxim's account of his own actions is "the only tentative statement about what happened that night"; he is "curiously unsure," whereas his account of the events and

---

[23] It is worth noting the contrast with Olivier's performance style up to this point in the film, which has a more brooding tone, reminiscent of Olivier's performance as Heathcliff the year before, as noted by Nugent (*The New York Times*) seeing both characters (Maxim and Heathcliff) as "a study in dark melancholy" (1940: 25).

Rebecca's words are "precise." She suggests that while the truth remains uncertain, there are signs that he might have actually strangled Rebecca, and that the camera's focus upon the coils of rope "seems to give the lie to Maxim's story" (Tatar 2004: 84).[24] It is perhaps impossible to unravel any final, concrete evidence in the film that could prove a case of strangling, specifically, but I agree there are signs that cast doubt on the explicit narrative being told in Maxim's monologue. Robin Wood had similar suspicions when he reconsidered *Rebecca* in *Hitchcock Revisited*: "Maxim de Winter, having killed Rebecca (we must I think accept the logic of the narrative against the 'evidence' of an accident imposed on it to pacify the censor), can relate only to a child-wife who unquestioningly adores him and over whom he can exert control" (Wood 2002: 231, endnote 7). Looking at plot formations in Hitchcock films, he comments that if the level of the woman's guilt means she has to die, there is no film in which the man directly kills her himself but that the "logic of *Rebecca* is clearly that he *did*" (2002, 244), despite the change from the novel. Wood adopts a position that implies two levels of understanding: the first, based around "evidence" (that there are no conscious pointers to denote that Maxim is lying), is thrown into disarray by the "logic of the narrative." These different readings help draw attention to the specific instances of cinematic ambiguity that emanate from Hollywood's resourceful management of the Motion Pictures Production Code.

The purpose of the Production Code was to ensure the maintenance of moral principles, declaring that no motion picture should incite sympathy with criminal activity.[25] However, as Richard Maltby observes, the Code also served to invite filmmakers to find "strategies of ambiguity"

---

[24] Tatar's suggestion (2004: 84) that if Rebecca did fall, she would have had to move behind Maxim to open the door would hold weight had the door previously been shut, and Tatar further speculates that the rope the heroine took when she previously went into the boathouse (to use as a lead for the dog) might have been the murder weapon. Tatar's argument that this would be a fitting Hitchcock motif is a compelling one that led me to re-watch the scene. Chillingly, I could not see in the shot of the rope on the heroine's first visit any hard piece of tackle—just rope. (Of course, there is always the chance that it is just out of the frame.)

[25] 'A Code to Maintain Social and Community Values in the Production of Silent, Synchronized and Talking Motion Pictures,' adopted by the Association of Motion Picture Producers, Inc. (MPPDA), at Hollywood, California, and ratified by the Board of Directors of Motion Picture Producers and Distributors of America, Inc., March 31, 1930.

that would enable different layers of understanding without presenting licentious material openly:

> Much of the work of self-regulation in the 1930s and 1940s lay in the maintenance of this system of conventions, which operated, however perversely, as an enabling mechanism at the same time that it was a repressive one. As Production Code Administration director Joseph Breen persistently argued, the Code was not so much a system of censorship as an alternative to one: a system by which socially sensitive subjects could be represented on the screen, with their censurable content coded and codified so as to avoid censorship. (Maltby 2003: 473)

The further layer to this is the knowledge that the film is an adaptation from du Maurier's book, which acts as a reminder of 'change' (from the 'original')–from murder to 'accident'—no matter how independently the film is considered. As Maltby (2003: 475) outlines, "In the case of adaptations from novels, the repressed of the text might often be the original story, the 'unsuitable' or 'objectionable' elements of which had been removed in the process of adapting it to the screen." Indeed, for many, du Maurier's work haunts the revelation sequence and the film as a whole, all the more so in the places of differentiation. There is a similar incidence in *Suspicion* (Hitchcock, 1941), a film (also starring Fontaine) adapted from Francis Iles' novel *Before the Fact* (1932). *Suspicion* is linked with the 1940s 'persecuted wife' cycle, but ends with the disclosure that, rather than plotting his wife's murder, Johnnie (Cary Grant) had been planning his own suicide—a final twist that never quite matches up to the build-up of the preceding narrative.[26] In *Rebecca*'s beach cottage sequence, there is a residual ambiguity, that Maxim is scripting or fixing a memory, that the whole framing of the sequence might be seen as staged by Olivier's performance, and—as a play on the restrictions of the Code—the overt cinematography used to vivify Maxim's monologue adds a further layer to the words he actually says.

At no point does the film openly pause to question whether Maxim should have struck Rebecca, but the threat remains (as an unspoken

---

[26]Waldman (1984: 33) observes that every newspaper reviewer groaned about the conflict between the ending and the rest of the film.

taboo): stray from the position of loyal wife and your life may be in danger. The heroine's words about Rebecca, instigated by the urge to soothe Maxim—"She can't speak... She can't bear witness..."—possess a chilling irony. In one respect, Rebecca *has* spoken (through Maxim). But in actuality we have not heard her version of events. As Tatar argues, "the heroine's words betray her own intuition that the victim might have a story very different from that of the husband" (Tatar 2004: 84). The grisly spectacle of the dead previous wives in the 'Bluebeard' tale triggers a double revelation: simultaneously the husband's brutal past and the new threat—the imminent death of Bluebeard's current wife. Opening the door is a performative act, the effect of which is highly dependent on the heroine's reaction. The horror of the 'other' (the spectacle) signals the threat to the 'self.' Opening the door is thus also a necessary process in order to survive. Knowledge of the husband's previous crime/s transforms the wife into both a potential victim and someone who can raise alarm. In *Rebecca*, the new Mrs. de Winter now knows the secret and can act upon it, in the sense that she gains confidence and starts to plan ways to ensure the stability of their marital relationship. Maxim now, for the first time in the film, finally declares his love, slowly—"I have loved you.... I will always love you"—(notably not using the present tense), as if perhaps finding the script, to bring his wife on board as his accomplice. This heroine stands stalwartly by her husband, but the decision also provokes a shudder. The heroine's complicity with a fantasy that maintains patriarchal structures means that she fails to break the cycle; she represses her desire to identify with Rebecca, and the idea that she could be like her. The horror is that she shows no conscious realization of this. Furthermore, the heroine's opportunities in life are extremely limited, as implied in Maxim's blithe but patronizing proposal of marriage near the start of the film, shouted at the heroine from the bathroom of his hotel suite in Monte Carlo, "Either you go to America with Mrs. Van Hopper or you come home to Manderley with me." Although she shows no sign of consciously realizing it, the myth of romantic love entwined with maternal concern that inclines the heroine towards supporting Maxim in the final stages of the film might be her only chance of survival.[27]

[27]That such a motivation is not illuminated in the beach cottage sequence as a survival strategy has led me away from interrogating further parallels in this instance with the Grimms' 'Fitcher's Bird,' a tale similar to 'Bluebeard' but for the detail that the heroine deceives Fitcher into believing she has not disobeyed the interdiction. As Pauline Greenhill (2008: 150)

The concept of a cyclical repetition continues through the 'persecuted wife' films of the 1940s. The parallels between wives in *The Two Mrs. Carrolls* are explicitly reinforced with the repeated pattern of Geoffrey (Humphrey Bogart) painting each wife as the 'Angel of Death' as he plots their murder.[28] His artwork is 'representational' of his changed perspective once the honeymooning period is over, casting a shadow of death, with each wife represented as more abjectly crazed or sexualized (dressed in black, baring skeletally defined flesh) than her real life counterpart, helping him justify his actions. The second wife, Sally (Barbara Stanwyck), plays quite an active role, working out that her husband's new mistress, Cecily, has visited, even though the maid denies this, and while helping Geoffrey's daughter, Bea, pack for her new school, in a series of revelations she finds out the first wife had not been "an invalid since the birth of her daughter" as her husband had claimed, but had been extremely active prior to becoming ill very suddenly. Together, Sally and Bea take the key and find 'The Angel of Death' that has been locked in Geoffrey's studio away from public view. It is thus the repetition (the painting's likeness with the painting of his late wife) that confirms her fear that he aims to kill her, and Geoffrey announces his intentions outright when he bursts through her bedroom window in a terrifying vampire-like intrusion of her privacy towards the end of the film. In *Secret Beyond the Door* (Fritz Lang, 1947), the bedroom of the new wife, Celia (Joan Bennett), is an exact replica of his late wife's. When Celia first encounters the murder room that her husband Mark (Michael Redgrave) has hidden in the forbidden 'Room 7,' it seems to be proof that he murdered his first wife. However, Celia spots that the candle has been burned down in precisely the same way that she had burned the candle in her own room, melting the wax to gain an imprint of the forbidden key. The murder room is a replica of her bedroom, rather than the late wife's, and thus in one uncanny moment she realizes

---

stresses, "Women's duplicity, feminine duplicity, is not only powerful; it is also a primary survival strategy." In addition, while the second Mrs. de Winter's decision to keep her visit to Rebecca's room secret from her husband also comes close to paralleling this duplicity, I suggest that her conscious survival motivation revolves around conformity rather than support of an autonomous sisterhood.

[28] In *Bluebeard* (Edgar G. Ulmer, 1944), the protagonist is also an artist, justifying his crazed behaviour for the sake of his art.

that her husband is intending to kill *her*. This switch of perception, to realizing that something 'other' is in fact linked to the 'self', mirrors 'Bluebeard' but also resonates with an anecdote by Sigmund Freud in 'The Uncanny' (first published in 1919) about a time when he was astonished to realize that "an elderly gentleman in a dressing gown and travelling cap" he saw entering his train compartment by mistake was not actually an "intruder" but in fact his "own image, reflected in the mirror on the connecting door" (Freud 2003: 162, endnote III 1). He suggests that the "displeasure" caused by such an unexpected image of the self indicates an ancient uncanny response to the "double" (Freud 2003: 162, endnote III 1). In both *The Two Mrs. Carrolls* and *Secret Beyond the Door*, drawing on 'Bluebeard,' the new wife's sudden realization of the identical features shared with the previous wife helps her confront, however uncomfortably, the threat to herself. We share this moment of realization and the horrifying sense of the uncanny it simultaneously provokes.

The sense of the uncanny works differently in *Rebecca*. The ominous threat to the heroine, implied by the uncanny doubling of the two Mrs. de Winters, can be sensed throughout the film, but the crucial moment of realization glimpsed in the beach cottage sequence is bypassed by the heroine, as Maxim's presence and narration of events steers her attention. Cristina Bacchilega (1997: 107) suggests a reading of 'Bluebeard' that focuses on the forbidden chamber rather than the bloody key, seeing the "central motif" as: "a process of initiation which *requires* entering the forbidden chamber ... The heroine's knowledge of her husband, of herself, and of sexual politics is what matters." In the beach cottage sequence, the second Mrs. de Winter survives merely by repressing knowledge, and Maxim's brutality is overshadowed by Rebecca's unspeakable deviancies, in a cycle of perpetual renewal. Witnessing the heroine's repression of the realization in the beach cottage makes the sequence all the more horrific, as our sense of the uncanny is not shared with the heroine.

While the heroine's point of view seems to frame the early parts of *Rebecca*, via the voice-over and dream sequence leading into the film as flashback, the film sees a breakdown of clearly identifiable roles. The heroine is not much of an active agent in her engagement and early marriage, but in Proppian terms she shares some alignments with the 'hero,' in common with the young wife in 'Bluebeard.' The "interdiction... addressed to the hero" (Vladímir Propp 2008: 26) occurs when Maxim shouts at his new wife earlier in the film, forbidding her to ever go down to the beach cottage again. Thus, when she does return, it could be said that the "interdiction is violated" (Propp 2008: 27). However, when she finds Maxim sitting calmly, it is almost as though he has prepared for her arrival; the lights are on; the door is not locked. While this might appear very different to the fairy tale 'Bluebeard,' in which the crux of suspense and horror forms around the wife's disobedience being found out, it also sheds light on the moral idiosyncrasies of Perrault's tale, because Bluebeard is clearly testing his new wife to see if she will disobey him, or be unfaithful.

Propp's findings also suggest that the 'villain' usually enters the story via the event of violating the interdiction (Propp 2008: 27), but distinct notions of 'villain' and 'hero' are shaken up in *Rebecca*, as a further set of repetitions come to the surface.[29] In the fairy tale, Bluebeard is exposed as 'villain' for murdering his previous wives, but in fearing for her own life, his wife is forced to hide her violation of his rules, and is thus exposed by him for going against his order. The young wife uses initiative to stall for more time, which finally brings about her escape, thus affirming the notion of Bluebeard as villain, and she remarries—this time "a man of true worth" (Perrault 2009: 103). Maxim, on the other hand, confesses by villainizing Rebecca, saying that Rebecca's behaviour probably drove him mad: "It doesn't bode for sanity does it—living with the devil." The way Maxim plays his confession by actively luring the heroine in, utilizing the props and his own body to aid the visualization of Rebecca's movements, blurs the boundaries further between hero and villain. Moreover, in one further twist, Maxim's narrative casts Rebecca in a role that likens *her* to Bluebeard, in the sense that he says the secret of Rebecca's hidden self ("Incapable of love, or tenderness… or decency") was only revealed just after they were married. With a lighthearted tone to his voice, Maxim reveals that the place where he and the heroine first met (on the clifftop) was the exact spot that Rebecca first told him all about herself on their honeymoon—"everything…"; things he says he "would never tell a living soul…". The comment passes scarcely noticed, played down by the relatively cheery scoring at this point. It is only in retrospect that it might dawn on an audience that it is odd for Maxim to return to the same area, if he is trying to forget, let

---

[29] Propp (2008: 27) suggests, "The villain(s) may be a dragon, a devil, bandits, a witch, or a stepmother, etc."

alone to propose to the heroine, fleetingly marry and have a repeat honeymoon there as well.

Sigmund Freud describes "unintentional return" as one feature of the uncanny "that recalls the helplessness we experience in certain dream-states," citing a time when wandering through a small Italian town he kept accidentally returning to the same red light district to the point where it drew unwanted attention (Freud 2003: 144). In *Rebecca*, it is only in retrospect that such knowledge provides an uncanny sense of repetition or circularity to their first meeting and a further nauseous dimension to the home movie of the honeymoon with its haunting image of the happy couple—a sensation that is not consciously shared by Maxim or the heroine. The retrospective awakening to the uncanny instances of repetition in *Rebecca* positions us outside the characters' conscious experiences, a cyclical position resonating with the heroine's dream of returning to Manderley at the start of the film.

The remarriage of the heroine at the end of Perrault's 'Bluebeard' signifies change. The new worthy husband replaces Bluebeard, who is represented as decidedly unique in his evil ways. Despite its conservative tendencies, *Rebecca* can be seen as ahead of its time so far as questioning strict, essentialist notions of good and evil with its complex, gothic levels of ambiguity that bring to prominence the cyclical elements of the fairy tale. In many films of the 1940s cycle, the 'persecuted wife' finds a new husband at the narrative's close, completing the happy ending. He must be seen to represent a pleasant (if sometimes more bland) alternative to the ogre she has been married to, thus reinforcing the ideology that she simply chose the wrong man, and that things will improve. Conforming to the classical versions of 'Cinderella,' 'Sleeping Beauty' and 'Snow White,' the male hero often saves the woman (*The Two Mrs. Carrolls*). Sometimes he solves the mystery as a detective pointing out to her the Bluebeard ways of her current husband (*Gaslight*, George Cukor, US, 1944)[30], or he is a trustworthy doctor (*Experiment Perilous*, Jacques Tourneur, 1944; *Dragonwyck*, Joseph L. Mankiewicz, 1946; and *Caught*, Max Ophüls, 1949).[31] However, in spite of this tendency for a conventional ending,

---

[30] In *Gaslight* (Thorold Dickinson, UK, 1940), it is the former detective who solves the riddle and 'saves' her.

[31] *When Strangers Marry* (William Castle, 1944) offers a notable twist on this arrangement: the husband who seems criminal turns out to be fine, and the seemingly benign friend (albeit played by Robert Mitchum) is the dangerous one.

repetitions in the cycle can sometimes be exposed, such as the seeming hastiness in the forming of the new couple, when as Waldman argues, "the narrative comes dangerously (is unintentionally) close to suggesting that the pattern will be repeated" (Waldman 1984: 37). As Waldman observes, *Experiment Perilous* ends with an "idyllic country scene" that virtually mirrors the earlier flashback of the courtship of the heroine with the previous (villainous) husband (Waldman 1984: 37). Thus, in some of the films of the cycle, as in *Rebecca*, there is an unspoken undercurrent that there is a repeated cycle, whereby the heroine may be susceptible to making the same mistake all over again.

Secret Beyond the Door pushes this sense of cyclical return to an extreme point when (like *Rebecca*) the wife is seen recoupled with the same husband: Celia 'solves' the mystery of Mark with a psychoanalytic reading, attributing his urge to kill her to a time when he mistakenly thought his mother had locked him in his bedroom when she went out on a date.[32] When Celia exposes this misunderstanding, she finds a way of understanding the tenderness beneath the dangers her husband poses to her, indicated in the new position they take at the end of the film, with Mark's head rested on Celia's lap, similar to illustrations and images of 'Beauty and the Beast.'[33] The pietà-like final image suggests that the tensions within marriage are to some extent resolved by the wife becoming the mother figure in the relationship, seemingly solving both the mystery of his changed relationship with his first wife since his return from the war, and his feeling of being hemmed in by women all his life, and having been abandoned.[34] The need for the mother figure can thus be seen in context of returning home from war experiences.[35]

[32] Some approaches to the film (Jenkins 1981; Doane 1988) see the point when Celia's voiceover is replaced by Mark's as the point when he replaces her as the central subject, marking the death of "female subjectivity" (Doane 1988: 151). By contrast, Tom Gunning (2000: 360) suggests that her interior monologue ends, because she finds a new active voice and can now voice "out loud."

[33] John Cocteau's *La Belle et la Bête / Beauty and the Beast* was released in 1946.

[34] The uncanny presence of the actor Michael Redgrave who plays Mark adds to the notion of the split identity, recalling the ventriloquist he played in the final 'segment' of *Dead of Night* (Alberto Cavalcanti, Charles Crichton, Basil Dearden, Robert Hamer, 1945).

[35] It is possible to suggest that Mark's contradictory feelings of having been abandoned by the mother and overpowered by women resonated with contradictory reactions to war at the time, as Walsh highlights: Christian Dior's 'New Look' (padded bra, tiny waist) caused women's picketing (Walsh 1984: 77) amidst a dominant ideology "stressing nurturance of and loyalty to the 'right man'" (Walsh 1984: 168).

In solving her husband's psychological disturbance, Celia has also "regained a sexually active husband" (Walker 1990: 26). Nevertheless, as Walker (1990: 29) goes on to conclude, "it is the husband's view of the wife/wives that is paramount beyond the door." Celia's own desires seem to be abandoned; her attraction to the stranger cannot be reconciled with the pietà-like final image. As Tatar (2004: 104) argues, Celia's desire is linked to danger, violence and death: "Mark represents the fulfilment of erotic desires in large part because he also represents the threat of death."[36] However, his taming at the end sees an end to the importance of Celia's erotic desires. The final arrangement envisages female desire as a threat that must be repressed by a cyclical 'return' to a maternal role. Moreover, in a striking reminder of *Rebecca*, the couple are in exactly the same location as their honeymoon near the start of the film and, as du Plessis (1990: 68) notes, the "boxed in quality" of the final scene is intensified by the repeated tolling bell and the same hacienda honeymoon fountain.[37] Thus, while the film ends with the honeymoon image, linking to a classical fairy tale 'happy ending,' the couple are also in a state of limbo—with an uncertainty about where they are going, suggesting the degree of stasis and confusion following the war.[38] The notion that the complexity of women's desires seems scarcely to have been explored appears to be expressed when in response to Mark saying that he still has a long way to go, Celia corrects him: "*We* have a long way to go."[39]

---

[36] Elizabeth Bronfen (2009: 145) also reads the film as Celia's desire for death: "her own alienness mirrored in her husband's behaviour"—a repressed side that is "strange to herself."

[37] Michael du Plessis (1990) also picks up on the sexual undercurrents, raising doubt over Mark's seeming final 'cure': "Mark's case is perhaps too easily opened and shut" (du Plessis 1990: 50). He also suggests that the film opens the door to Mark's latent homosexuality only to close it again by the end of the film: "*Secret Beyond the Door* keeps its secrets secret" (du Plessis 1990: 65).

[38] The cyclical theme can be traced back in cinema history to *Barbe-bleue / Bluebeard* (Georges Méliès, 1901) when the dead women revive and immediately receive new husbands.

[39] Hitchcock's *Rebecca* haunts *Secret Beyond the Door* as much as Rebecca haunts *Rebecca*; Celia's opening of the curtains has the chilling effect of repetition, with the bricked up window marking a change from the open window that faces the heroine in Rebecca. Here Celia is blocked in, and cannot jump out of the window.

The cycle of repression and desire is crucial in *Rebecca*, explored through the differences between the female characters, but also through the blurring of boundaries between them. By virtue of her seeming kindness (as noted by Frank), the heroine, akin to Cinderella and Snow White, survives to the end. However, while the foundations set up to identify with the young and inexperienced heroine, ostensibly casting Rebecca as external threat, fixed notions of the innocent new wife versus a duplicitous predecessor break down as parallels between the two wives emerge. Polarities associated with classical fairy tales are frequently undercut through the blurring of roles and, as Pauline Greenhill (2008: 164) argues, "Multiple experiences make for multiple knowledges" and "the multiple reflections and reproductions in fairy tales implicate multiple truths." The heroine makes tentative steps to express a more active side—we see her sketch the notably iconic, androgynous female hero Joan of Arc and then cross the image out as a possible idea for the costume ball.[40] The doubling of the two Mrs. de Winters is visualized in the subversion of the classical Cinderella fairy tale at the costume ball. On Danvers' advice, the heroine copies the outfit worn in the portrait of Caroline de Winter, inadvertently infuriating her husband by mirroring Rebecca who had dressed identically at a previous ball, and causing Maxim's sister Beatrice to exclaim 'Rebecca!' On one level, the return of the repressed relates to Maxim:

> It's as if the trauma of seeing the heroine as Rebecca's 'ghost' triggers the return of the repressed. And it is this which prompts Maxim's confession to the heroine, a confession in which, we note, he shows no contrition. (Walker 2005: 209)

As Walker notes, the doubling brings the couple closer, but also emphasizes how much like a villain Maxim really is, showing "no contrition" (2005: 209). Taking this further, I suggest that the doubling of the women multiplies as it also highlights the similar predicaments facing the three female de Winters (Caroline, Rebecca and the unnamed heroine),

---

[40] See, for example, Marina Warner's examination of Joan of Arc as a figure whose multiple roles and representations highlight the "present classification system" of strict female types: "She is anomalous in our culture, a woman renowned for doing something of her own, not by birthright. She has extended the taxonomy of female types; she makes evident the dimension of women's dynamism" (Warner 1981: 9).

and beyond this working through multiple generations of females, bringing to mind Freud's final postulation on the uncanny and the compulsion to return and repeat: "the constant recurrence of the same thing, the repetition of the same facial features, the same characters, the same destinies, the same misdeeds, even the same names, through successive generations" (Freud 2003: 142).

Rebecca's lover, Favell, is a key figure in casting doubt on many of the fairytale myths and fixed, essentialist roles perpetuated through the course of the film. As a car salesman, he functions on one level as the villainous capitalist predator whose blackmailing threatens the security of the new couple but, as he tells the heroine, he is not such a "big bad wolf." He also offers a cunning insight into and critique of established behaviours and traditions: he shows that Maxim has a violent temper by easily inciting him to punch him; he recognizes that the second Mrs. de Winter is not such an innocent 'Cinderella' and speaks candidly in front of her; he hints that there was some interest from Maxim's 'loyal' friend Frank towards Rebecca and that it was possible that he had been shunned by her rather than the other way round. He knows exactly how Maxim, "George Fortescue Maximilian de Winter," would react to Rebecca's taunt, concluding, "Like the gentleman of the old school that he is—he killed her." His authentic shock at the suicide verdict in connection with Rebecca's death is evident in his mocking tone when he telephones Danvers: "Now Max and that dear little bride of his will be able to stay on at Manderley and live happily ever after." The irony that we witness here is that Maxim's "dear little bride" cannot be contained forever; Favell's comment at once reinstates the myth that the honeymoon period has not ended and reminds us of Maxim's attempts to freeze his wife's youth and inexperience.

In the final scene of the film, the couple embrace as someone calls out, "Look! The West Wing!" There is a cut from them turning to look, to a shot of the flames with the silhouette of Danvers at the window. The camera tracks along the outside from window to window with Danvers moving, arms waving, through the flames, until she pauses at an open window, and stands still, looking up. There is a cut to her viewpoint of the glowing timbers falling down above her, followed by a shot across Rebecca's room. The camera tracks forward through the flames, past a table and chair, against the sounds of the crunching flames and crashing furniture, as the camera arrives at the grand bed, which dissolves to the nightgown case embroidered with the letter 'R.' The 'R' creeps back through the flames, resistant, until "The End" materializes before the blaze. As Fletcher argues, "despite the erasure of Rebecca at the level of the plot, the film returns in its closing shots to that negligee and its embroidered cover… the site of its most highly charged and most taboo moment." (354) The reigning 'R' registers the eponymous but absent Rebecca, suggesting both the repression and irrepressibility of the past.

It is apt that the film should end with the burning of Rebecca's room, reminding us of a further doubling in the sense that there are two Bluebeard rooms in the film. When Maxim goes to London on business, the heroine enters what to her seems the forbidden territory of Rebecca's bedroom in the grand West Wing overlooking the sea. The rooms of the suite engulf her in their enormity and modern, pristine white grandeur. The heroine enters alone. There is a close up on the keyhole and door handles, of the two dwarfing white doors, as she passes first through the unlocked doors, and then through the floating floor-to-ceiling transparent lace screen that partitions the room (peeping through it as if it were an enormous wedding veil, or slip), past Rebecca's bed. Rebecca's potency as the mature, sexual mother figure overwhelms the heroine. In entering this room, the heroine feels she is trespassing and confronts what she dreads most—evidence of Maxim's passionate love for Rebecca—but we also witness the heroine's desires to discover everything about Rebecca's intimate life. She opens the curtains halfway letting in some light, and then a window as if to sense the breeze that Rebecca would have felt. Following the sudden tapping of the window against the sill, Danvers' abrupt appearance is unsettling, and fills the heroine with renewed dread. Danvers' dark silhouetted appearance through the transparent screen is represented as sinister, and almost predatory, as she enters through to the private bedroom, opening the other curtains fully, in an act of unadulterated exposure. However, Mrs. Danvers ('Danny' to Rebecca and Favell) must be seen as a conduit for the heroine's desires as well as her fears, appearing not only as a demon to haunt her but also as a summoned genie, demanding: "D'you wish anything madam?" The tour she provides of the room, tempting the heroine to look closely at Rebecca's private items including her lingerie, speaks to the heroine's uncomfortable desires to know, and get close to, Rebecca's secret sexuality.

Although largely quashed by the end of the film, strong inferences can be drawn from this sequence regarding the possibilities opened up by multiple identities, expressed here by Mrs. Danvers' homosexual desire for Rebecca, coded carefully to play along with the guidelines of Joseph I. Breen, who administered the Production Code. Breen had stipulated in a letter to Selznick:

> [I]t will be essential that there be no suggestion whatever of a perverted relationship between Mrs. Danvers and Rebecca. If any possible hint of this creeps into this scene, we will of course not be able to approve the picture. Specifically, we have in mind Mrs. Danvers' description of Rebecca's physical attributes, her handling of the various garments, particularly the night gown. (Breen, cited in Rhona J. Berenstein 1998: 18)[41]

Rebecca meets this challenge in a bizarre fusion of codes: matching those of transgressive suggestion with religious purity. The sequence provides, in abundance and excess, an exhibition (if not a consummation) of the heroine's repressed desires. Danvers keeps the room preserved as it was on the last night, replenished with fresh flowers, but it is also a preserved image of bridal perfection embalmed before the heroine in a synthesis of both the expected sacrosanctity and passion traditionally associated with new marriage. Allusions to sex are filtered through the euphemism of ritualized marriage—enforced by the tall church-like windows, the alter-like dressing table, and the photograph of Maxim perched like an altered icon, duplicated in Rebecca's glamorous mirror, returning the heroine's gaze, as the heroine picks up and then quickly replaces the hairbrush. The heroine turns away when she sees the photograph. Despite the heroine's fears of transgression, Danvers states that she has never been barred from this room:

> You've always wanted to see this room haven't you madam. Why didn't you ask me to show it to you? I was ready to show it to you every day.[42]

---

[41] Letter from Joseph I. Breen to David O. Selznick dated 25 September 1939, Motion Picture Association of America (MPAA) file, Margaret Herrick Library, Los Angeles, cited in Rhona J. Berenstein (1998: 18).

[42] Indeed, as Walker (2005: 276) observes, there are no references to any house keys in *Rebecca*. This omission may be to protect "Maxim's status as patriarch: Danvers's power is not a threat to him" (Walker 2005: 277). It also suggests that it is the heroine's own repressed fears that make her hesitate about entering the room rather than any physical barrier.

Danvers' words imply a freedom of choice that has always been there. As she shows the heroine Rebecca's dressing room, strong sensual suggestions underline the touching of Rebecca's fur coat to her own face (to the gentlest score of bell music) and then to the heroine's. Danvers' next three statements, consisting each of two short sentences, contain a remarkable exhibition of coded creativity and constraint. The first sentence (if spoken in isolation) is subversive. The second comes in to rescue or legitimate the first, stamping out the subversive reading, like a punchline:

> Feel this [*she touches the fur to their faces*].[43] It was a Christmas present from Mr de Winter.
>
> I keep her underwear on this side. They were made especially for her by the nuns of the convent of St Clare.
>
> I always used to wait up for her no matter how late. Sometimes she and Mr de Winter didn't come home until dawn.

The reference to the nuns of St. Clare seems to provide a near-comical appeal to Breen's Catholic sensibilities, and a further nod to Hitchcock's own Catholic background. Danvers herself is also dressed slightly like a nun from that order.[44] Her closeness to Rebecca is also indicated by her revelation that she embroidered the nightgown case herself. As she brings out the nightgown from its case, her comment about it being delicate masks the sexual dimension of its see-through quality: "Did you ever see anything so delicate? Look you can see my hand through it."

As Yvonne Griggs argues, Mrs. Danvers' taunting of the heroine with Rebecca's silk underwear "provides a subtle yet powerful exploration of the novel's sexual dalliance with homosexual desire at a time when such matters could not be addressed openly" (2016: 51). Nevertheless, there are hints that on the film's release, newspaper critics picked up on a hidden element to Mrs. Danvers' devotion to Rebecca. For instance, Frank S. Nugent (1940: 25) in *The New York Times* asserts that du Maurier's novel "demanded a film treatment evocative of a menacing

---

[43] The words in italics indicate my own description of Mrs. Danvers' actions.

[44] This is perhaps another subtle jest, but can also been read in relation to the notion that joining a convent offered sometimes one of the few alternative lifestyles (or means to survive) for women.

mood, fraught with all manner of hidden meaning" and later suggests that Judith Anderson's spine when playing Mrs. Danvers is "menacingly rigid." The term 'menace' was used frequently in reviews of the film and specifically in relation to Danvers' taunting of the heroine, suggesting a meaning beyond simply a danger or threat; Desley Deacon (2012: 48) argues that: "'Menace,' indeed, seems to act as a codeword for 'lesbian'".[45] In a more broad way, 'menace' denotes notions of a dangerous or taboo attraction that takes over, linked as much to fantasy and desire as to fear. Maxim's absence from Rebecca's room, apart from the photograph that speaks through to the heroine's conscience, means that alternative readings can be made of the fetishistic possessions (than mere male disavowal in a psychoanalytic sense), as Rhona J. Berenstein argues: "The fetishization of Rebecca's personal property does not quash Danvers's and Fontaine's castration anxieties—why indeed would they have castration anxieties?—but serves, instead, to fuel Danvers's enamored reminiscences of the woman she adores and to reinforce Fontaine's feelings of fear and desire for Max's alluring and powerful first wife" (Berenstein 1995: 260, endnote 34). The threat of the visit being found out causes the heroine to summon Mrs. Danvers to the Morning Room to demand that she destroy all "these things," gesturing to Rebecca's stationery, with the afterword, "Mrs Danvers – I intend to say nothing to Mr de Winter about Mr Favell's visit. In fact I'd prefer to forget everything that happened this afternoon." Thus, the heroine blackmails Mrs. Danvers, and at the same time closes the door on the desires and fears opened up by the tour of Rebecca's room.

Rebecca can be read as an expression of the second Mrs. de Winter's 'other' side. In her absence, Rebecca embodies the multiple identities and unlimited bounds that might be open to the heroine were she to embrace them (suggested to some degree by Danvers, who implied the private room was never locked—she was always ready to show it to her every day). Rebecca's death is also an unremitting sign of the containment of female desire. The many voices that describe Rebecca through the film go some way towards reimagining Rebecca's many roles, as evidenced in

---

[45] Deacon (2012: 48) argues that while initial publicity focused on the Olivier/Fontaine couple, "photographs of Anderson 'menacing' Fontaine soon rivalled those with Olivier." She states, "*Los Angeles Times* put it succinctly in an article titled 'Rebecca Has Novel Menace'": "Menace consists of a night gown, lingerie, boudoir, slippers and a $25,000 fur coat." *Los Angeles Times*, 24 May 1940: 28 (cited in Deacon 2012: 48).

her adoption of Mrs. Danvers' name at her London doctor appointments. Rebecca represents a life of fluidity, ridiculing boundaries of class, gender and sexuality, a trait that Danvers praises: "She had a right to amuse herself didn't she... Love was a game to her... only a game. It made her laugh I tell you... She used to sit in her bed and rock with laughter at the lot of you." As Modleski (1988: 54) argues, there is a "hint at what feminine desire might be like were it allowed greater scope." Through gothic doublings, the film offers the suggestion of an alternative way—of a lifestyle unshackled by constraints—even as it represses this alternative way.

Rebecca illuminates the tensions between Maxim's desire for an innocent young bride and the heroine's fantasies of venturing beyond these restrictive boundaries. The dominant discourse coaxes the heroine into a supportive, maternal role, starved of her own desires. In his article on 'The Uncanny,' Freud makes two broad observations:

> [I]f psychoanalytic theory is right in asserting that every affect arising from an emotional impulse – of whatever kind – is converted into fear by being repressed, it follows that among those things that are felt to be frightening there must be one group in which it can be shown that the frightening element is something that has been repressed and now returns... In the second place, if this really is the secret nature of the uncanny, we can understand why German usage allow the familiar (*das Heimliche*, the 'homely') to switch to its opposite, the uncanny (*das Heimliche*, the 'unhomely')... for this uncanny element is actually nothing new or strange, but something that was long familiar to the psyche and was estranged from it only through being repressed. (2003: 147)

The heroine almost leaves the beach cottage to take stock of the knowledge she has gained; she is poised at the door, but the strain of the romantic impulse to return refocuses attention onto solving Maxim's predicament. A part of the heroine dies in the beach cottage sequence when she shuts out some of the unspoken fantasies that have preoccupied her. During the 'confession' or 'revelation' interchange there is a brief and uncanny release of repression, heightened by the distancing effects during Maxim's monologue—uncanny in the sense that it was "intended to remain secret and hidden and has come into the open" (Freud 2003: 132). The horror is that knowledge of this secret is not openly realized by the characters; the sense of the uncanny is not shared by the heroine. It is repressed in a cycle of renewal. The design of strategy and initiative rooted in the fairytale hero's rite of passage is here quashed. It is displaced by the heroine's renewed mission to support and protect the husband—as a mother might protect a child—no matter what he has done, in contrast to Bluebeard, who declares, "there is no knowing what I might do, so angry would I be." The heroine, in treading the expected path, represses knowledge that there are alternative ways of living geared towards female fulfilment and autonomy within as well as beyond the home.

I see *Rebecca* as a horror film, but not for the threat Rebecca poses by her haunting return. The horror lies in the heroine's repression of knowledge beyond the door and of the doubt cast over Maxim's narrative. That she shows no conscious realization of this repression is a further horror. To counter Perrault's first 'moral' caution (2009: 113), directed to female readers, at the end of 'Bluebeard': the knowledge looked for is well worth the cost. Reading *Rebecca* through the lens of the 1940s 'persecuted wife' cycle, and particularly *Secret Beyond the Door* (a film that is as haunted by *Rebecca* as *Rebecca* the film is haunted by du Maurier's novel), enables a broader contextualisation. World War II would provide access to the familiar but repressed knowledge, that women were not only able to take on the same positions in the workplace as men but that restrictive roles and identities within the home had reached stifling proportions, a secret that would be revealed and repressed through the decade, in a perpetual cycle of return and renewal.

The finale, in which the West Wing burns, both destroys traces of Rebecca's bedroom physically and reminds us of it. Ostensibly, if we accept the terms that Maxim uses, and that his new wife adopts from the beach cottage sequence onwards, to demonize Rebecca, it might seem like the only way that Rebecca has 'won' is as the monster that returns to haunt the new couple. In such a light, Mrs. Danvers' actions are driven by compulsive jealousy as a means to extinguish the couple's happiness—by attempting to kill the heroine and by destroying the home that she sees as Rebecca's. Danvers' "sinister" behaviour and eventual suicide completes the film's regressive recourse to the familiar Hollywood treatment of a lesbian-coded figure.[46] However, on a more subversive level,

---

[46]There is a dominant discourse in the film that aligns homosexuality with monstrosity. In conversation with François Truffaut, in a section notably entitled, "'Rebecca': A Cinderella-like Story," Hitchcock misses Truffaut's hint that the film could be likened to 'Bluebeard,' but later declares: "The heroine *is* Cinderella, and Mrs Danvers is one of the ugly sisters" (Truffaut 1986: 183). Earlier he says that he did not want to "humanize" Danvers (Hitchcock in Truffaut 1986: 180). Later, Hitchcock goes on to suggest that she is the "villain" (Truffaut 1986: 183).

despite many of the film's more reactionary structures, it is important to note that Danvers' handiwork (the nightgown case) is conveyed through the independent gaze of the camera, unseen by the characters on screen.[47] The resistant 'R' returns to the absent first wife who in living autonomously on 'home' ground and threatening the bloodline brings about her own death. Read in this light, the burning house is testament to the force needed to uproot firmly engrained traditions whereby the home is passed down from father to son. Underlying this is the threat posed upon women through a succession of generations that brings with it a cul-de-sac of opportunity or deep entrapment within marriage.

References

Bacchilega, C. (1997). *Postmodern Fairytales: Gender and Narrative Strategies* (Philadelphia, PA: University of Pennsylvania Press).
Benson, S. (2000). '"History's Bearer": The Afterlife of "Bluebeard"', *Marvels and Tales*, Wayne State University Press, 14: 2, 244–267.
Berenstein, R.J. (1995). '"I'm not the sort of person men marry": Monsters, Queers, and Hitchcock's *Rebecca*', in C.K. Creekmur and A. Doty (eds.) *Out in Culture: Gay, Lesbian, and Queer Essays on Culture* (London: Cassell), pp. 239–261.
Berenstein, R.J. (Spring 1998). 'Adaptation, Censorship, and Audiences of Questionable Type: Lesbian Sightings in "Rebecca" (1940) and "The Uninvited" (1944)', *Cinema Journal*, 37: 3, 16–37.
Bronfen, E. (2009). 'The Enigma of Homecoming: Secret Beyond the Door—Film Noir's Celebration of Domestic Anxiety', in G. Pollock and V. Anderson (eds.), *Bluebeard's Legacy: Death and Secrets from Bartók to Hitchcock* (London and New York: I.B. Taurus & Co Ltd), pp. 133–172.
Britton, A. (Winter 1986). 'Blissing Out: The Politics of Reaganite Entertainment', *Movie*, 31/32, 1–42.
Deacon, D. (2012). 'Celebrity Sexuality: Judith Anderson, Mrs Danvers, Sexuality and Truthfulness in Biography', *Australian Historical Studies*, Routledge, 43. 1, 45–60.
Doane, M.A. (1988). 'Female Spectatorship and Machines of Projection', *The Desire to Desire: The Woman's Film of the 1940s* (Basingstoke, Hampshire and London: Macmillan Press, 1988), pp. 155–175.

---

[47] We might note the similar independent camera technique that draws attention to 'Rosebud' at the end of *Citizen Kane* (Orson Welles, 1941).

Doane, M.A. (1988). 'Caught and Rebecca: The Inscription of Femininity as Absence' in Constance Penley (ed.), Feminism and Film Theory (New York and London: Routledge and BFI publishing), pp. 196–215.
Du Maurier, D. (1975). Rebecca (London: Pan Books Ltd).
Du Plessis, M. (1990). 'An Open and Shut Case: Secret Beyond the Door', Spectator: The University of Southern California Journal of Film and Television Criticism, 10: 2, 58–77.
Elsaesser, T. (1972). 'Tales of Sound and Fury: The Family Melodrama', Monogram, 4, 2–15.
Fletcher, J. (Winter 1995). 'Primal scenes and the female gothic: Rebecca and Gaslight', Screen, 36: 4, 341–370.
Freud, S. (2003), 'The Uncanny' (1919), in The Uncanny, translated by D. McLintock (London: Penguin Classics), pp. 123–162.
Gallafent, E. (Summer 1988). 'Black Satin: Fantasy, Murder and the Couple in Gaslight and Rebecca', Screen, 29: 3, 84–103.
Greenhill, P. (2008). '"Fitcher's [Queer] Bird": A Fairy-Tale Heroine and Her Avatars', Marvels and Tales (Erotic Tales), 22: 1, 143–167.
Gunning, T. (2000). The Films of Fritz Lang: Allegories of Vision and Modernity (London: BFI).
Griggs, Y. (2016). The Bloomsbury Introduction to Adaptation Studies: Adapting the Canon in Film, TV, Novels and Popular Culture (London and New York: Bloomsbury).
Hanson, H. (2007). Hollywood Heroines: Women in Film Noir and the Female Gothic Film (London, New York: I.B. Taurus).
Harbord, J. (Summer 1996). 'Between Identification and Desire: Rereading Rebecca', Feminist Review (Speaking Out: Researching and Representing Women) (Palgrave Macmillan Journals) 53, 95–107.
Jancovich, M. (Summer 2013). 'Bluebeard's Wives: Horror, Quality and the Gothic (or Paranoid) Woman's Film in the 1940s', The Irish Journal of Gothic and Horror Studies 12, 20–43.
Jenkins, S. (1981). Fritz Lang: The Image and the Look (London: British Film Institute).
Leff, L.J. (1987). Hitchcock and Selznick: The Rich and Strange Collaboration of Alfred Hitchcock and David O. Selznick in Hollywood (Berkeley, Los Angeles, London: University of California Press).
Light, A. (Summer 1984). '"Returning to Manderley": Romance Fiction, Female Sexuality and Class', Feminist Review, 16, 7–25.
Maltby, R. (2003, 1995, second edition). Hollywood Cinema (Malden, Oxford, Melbourne, Berlin: Blackwell.
Modleski, T. (1988). 'Woman and the Labyrinth: Rebecca', The Women Who Knew Too Much: Hitchcock and Feminist Theory (New York and Abingdon, Oxfordshire: Routledge), pp. 43–55.

Nugent, F.S. (29 March, 1940). 'The Screen: Splendid Film of du Maurier's 'Rebecca' Is Shown at the Music Hall', *The New York Times*, p. 25.
Perrault, C. (2009). 'Bluebeard' (1697), in C. Perrault (2009) *The Complete Fairy Tales*, translated by C. Betts, with illustrations by G. Doré (Oxford and New York: Oxford University Press), pp. 104–114.
Propp, V. (2008, revised second edition). *Morphology of the Folktale*, translated by L. Scott (Austen: University of Texas Press, revised second edition).
Tatar, M. (2004). *Secrets beyond the Door: The Story of Bluebeard and His Wives* (Princeton and Oxford: Princeton University Press).
Truffaut, F. (1986, 1978, revised edition). *Hitchcock by Truffaut: The Definitive Study* (London: Paladin).
Waldman, D. (Winter 1984). '"At Last I can tell it to someone!": Female Point of View and Subjectivity in the Gothic Romance Film of the 1940s', *Cinema Journal*, 23: 2, 29–40.
Walker, M. (1990). '*Secret Beyond the Door* (1947)', *Movie*, 34/35, 16–30.
Walker, M. (2005). *Hitchcock's Motifs* (Amsterdam: Amsterdam University Press).
Walsh, A.S. (1984). *Women's Film and Female Experience 1940–1950* (New York and London: Praeger Publishers).
Warner, M. (1981). *Joan of Arc: The Image of Female Heroism* (New York: Alfred A. Knopf).
Wood, R. (1989, revised edition 2002). *Hitchcock's Films Revisited* (New York and Chichester, W. Sussex: Columbia University Press).

CHAPTER 5

Encountering the Werewolf—Confronting the Self: On and Off the Path to *The Company of Wolves*

The werewolf of folklore, fairy tale and fictional texts is a mutable beast, whose habitats and origins vary at the story teller's discretion. Once bitten, infected or born into the state, the werewolf exists as an indeterminate being, somewhere between the realms of wolf and human but depicted usually as a 'cursed' human who transforms into beast form. Thus, the human is contrasted with the animal, but the myth can also prompt thoughts about the confluences between human and animal, and about the human as animal. The werewolf never entirely leaves or remains in either realm, but is burdened with the curse, and death is usually the only 'cure.' Despite the fluidity of werewolf narratives, certain traits have become popular, such as the beast emanating from the forest or the margins of civilization, the full moon monthly transformations and death by a silver implement or bullet.[1] Etymologically half person, half wolf, the werewolf transforms physically from one to the other—from person to (were)wolf and back to person. It is the transformation from human to (were)wolf guise that cinema dwells on as the most visually horrifying, generating the most expensive special effects. Often the

---

[1] Transformations triggered by the full moon can be traced back to *Werewolf of London* (Stuart Walker, 1935). In Guy Endore's novel, *The Werewolf of Paris* (1933) and George Waggner's film, *The Wolf Man* (1941), silver alone can kill a werewolf, as other films and magazines went on to emulate. However, as Chantal Bourgault du Coudray (2006: 77) notes, silver had been listed among other methods for a long time, for example Frank Hamel's book *Human Animals* (1915).

© The Author(s) 2018
L. Hubner, *Fairytale and Gothic Horror*,
https://doi.org/10.1057/978-1-137-39347-0_5

transformation to the human guise is not shown on screen, until death signals the removal of the curse as the freeing of the soul.

Within some of the werewolf narratives, fears associated with evolution (or recidivism) coincide with ideas of the unconscious, whereupon animal origins might be seen to lie dormant from the past, as a repressed or hidden ancestry that threatens to surge upwards and outwards from deep within. In a psychoanalytic sense, the conscious self is allied with the rational and the unconscious with the primal or instinctual—or the irrational that has been repressed or hidden with the threat to return. The hybrid nature of the werewolf stimulates reflection on what makes us human, or animal, and the liminal zones between the bounds of human and animal, person and beast, the civilized and the monstrous, the repressed and the liberated.

Werewolf mythology is predicated upon a dualistic understanding of the world, and self. As Chantal Bourgault du Coudray (2006: 3) outlines, "This conceptualisation of the self was reinforced and elaborated within Enlightenment philosophy through further, parallel, oppositions: particularly that of nature-culture." While gothic texts might explore nature as a threat to civilized society, an ambiguity remains whereby the tensions brought about by a nature–culture dualism remind us of the wild side within that responds cumbersomely to being overly repressed. R.L. Stevenson's *The Strange Case of Dr Jekyll and Mr Hyde* (1896) is a useful parable for exploring the concept of the werewolf as beast within, and many cinematic werewolf representations draw inspiration from Jekyll/Hyde style oppositions. Hyde is conceived as the 'other' within thrust outwards by repressed libidinal drives, concealed by the acceptable (public) face of the doctor. Here the split self is cast in relation to a veneer/interior dualism. Such a dualism challenges the concept of a unified finite self. While Hyde carries out deeds deemed criminal (stealing, violence), as a gothic text Stevenson's work also functions as an "allegory of Victorian hypocrisy and repression" and "draws attention to 'evil' as a relative moral category, as a notion imposed upon natural disorder" (Jackson 1991: 114). Similarly, societal repression is often a main concern in werewolf movies, which have the potential to give voice to marginalized ideas and identities.

Looking at British werewolf films up to *The Company of Wolves* (Neil Jordan 1984), the focus of this chapter is twofold. It involves analyzing British and British-American werewolf movies, but also werewolf films in which Britain is fundamental in terms of setting. I aim to explore where the beast comes from, resides, bites, infects and dies, and how the location or environment changes as notions of self and other, but also the split self that the werewolf embodies, take prominence. This involves looking at how notions of internal and external affect who is or becomes the film's central protagonist, and how fears and desires are manifested. Using *The Company of Wolves* to help frame debates, I suggest that boundaries in earlier British werewolf films (prior to the 1980s) have tended to be more fixed, both in terms of how setting draws on secure distinctions between civilization and wilderness, but also how these infiltrate binaries such as femininity/masculinity; violence/gentleness; innocence/lust; corruption/purity; holy/cursed. Nevertheless, sympathy with the monstrous adds a gothic dimension of ambiguity, in which the werewolf is precariously positioned as a tragic hero. Universal Studios' werewolf films of the 1930s and 1940s ensure that the werewolf is quashed at the end, but not without venturing off track to unveil the secretly repressed, and the unconscious synthesis of dread and desire that lies within. I suggest that, while *The Company of Wolves* in focusing on a teenage heroine's coming of age narrative sets out to play with, and sometimes shatter, binaries and dualisms in a complex and fluid way, certain tensions remain.

As Bourgault du Coudray (2006: 4) argues: "some Gothic monsters are constructed as an externalized other threatening the self, while others are shown to well up from within the realm of the self." She goes on to assert that the werewolf embodies both; in its lupine form the werewolf is usually represented as a foreign entity threatening society. When the monstrous rises from within the self (frequently the central protagonist of the film), it is often a sign of deep angst, an expression of the incompatible relationship between the conscious and the unconscious:

> Representations of the werewolf have reproduced such attitudes, showing the lupine instincts of the wolf or 'beast within' (an analogy of the unconscious) to have a damaging and negative impact upon the inflicted individual (an analogy of the conscious self). (Bourgault du Coudray 2006: 6)

The wolf is associated with 'the other,' the wild side, the untamed or uncultured and, in Freudian psychoanalysis, the repressed. The werewolf is an apt metaphor for the beast within, an expression of repressed drives and desires that surge, often at predetermined intervals, inevitably and unremittingly. While the wolf half of the werewolf tends to denote nature and the human half culture, in a relationship that revolves around notions of internal and external, such notions are complicated by the very ontology of the werewolf, whereupon the beast (physically) erupts out of the human, shattering boundaries between external and internal, or a 'true' and 'alien' identity.

While the werewolf tends to be something to be feared, and can operate as something externally monstrous to be encountered or that might infect us, association spreads to include that which is liberated from the shackles of society or the strict codes of civilization. In this sense, the notion of joining the company of wolves can be a means to express a necessary initiation or rite-of-passage into the woods to become wise to the animal within us, shattering fixed notions of self and other. More radically and less commonly, it might entail giving up the restrictive codes of culture entirely, as a means to explore a more liberated sense of being. *The Company of Wolves* is unique among the films explored in this chapter for conveying the realm of the werewolf through the dream visions of a teenage girl (Sarah Patterson). The fairy tale 'Little Red Riding Hood,' which can be traced back to a werewolf story and frequently appears on the peripheries of werewolf movies, becomes the central focus of *The Company of Wolves*.

The evolution of 'Little Red Riding Hood' continues as multiple variations, revisions and inversions of the tale abound. The first literary (published) version of 'Little Red Riding Hood,' 'Le Petit Chaperon Rouge' by Charles Perrault in *Histoires ou contes du temps passé / Stories or Tales of Past Times* (1697), introduces the red hood, indicating the girl's spoilt or sexually ostentatiousness nature. This version, in which both Granny and the girl are eaten, following the girl's flirtation with the wolf, and her prolonged dawdling along the path, adds a sense of blame to her unfortunate outcome. Perrault also adds the *verse moral* at the tale's end consistent with his usual style warning that girls "especially beautiful well-bred, nice young ladies"[2] should never talk to strangers lest they get eaten by the wolf (implicitly—seduced or raped). He points out that there are various kinds of 'wolf,' warning that those who are charming, tame and sweet are the most deadly of all, quietly pursuing young ladies to their parlours.

---

[2] My translation from the French, 'Surtout de jeunes filles Belles, bien faites, et gentiles'.

However, accounts also document a folklore tradition that seems to predate Perrault's version.³ Oral versions of the tale, researched by Paul Delarue, recorded in Nièvre in about 1885, entitled 'The Story of the Grandmother' concern a girl who at the crossway on her route to her grandmother's with bread and milk meets "*bzou*, the werewolf."⁴ When the werewolf asks her if she is taking the path of the pins or needles, she says she will take the path of the needles, which Jack Zipes interprets as indicating "she is on her way to becoming a seamstress" (Zipes 2000: 301), and thus puberty; this is a coming of age tale.⁵ Arriving first via the path of the pins, the wolf devours the grandmother, putting aside some of her flesh and blood, that he then offers to the girl as meat and wine on her arrival before inviting her to his bed. There is a ritualistic undressing of the girl in most of the versions, like a striptease, and the series of her questions pertaining to his hairiness and enormous size, culminating with the teeth ("The better to eat you with my child!"). At this point, the girl insists she must go outside to urinate, and in some versions, when the werewolf says she can do this in bed, she states that she also needs to defecate. He allows her to go outside, attached to a rope, which she then ties around a tree and manages to escape.

This oral tale, that probably precedes Perrault's cautionary tale, and that bears no mention of a red hood, is a rite-of-passage narrative about using initiative to fend off attackers. It indicates the importance of using any means possible to survive, even to the point of breaking through barriers of etiquette. Yvonne Verdier (1997: 110) argues that the eating of the grandmother's flesh and drinking of her blood symbolizes the girl's replacement of the grandmother, as part of life's inevitable rejuvenating cycle: "the necessity of the female biological transformation by which the young eliminate the old in their own lifetime." It also bears some resemblance to ancient rituals of taking communion, together with a child's first taking of the Holy Communion in Christian Confirmation

---

³Paul Delarue, Robert Darnton, Alan Dundees, Maria Tatar, Catherine Orenstein and Jack Zipes all consider this folktale to be much older than Perrault's (Andrew Teverson 2013: 3). On this basis, Teverson (2013: 4) argues that it is "highly likely."
⁴The tale is reproduced in Jack Zipes (1993: 21–23).
⁵While other interpretations are possible, from denoting the material of the ground / path (e.g., pine needles) through to different stages of life or materials linked to the telling of the tale, critical consensus rests on the choice indicating those linked with emerging womanhood.

traditions. There are sharp distinctions between the smart outspoken peasant girl and Perrault's spoilt vulnerable girl, led by the conceit of her own amusements. As Zipes (1993: 27) argues:

> Whereas the oral tale referred direct to actual conditions in the country faced by peasants and villagers, Perrault's literary version assumed a more general aspect. It talked about vanity, power, and seduction, and it introduced *a new child*, the helpless girl, who subconsciously contributed to her own rape.

Jacob and Wilhelm Grimm's first published version 'Rotkäpchen' ('Little Red Cap') in *Kinder—und Hausmärchen / Children's and Household Tales* (1812), introduces a huntsman to save the girl and grandmother, and Little Red Cap is instructed to stay on the path by her mother. The fairy tale through all its phases concerns the journey of a girl on the cusp of womanhood facing life choices as determined by nature and culture. The choice of which course to take is vital, but the outcome differs depending on the version. The Grimm brothers' and Perrault's versions, which have been reprinted in countless forms, mostly as a children's tale, still infiltrate the market. Despite multiple variations, revisions and inversions, the instruction to stay on the path subsists; take the conventional route as culture dictates. The 'classical' tale tells us that veering into the woods (the realm of the wolf) results in victimhood and can also be a sign of unbridled libido that should be kept in check. The heroine becomes not only an endangered prey but also a siren (or provoker) of that danger. This is a devaluation that the cinema has had a tendency to exploit.[6] The story of the fairy tale's evolution, in which the villainous (culturally shaped) literary versions vanquish the pure untamed folktale, has become a myth of our own time, seeping into revisionist versions of the tale. But the story helps to illuminate the multiple ways that codes of femininity have been shaped by societal shifts.

---

[6]Tex Avery made this element his central fixation. In his animation *Red Hot Riding Hood* (1943), the protagonist is a blonde striptease artist in a Hollywood nightclub. The wolf is a gentleman in top hat and tails whose eyes pop out on stalks at her provocative performance—the joke being that the wolf ends up being chased by a sexually besotted grandmother. As Catherine Orenstein (2002: 115) argues, "The showgirl and her lascivious partner were not just a girl and a wolf, but the characters and symbols of the human sexual drama." The representation perpetuates the notion that sexual desire is defined by the male voyeur's active objectification.

The Company of Wolves (Neil Jordan, 1984) draws on numerous werewolf tales, historical accounts and mythologies, intertwined with multiple versions and strands of 'Little Red Riding Hood,' also offering new ways of envisioning the fairy tale. The screenplay was co-written by Jordan and Angela Carter, adapted from Carter's short story, 'The Company of Wolves,' with inspiration from her other stories such as 'The Werewolf' and 'Wolf-Alice.' 'The Company of Wolves' is clearly the most influential, and different stages of development can also be traced through Carter's radio play that bears the same title and the screenplay, both of which bear interesting distinctions from the finished cut of the film.

Wolves and werewolves take on many different forms and meanings in *The Company of Wolves*; there is no definitive representation. The film is set mainly in the heroine's dream world, positioned between an opening and closing frame, which is set in contemporary (1980s) England. The film opens with the heroine's parents returning from a shopping trip to their large white Georgian house, and her older sister coming up to the heroine's attic bedroom to see why she is hiding away. The younger sister slips off to sleep and the camera tracks through her bedroom window to the woods beyond (signalling her dream, which is interspersed at the beginning with residues of items around her bedroom, such as a large doll's house and a grandmother modelled on one of her dolls). Within the dream world, there are a number of stories, made up from various werewolf tales and old wives' tales, as well as the unfolding narrative that takes over the rest culminating with Rosaleen, the heroine figure in dream form, as a revised Little Red Riding Hood visiting her grandmother (Angela Lansbury) through the woods and encountering the werewolf. Apart from a few brief glimpses of the sleeping heroine, the film remains in the dream world, until it returns in the final frame to the house of the opening frame. The dream world ruptures the 'real' world when wolves burst into the large house through an ancestral portrait and a lone wolf crashes through the heroine's bedroom window.

The film contains numerous revisions of the classical 'Little Red Riding Hood.' For example, in the culminating narrative of the dream world, Rosaleen encounters a gentleman huntsman (Micha Bergese) in the woods, who then later at her grandmother's transforms into a werewolf, a reworking of Perrault's gentleman seducer and a twist on the huntsman as rescuer added by the Grimm brothers. Shifts in generational attitudes to the female role are emphasized in the comments made by the grandmother and Rosaleen in response to her older sister Alice's mutilation by wolves:

> *Grandmother:* Your only sister all alone in the wood and nobody there to save her—poor little lamb.
> *Rosaleen:* Why couldn't she save herself?

Rosaleen's response functions as an incisive rejection of Grimm's huntsman rescuer, sourcing further back to rekindle the value of initiative in the oral version.

The grandmother tells two stories, notably built on fear and caution. The first tells of a husband going outside into the woods to take a pee (a refocusing of the girl's action in the oral tale) and being attacked by wolves. After a prolonged absence, and his wife's remarriage, he returns as a werewolf wanting to take back what is rightfully his. The second husband slices off his head. It lands in the milk and transforms into human form surrounded by blood. The vision is an abject remixing of the red/white motif in fairy tales, but the wife is notably unfazed, simply seeing her husband as he was. She kisses his head, inciting her second husband to beat her. The story prompts the grandmother's warning that once the bloom of new marriage has gone, the beast comes out. But Rosaleen's response is adamant; she will never let a man strike her. The grandmother's second story ends with the grandmother's warning to run if a naked man is seen in the woods. The story builds on the notion that man unclothed is a violent sexual predator, that layers of civilization will quickly erode if a man is naked, taking him back to a prior state.

The grandmother's stories are not given any finite worth over others in the film. It is the grandmother who tells Rosaleen not to stray from the path (a change from the mother in the Grimms' version). With respect to sexual passion, a different perspective from the grandmother's is offered to Rosaleen by her mother, who speaks of reciprocity: "If there is a beast in man it meets its match in women." Rosaleen is able to reinterpret her grandmother's stories, as new generations have with fairy tales. When she recounts her grandmother's tale of the peasant girl "witch" who (pregnant with his child) confronts her ex-lover at his aristocratic wedding, she revels in the woman's power to transform (back) the guests to their wolf-like state in a powerful class attack (of Swiftian nature).[7] Those of a lower social status (the waiters and servants) remain as

---

[7] That the setting is also the grounds of the dreaming girl's own grand home (introduced in the opening frame) gives a further unsettling depth—especially since her fantasy of herself in the dream is that of a poor village girl.

humans. When asked by her mother what can be gained by the woman having the wolf-guests serenade her and her baby with their howling, Rosaleen replies: "the power it gave her." She identifies with the woman rather than alienating her as "witch." Rosaleen's new takes on the old tales are a reminder of the folktale 'The Story of the Grandmother' in which the girl replaces the grandmother.[8]

Having visited the grandmother in the culminating narrative, and seen the spectacular werewolf transformation, Rosaleen wounds the werewolf with a gunshot and then sympathizes with him, telling her own story about a wounded she-wolf. The final image within the dream world shows Rosaleen as a wolf leaping out the window of the woodland cottage into the woods to join the company of wolves. While this might be viewed as a marked celebration of the female's wild, untamed desires, the fantasies remain contained, or framed, within the contemporary location as made clear by the stark return to the large house (the location of repression) at the film's end. I suggest that while the final frame, which I return to at this chapter's close, invokes many of the tensions that pull at the film's transgressive core, the opening introduces the dualities of nature and culture that fuel the heroine's dreams. A brief analysis of the opening frame also helps to initiate an exploration of themes that resonate through British werewolf films prior to *The Company of Wolves*.

The film opens among woodlands that engulf the road leading to the house. The camera tracks the family's large German Shepherd Dog, or Alsatian, sniffing leaves and racing through trees, at times towards the camera, at others leaping over wildlife, dislodging a toad and a crow, as the family Volvo emerges on the road, intercepting a rat. Made clear from the start is the polarity between culture and nature, together with their intermingling. The dog intersects and disturbs nature, making its way to the house, racing at high speed, reminiscent of its wolf nature, but also foregrounding its domesticated return. Wolves are unable to be tamed—unable to live alongside people in a sustainable way like dogs do.[9] This difference from dogs that wolves represent makes

---

[8] In the (1984) Channel 4 Visions series about *The Company of Wolves*, Carter says she does not fear the wolf, but does see the grandmother as a terrifying figure in her desire to have the girl for herself.

[9] However, the threat of going feral remains with certain breeds; if left to live in the wild, it does not take long for most dogs to lose the aptitude for being controlled by humans.

them a fitting motif for the boundaries between nature and culture. The uncanny similarities between wolves and dogs helps elicit thoughts of the encroachment of nature on culture and vice versa.

The heroine's older sister runs across the manicured lawn, in a white Confirmation-style dress with a crucifix necklace, greeting the parents as they drive through the gothic iron gates, the dog following eagerly behind. We share its eye-level viewpoint. The mother gives the older daughter a parlour palm, a cultivated garden centre plant that contrasts with the wilderness of the previous shots. As they unload Sainsbury's shopping bags, the younger sister's tummy ache is discussed, her antisocial mood the topic of her big sister's annoyance, when the mother reminds her that she was also a "pest" once and tells her to go and wake her sister. The father carries in an enormous bag of dog food, a clear sign of the hunting animal's domestication. Eager to see the heroine, the dog runs into the house and up the stairs, followed by the older sister who dumps the plant and bags (quickly forgotten consumables). The dog makes its way through maze-like corridors to the heroine's attic room. Nature encroaches on the upper parts of the house, as doves wander on the shabby rug, among discarded portraits, boxes and old cases, and a dog's eye view leads us to the heroine's room, as it sniffs the closed door. Hidden away in the attic, where nature infringes, the heroine has an affinity with the dog, whose instinctual wild side lingers. As a young teenager, the heroine is represented as a liminal figure, between childhood and adulthood, her white dress hanging on her bedroom door, yet to be worn.

From inside the heroine's bedroom, the sister's bossy voice and constant knocking are heard over the slow tracking shot of childhood remnants—fairy tale books and illustrations (such as Gustave Doré's Little Red Riding Hood meeting the wolf)—mixed with teen merchandise and pop music posters. First shown in the mirror next to scrunched tissues indicating she has been trying on lipstick, the heroine tosses and turns in a drowsy sleep. As the camera pans round to face her, a copy of a teenage magazine, *My Weekly*'s 'The Shattered Dream,' comes into focus on her pillow, a picture of a girl screaming, her arms raised above her head, on its front cover.

The older sister's words "pest, pest, pest" dissolve as winds blow, ornaments come to life and the camera tracks through the heroine's window to dark woodland beyond. George Fenton's orchestral score mixes with shattering glass sounds and wolf howls. The heroine dreams of her sister running through a now decayed iron gate, chased by an animated doll, and grabbed by an outsized teddy bear. There are brief returns to shots of the sleeping heroine. The sister encounters a rat-infested dolls house,

Fig. 5.1 The heroine smiles—*The Company of Wolves* (Neil Jordan, 1984)

a hanging white dress, large fairytale mushrooms and a grandfather clock with wayward hands as the sequence cross-cuts to the photograph of the heroine snuggling up with the family dog, highlighting their alignment—their shared wild side. The sister is cornered by wolves, their red eyes penetrating the darkness, as the music builds to a crescendo and she screams piercingly, her mouth wide open and her arms raised above her head, mirroring the girl on the magazine cover. As the sister sinks screaming to the floor, the shot fades to the sleeping heroine, who turns over, her blood-red lipstick-smeared mouth briefly smiling (see Fig. 5.1).

This is a brief glimpse of the heroine's taboo fantasy and aggressive desires, reacting against her sister's controlling influence, allowable in dreamscape but disturbing in her conscious life.[10] Her face becomes serious again as she briefly stirs before the film returns via the window to the dream world. It is now day time, and the funeral of her sister Alice takes place in the forest clearing. Up to this point, the heroine has only been referred to (in an objectified manner) as "she" and "her" in the 'real' contemporary family setting. In the dream, she has a name—Rosaleen—and thus gains an identity, but also invokes, as Keith Hopper (2003) and Sharon McCann (2010) have noted, "Dark Rosaleen," the

---

[10] As Pauline Greenhill (2008: 143) observes, the notion of younger sisters learning from older sisters' mistakes is an established fairytale trope.

figure from Irish 'aisling' poetry that has allowed writers to use an allegorical subtext of tensions that cannot be expressed openly.

The framing of the dream world, through the window, allows for a licensed elastic space, extending diegetic boundaries, of fantastical happenings, distorted narratives and unsayable imaginings. As Jackson (1991: 180) argues, "fantasy hollows out the 'real,' revealing its absence, its 'great Other', its unspoken and its unseen." Fantasy can operate on a metaphoric level, allowing the unmentionable to push its way into the public sphere. The location of the heroine's internal, unconscious visions is an indeterminate 'Once Upon a Time' medieval-style village on the edge of a forest. At the scene of Alice's funeral is a stork, symbol of births; however, the vicar says, "Amidst life we are in death," again dissolving boundaries between strict poles. The stork suggests a continental setting, providing an exoticness that contrasts with the contemporary British framing. Halfway through the film, a Rolls Royce passes through the woods (a residue of the white vintage toy car on the heroine's dressing table in the opening frame) reemphasizing the impression of the elastic set where anything is possible within the story-within-dream framework. Thus, while the framing of the film is more specifically set in a country house in contemporary Britain, the dream world—where the werewolf resides—is presented as an exotic other world, inspired by European fairy tales but flexible in its interpretations.[11]

Prior to *The Company of Wolves*, British werewolf movies tended to be set outside the UK, and usually in the past. Set in Spain during the late eighteenth and early nineteenth century, *The Curse of the Werewolf* (Terence Fisher, 1961) is testament to Hammer Films' increasing interest from the late 1950s through to the 1970s in making historical, costume horrors.[12] The term 'historical' is perhaps a loose one. Bearing

---

[11] Carter and Jordan's screenplay (1997: 189) describes, "*peasants out of any number of fairy-tales, redolent of the late-eighteenth century, perhaps, the world of the Brothers Grimm, but much else besides.*"

[12] The dates "1740–1840" are handwritten a number of times on the Shooting Script front cover and preliminary pages; the description of the location is general, "A small Spanish Farming Town. The Square" (Elder, August 1960: 1). With thanks to Professor Steve Chibnall and the Hammer Script Archives, De Montfort University. Sue Harper (1998: 110) observes that while Hammer Films' pre-1957 productions had "modern settings," *The Curse of Frankenstein* (1957) and *Dracula* (1958) launched the new Hammer horror cycle with historical settings: "Over half the films produced between 1957 and 1974 had historical settings." Hammer Films received the Queen's Award for Industry in 1968 for international profits.

in mind inconsistencies in *The Curse of the Werewolf*, like the narrator (Don Alfredo Càrido) declaring that events happened "some two hundred years ago..." which would make him ancient, Bruce G. Hallenbeck and Jan Van Genechten suggest the film should simply be regarded as a "definitive example of Fisher's description of his horror films as 'fairy tales for adults,'" and that the opening words might just have easily been "Once upon a time" (2001: 85). As Sue Harper argues, the "costume" element in Hammer's horror films played a key role in their profits, as they sought to offer productions that were distinct from America's home-grown horror:

> In what looks like a classic two-hander, Hammer packaged European history so as to give American audiences a strong flavor of the exotic, and to give everyone else a version of the past that retained some familiar elements. The two-hander paid off. Only a third of Hammer's considerable profits came from Britain; another third came from America, and the rest from other overseas sources.

Universal had encouraged Hammer to remake a werewolf movie based on Guy Endore's novel *The Werewolf of Paris* (1933). Ted Newsom (1992: 80) notes, "Hammer was saddled with the 'source', *Werewolf of Paris*, because Universal wanted to write off the cost. Thus, Hammer had to account for Universal's 25-year-old acquisition of the Guy Endore novel in their scanty budget." To accommodate the hefty title costs, the producer Anthony Hinds also took on the role of scriptwriter, under the pseudonym 'John Elder.' *The Curse of the Werewolf* was originally intended to be set in Paris. However, because Columbia Pictures decided to discontinue with the film that was supposed to precede it, *The Inquisitor* (also known as *The Rape of Sabena*), apparently fearing the reaction of the Catholic Church's 'Legion of Decency,' Hammer resourcefully used the set that was already there.[13] The ease with which Hinds exchanged character and place names from French to Spanish ones suggests that any European period setting might give the exotic appeal required.[14]

---

[13] *The Inquisitor* concerned the Spanish Inquisition taking root in a small town.

[14] Although the basic structure was kept, much of Endore's novel would have needed to be removed anyway due to its heavy descriptions of political and historical context, and allegorical themes.

The werewolf 'curse' originates from the margins of society, and the film represents strict boundaries between righteous (Christian) civilian life and that which is lost on the peripheries. The werewolf, Leon (Oliver Reed), is born with the curse, triggered by a succession of ill-fated events following a homeless beggar's arrival in town in search of charity. The extreme high-angled shot from the bell tower looking down on the square stresses that he emerges from the outside, entering in through the arch. Treated like a dog and then thrown into jail by the evil Marques Siniestro, the beggar rapes the mute servant girl who is placed in the same cell temporarily for her inability to respond to the Marques. The illiterate and impoverished beggar is represented as a lower species. While prison makes him grow visibly beast-like (with hair growing across his body and face), there remains an essentialist suggestion that such a figure is inclined to revert backwards. His untamed hunger is linked regressively with lust, borne out by his attack on the servant girl and the subsequent 'curse' that the offspring is born with—on the ill-fated Christmas day. Marginal figures are thus represented as a threat to stable civilized society.

Indeed most of the characters have a two dimensional quality, as strict types that conflict with each other, as implied by the scarcely veiled names: Siniestro (sinister); Teresa (Alfredo's saintly servant); Cristina (the angelic girl in love with Leon). This is in keeping with the "sharp oppositions" that Harper observes in Hammer's historical films of this period, for example between weak and strong, dark and fair, virgin and crone, male and female (Harper 1998: 113). Similar strict tensions between light and dark are evident within Leon (the inversion of 'Noel'). When he first goes hunting with Pepe and tastes the blood from the injured squirrel he kisses, he is torn between the innocent boy who cannot bear animals suffering and the longing to taste more blood. There are also the bad dreams that he knows nothing about in his waking (conscious) hours. Later, these tensions grow to monumental proportions when werewolf monthly outbursts conflict with the daytime civilized man who wants to earn a wholesome living and marry Cristina. The 'curse' is cast prior to birth and, having lain dormant since his loving parental figures fixed restraining bars on his windows, it is destined to return in adulthood, triggered by the full moon but associated with sexual desire. As Peter Hutchings (1993: 69) asserts:

> Leon's unwilled transformations into a ravening beast are linked with sexual desire, with one of these transformations actually taking place inside

a brothel. Indeed the circumstances of his conception are also connected with a male sexual desire that is seen as animal-like and corrupting; this takes the form of both the degenerate beggar who rapes Leon's mother and the syphilitic nobleman who makes advances to her.

Leon is positioned as central subject. By being allied to male arousal the prostitutes are 'othered' as a sign of lust, functioning in strict opposition to the pure Cristina in accordance with a stereotypical 'virgin/whore' dichotomy.[15] At the brothel, Vera becomes victim of the brutal attack, but can be seen as the trigger, because she has invited Leon to her bedroom and shows some initial enjoyment in the embrace (until it becomes violent). When Leon's co-worker, Jose, tells another prostitute he is going to look for Leon, she laughs, "Don't speak to any strange men!" The allusion to the fairy tale implies that, like Perrault's Little Red Riding Hood, Vera should not invite men to her bedroom, and more broadly she is punished because she has taken the pathway of prostitution.[16]

The servant girl is similarly disposable. 'Found,' nearly drowned, by Don Alfredo, she resembles the Victorian fallen woman who has nothing left to live for.[17] While taken in by Don Alfredo and Teresa in a Christian pseudo family unit, the colour palette denotes her separateness, drawing on superstitious qualities surrounding female sexual maturity and childbirth. In contrast to Alfredo and Teresa's blue clothing, the red of the

[15] The Shooting Script (August, 1960) reveals a regressive conceptualization of women: "fat and raucous, and the music is loud and bad; but it makes up for any deficiencies by a rowdy 'Hogarthian' good humour. In fact, the combined noise of the girls' piercing laughter, the shouts of the happy CLIENTS, and the blaring of the musicians, is almost deafening." The "madam" is described as a large woman, and later "JOSE bursts back with two large, laughing strumpets" (Elder 1960: 70). The hand-drawn sketch on the right margin of the script depicts three cartoonlike women, bulging over tight corsets. Thanks to Professor Steve Chibnall and the Hammer Script Archives, De Montfort University for reprinting this copy for me. The film's bordello dancing girls, different from the script, are attractive, sexualized Spanish dancers. Although Jose introduces them as two good friends he does not know their names, exposing their disposability in his mind.

[16] There are red tinges to the lighting in the brothel, the sky is notably red when Leon is imprisoned; the Shooting Script describes it as having "deepened to a blood colour" (Elder 1960: 77).

[17] Victorian art perpetuated this fantasy of a 'found' fallen woman, who had drowned herself in despair—for example, the painting *Found Drowned*, GF Watts, c. 1850. Don Alfredo as narrator notably declares that it is here (in the lake) that he "found her."

servant girl's dressing gown and the drapes around the bed stand in for gore, contrasting with the white bed linen, a reminder of fairy tale's use of red and white (such as the blood on snow or milk in 'Snow White' to symbolize the loss of innocence). As the girl sits up holding Leon, the painting of the Madonna and child is visible behind the bed, but moments with her new-born are cut short by her inevitable death following childbirth. The revenge she sought by stabbing the Marques has come full circle to complete her own doomed fate.

Exploitative elements of the film are taken to the extreme in its marketing. For example, one poster depicts the servant girl in the werewolf's arms, collapsing backwards in her red dress blurring with the flames of lit torches carried by the crowds. Another depicts two versions of the servant girl shrieking back in terror, beneath the caption "Half-Man…Half-Wolf." One version of the girl is draped across a hilltop in her low-cut red dress with skirts lifted above her legs as she retreats in terror that again blurs into the flames of the men's torches, before a skeletal tree and full moon. The other version of her is positioned to the far right looking in terror, with the flames gathering around her shoulders as if a red cloak and hood. The werewolf's face is between them creating the stir; below in the bottom corner is Leon's face, stern and melancholy. These are not only scenes that never occur in the film, but also ones that do not fit logistically—the servant girl being Leon's mother, and dead immediately after his birth.[18] The terror of the wild beast out of control is thus linked with the dangerous female, plus also with the woman leaning out to the woods there is the idea of straying, only to encounter the werewolf, which adds to the fairytale mythology of the film and the appeal to the largely teenage male audience, but connects in no way to the narrative.[19] The servant girl's cleavage that had been emphasized in the shooting of the rape sequence is again given prominence in many of the black and white publicity stills in which Reed as werewolf carries her off, strangles her, leers over her on the floor, and approaches her from behind, blurring sex and violence, but in an arrangement of scenes

---

[18] While incest between mother and son is a feature in Guy Endore's *Werewolf of Paris*, it is clear that there is no allusion to this in these images.

[19] This recalls Bourgault du Coudray's observation: "Little Red Riding Hood's diversion from the path among the trees signals her liability to sensual abandonment even before she meets the wolf, who focuses the diffuse dangers of the forest in an obviously sexualised and gendered way" (2006: 116).

that never take place in the film. It was a case of making the most of the actors to hand, and those who clearly contained the strongest sex appeal (and chemistry): Yvonne Romain who played the servant girl had previously appeared in *Corridors of Blood* (Robert Day, 1958) and made a fitting match for Reed's dark, brooding, broad-shouldered werewolf.

The film is propelled by an overt conflict between untamed primitiveness and the force of Christian purity. The priest ordains that Leon should reside at a monastery to contain the curse, and the model of Christian sacrifice prevails when Alfredo (the father figure) shoots the werewolf with the silver bullet melted down from the crucifix, as Leon had finally requested. The arms of the loving Cristina could only temporarily abate Leon's lupine urges. In this sense, the film is not gothic, but rather a tragic love story tinged with fairytale qualities, reinforcing essentialist binaries of masculine and feminine, self and 'other.' Teresa and the well-read, middle class Don Alfredo represent the virtue of following the straight course. The ending sees a return to the bell tower where the film opened. The fairy tale is over, as the beast lies dead, and Alfredo covers it with his cloak, leading to the final shot of Cristina and Teresa embracing below, with no suggestion of a gothic ambiguity or return of the repressed. Earlier in the film, the priest had declared that with death, the soul (of the person) wins over the spirit (of the werewolf), thus bringing an end to the tragic battle. However, pushing against this is the relentlessness of a crucial moment just prior to the film's end, when a tear falls slowly from the werewolf's eye as he lies on the floor dead (see Fig. 5.2).

Significantly, this was also a highly contested image that took a long time to be shown on British screens. The British Board of Film Censors (BBFC) had been harsh on the film, resulting in the removal of two minutes from the final British print. This was due to the context. The script arrived with the BBFC in August 1960 just two months prior to *Psycho* (Alfred Hitchcock) opening to a stir at the Plaza, Piccadilly. Coming straight after *Peeping Tom* (Michael Powell, 1960), *Psycho* "only served to reignite flames of indignation" concerning excesses of sex and violence (Hallenbeck and Van Genechten 2001: 83). The BBFC were fearful of creating more of a commotion. Violent scenes that caused particular contestation were those outside the supernatural realm, when brutality took place in everyday life, such as the Marques' sadistic treatment of the beggar. Parts of the brothel scenes and shots of Vera's dead body smeared in blood were also disputed. However, more surprisingly, this shot of the werewolf's tear also remained a strong sticking point. It seems the BBFC

Fig. 5.2 The werewolf sheds a tear—*The Curse of the Werewolf* (Terence Fisher, 1961)

were concerned that any compassion for the werewolf would make the film's message less certain, but Hinds fought back arguing that horror films were "only dangerous if there were a complete lack of sympathy for the 'monster'" (Hinds, cited in Mike Murphy 1999: 9). Retaining the tear was thus seen as crucial by Hammer, and after a long debate over many months, the film was finally passed with the 'X' certificate including the reinsertion of the tear shot. Unfortunately, though, the film was released without this vital moment (a simple omission, through no fault of the censors), and was not included until 1993, when the BBC transmitted a restored version containing previously cut scenes.[20] This moment represents a vital move forward in British cinema, allowing for a more complex layering of the werewolf figure. The release of a tear from the strikingly blue eyes provides an uncanny vision of the human within the beast. While the change of the werewolf's eye colour (from brown in the opening sequence to Reed's/Leon's natural blue colour) is due to practical rather than artistic reasons, because Reed had an allergic reaction to the contact lenses so ceased to wear them through the remainder

---

[20] A restored version was made for the BBC in 1992, but accidentally the old print was shown.

of the film, the effect of humanizing the monstrous is unarguable, as is evident from the level of debate triggered by this final scene. The face looks old, bearing the toll of physical change brought about by the spiritual curse. The werewolf does not transform back to human when killed as it does in many endings to werewolf movies when the soul is released. Here, Leon as werewolf remains fixed in a tragically frozen state of limbo, wrought by external forces. The moment is horrific because it lingers on the deeply troubled person within.

Carrying on the tradition, *Legend of the Werewolf* (Freddie Francis, 1975) is also conveyed through the screen of a European past—in this instance, late nineteenth-century France.[21] Etoile (David Rintoul) is the offspring of a Central European couple who are among the thousands fleeing a tyrannical state. He is born in the woods on Christmas day, but left orphaned and alone when his mother dies in childbirth and wolves kill all the refugees including his father. Etoile is raised by the pack through the first part of his childhood, before joining a circus, and then taking up residence in France as assistant to a zoo keeper (Ron Moody). Problems arise as Etoile tries to sustain a contained veneer in his adult life. Thus again, while it takes a particular fusion of fate and superstition to bring about the werewolf condition, the 'curse' originates from the outskirts of society, seemingly incited by the crossing of borders during a period of change, marked by the flight from a previously 'civilized' society into the unknown wilderness.

The first words ("many years ago… ") of the male voice-over that opens *Legend of the Werewolf* conveys the fairytale universality of the woodland location by not stating a precise date. However, the Paris setting of the remainder of the film is important for visualizing the environment, as the film's art director, Jack Shampan, explains: "the lovely period was the nineteenth-century, Toulouse-Lautrec, that sort of feel, especially with brothels and all that" (Shampan, cited in Edward Buscombe 1976: 12–13).

---

[21]Of the other British 1970s films, the (Amicus Productions / British Lion Film Corporation) whodunit *The Beast Must Die* (Paul Annett, 1974) is set in a mansion on a non-specified island, where Britain is mentioned only in passing as a place free from werewolves or werewolf belief. Generically, the werewolf is thus 'othered' rather than set up in relation to a self/other duality. By contrast, *Demons of the Mind* (Peter Sykes, 1972) portrays the decadent Baron Zorn imagining himself as a wolf running wild in the forest, thus focusing on the psychical over the physical transformation—an image that is later rekindled in *An American Werewolf in London* (David Landis, 1981).

Hinds, as 'John Elder,' was once again commissioned as scriptwriter, and aesthetic inspiration was sought from *Moulin Rouge* (John Huston, 1953), for which Freddie Francis had been camera operator.[22] Like *The Curse of the Werewolf*, the environment of violence in *Legend of the Werewolf* is linked with sex via the mythologized, and safely historicized, screen of bordello life, but in this instance heightened by popular conceptions of the French art world. It is sexual jealousy that triggers the violent attacks carried out by the afflicted Etoile, mainly on the gentlemen visitors to his girlfriend, Christine, at the brothel. A further victim is the streetwalker on the wrong side of town. Like Leon in *The Curse of the Werewolf*, Etoile's daytime persona is innocent of his actions. Until the end, Etoile's transformations are not shown, but represented merely via a surge of rage, intersected by shots from his transformed viewpoint in which everything is depicted through a red lens to suggest lupine vision, recalling the same hued shots of the film's opening as wolves traverse woodland. The red-lens tracking shots position the audience as wolves but once aligned with the werewolf also reinforce a reductive viewpoint of sexual desire as distinctly masculinized and which, fuelled by fetishized rage, is based upon the sexual desirability of women. The streetwalker is not simply represented as a symbol of (male) lust, but also a sign of disposability.

However, the film openly critiques the hypocritical lifestyles of the gentlemen who frequent the brothel, including that of the Prefect of Police who becomes the first victim. It also provides insight into the day-to-day lives of the prostitutes. The love-interest, Christine, again bearing a name that marks her (Christian) purity, resides within—rather than external to—the brothel. Although her additional back-story of being forced into the trade by becoming orphaned makes her distinct from the other residents, there is nevertheless the hint of a breakdown between the usual fixed binary of nice girl and predatory vamp. In addition, Christine is practical, being fully aware that societal restrictions prevent her from marrying Etoile, and the brothel Madame maintains a reasonable balance between strong business sense and a concerned loyalty to the girls. It is also significant that, drawing on the tradition of 1930s and 1940s Hollywood werewolf movies, Christine sees the werewolf transform back to the young handsome Etoile, thus gaining final confirmation of his duality.

---

[22] A relatively large percentage (16.5%) of *Legend of the Werewolf*'s modest budget was spent on "Sets and models" (Buscombe 1976: 30).

Since British films about werewolves had up to this point tended to be set elsewhere, American filmmaking had not been averse to making *Britain* a haunt for werewolves. While key city landmarks are not flaunted in Universal Studios' *Werewolf of London* (Stuart Walker, 1935), contemporary London is the main setting and plays an important role in shaping how the realm of the werewolf is conceived in the film. The city's idiosyncratic features are brought to life by Miss Ettie Coombe's descriptions of the Thames lapping at her "very threshold," as she stands on the balcony of her high society home—couched between pubs and slums bordering on the "worst district" of London—where the beast launches its first attack. Providing a firm basis for law and order, the London-based institution, Scotland Yard, symbolic of the British police force itself, is brought in to solve the vicious and peculiarly animal-like killings. London provides a reliable haven for American audiences, being at once familiar, with respect to language and ancestry, and also strange. Werewolfery is positioned safely across the other side of the Atlantic. The London setting encapsulates broadly a history of European folklore and specifically a city synonymous with split-self gothic narratives such as *Jekyll and Hyde* and Oscar Wilde's *The Picture of Dorian Gray* (1890). Significantly, however, the werewolf originates from the more exotic location of Tibet, where at the start of the film the obsessive scientist Dr. Wilfred Glendon (Henry Hull) gets bitten on the arm by a werewolf, Dr. Yogami (Warner Oland) in werewolf form, when collecting a rare flower, the *Mariphasa Lupino Lumino*.[23] He first meets Yogami in human form back in England, during the garden party reception he and his wife Lisa (Valerie Hobson) host for the Botanical Society. Yogami tells him about their shared werewolf condition and that the juice of the Mariphasa is the only remedy to hold back a werewolf transformation. It is only a temporary antidote, rather than a cure. If not taken, the werewolf must kill at least one person each night of the full moon or become permanently afflicted. Glendon is resistant to the news at first, dismissing it as fairy tale, but following his first transformation he remains aware of his actions and ends up going to great lengths to lock himself away so that he cannot repeat. The uncontrollable, wild urges that befall the doctor against his will during the full moon generate a terror and shame that

---

[23]The film introduced the trend for depicting the condition being passed on by the bite of another werewolf; according to Bourgault du Coudray (2006: 77), this idea did not feature in fiction or folklore before 1935.

he cannot reconcile with his 'human,' civilized self. Nevertheless, the representation of a prohibited nocturnal world also articulates repressed sexuality—both the scientist's own repressed identity and the correlating developments of Lisa's reunion with her childhood sweetheart, Paul, having been neglected by her compulsive husband. Whatever is repressed must return.

In some respects, *Werewolf of London* reinforces regressive stereotypes, representing 'other' nations and classes as having a "primitive" affinity with nature, rather than culture. Glendon plucks the Mariphasa, the rare flower that blooms only in moonlight, seconds after he receives the bite in the forbidden valley in Tibet, suggesting that, as Emily D. Edwards (2005: 151) argues, the condition stems from the "infectious violence" of "primitive" cultures. Working class London is also depicted as a more apt environment for Glendon's nightly activities. By conveying Glendon during the full-moon period adorning (Hyde style) cap and gown to seek refuge in the rough East End, the film continues a tradition of representing a London underclass that is driven by primitive behaviour, debauchery and crime. Under this guise, he rents a room from an alcoholic landlady, first seen in double act chattering with another old lady, both hooked on gin. When Glendon asks how she would respond if he told her a man could turn into a werewolf, she laughs: "I'd say I was Little Red Riding Hood!" While a minute grain of social consciousness underlies the point that her abusive former husband who left for Australia years ago might have caused her 'ruin,' largely the thought of her being any kind of Red Riding Hood is ridiculed by her pronounced cockney accent and crone-like cackling. The landlady scenes set up a comical interlude, reinforcing the notion that this end of London and the people inhabiting it are essentially more open to corruption, with little sympathy for their difficulties. The comedy juxtaposes the ensuing horror as the newly transformed Glendon sets out on the prowl. Moreover, Glendon's first victim to be killed, the beggar woman on the street, is not given a back-story but becomes easy prey, similar to the prostitute-victims in *Curse of the Werewolf* and *Legend of the Werewolf*.[24] The paper headlines the

---

[24] She might easily be mistaken for a prostitute, her staggering gait across a street at night-time mirroring that of stereotypical cinematic representations of prostitutes. Robert Spadoni (2010: 55) describes the care taken, after she was changed from prostitute in the script to beggar woman in the film, to distinguish her from a prostitute to appease the Breen Office, but that even so she was still read as one by a critic.

next day highlight her disposability: "Mysterious Goose Lane Murder… unidentified girl horribly murdered."

At the start of the film, as Glendon approaches the valley where the rare flower grows, he encounters a Christian missionary who tells him that he and his assistant are the first white men he has seen in 40 years, and warns that some things are best left alone: "I've never been into that valley and I've never known a man to return from it." In ignoring this warning, a polarity is set up between Christian (light) and an alternative, forbidden route "just off the trail" into darkness. Alone, Glendon climbs down to see the flower, and is bitten on the arm. Thus, Glendon, like Red Riding Hood, is warned against going off the trail. On an unconscious level, he brings on the affliction himself or has always had a leaning towards the taboo, 'dark' side.

The conflict between Glendon's hidden and external sides is represented in the geographical layout of his home, and his positioning within this. Although the Botanical Society reception is going on outside in his garden, a high-society occasion bathed in sunlight, the first shot of Glendon at home is in his lab coat within the windowless space of his workshop, putting out the light to investigate his flower. He uses a large lamp attached via a steel arm to the ceiling as an artificial moon, and we share his microscope's viewpoint of the flower bud. Clearly, there is a tension throughout the film with respect to the acceptable, polite behaviour Glendon must endure at social events and the wild afflictions he bears as the werewolf transformations take effect. The close-up viewpoints we share with Glendon, here and earlier when he first sees the Mariphasa through binoculars, suggest such a dualism is complex with respect to notions of 'self' and 'other.' While nature takes over the doctor as a result of his curiosity, there is also a clear sense that he is trying to control it, and to affect its changes artificially.

Glendon's alienation from the outside world extends to his increasing withdrawal from his marriage. When his wife approaches the conservatory adjoining his laboratory, the arrival triggers an abrupt buzzer and flashing light that causes Glendon to switch on a screen revealing Lisa dressed in bright white with a large brimmed hat and flowing sleeves (see Fig. 5.3).

The distance between the couple is emphasized by the separate spaces, as Glendon looks on from the darkness at his wife outside, aglow in the sunlight. She walks forwards as if directly addressing Glendon (and us). At first, it seems as though she is looking at him, but they are in separate

Fig. 5.3 Voyeur on the outside world—*Werewolf of London* (Stuart Walker, 1935)

parts of the premises, with the lively party continuing on behind her. Glendon returns to the other side of the room to switch the light back on, as if his wife's presence has violently intruded upon his work, and privacy. Lisa moves to the next door, between the conservatory and the laboratory, but it is locked. Later in the film, she tells a guest that even she does not possess a key. As Robert Spadoni (2010: 59) argues, "The reinforced interiority of the lab, and the enclosed nature of the conservatory adjacent to it, invites us to read the lush contents of these spaces as representations not of the great outdoors but of Glendon's inner nature." This secret nature is kept from Lisa, emphasized by the cut from her at the door, marked 'PRIVATE,' trying the handle, to the shot split by the door's frame showing Glendon inside replacing his lab coat with his dinner jacket, pulling up the blind and opening the door to meet his wife on the other side. He is physically pulled from his trancelike state back into the blinding light and the everyday formalities associated

Fig. 5.4 Between the laboratory and the garden party—*Werewolf of London* (Stuart Walker, 1935)

with his wife. Filmed in such a way, it is a wrench we share, at the same time sensing that the wife, like the white Mariphasa flower, is objectified by her husband through a lens, an unwieldy specimen he is unable to control. As Glendon passes from the locked, darkened space through to the civilized world, the camera is positioned as if the wall is sliced down the middle, accentuating the firm barrier between the two worlds (see Fig. 5.4).

The sexual intimacy of their marriage is over, as made clear by Lisa's comment, "Nothing interests you anymore, except your mouldy old secrets in there – not even your wife!" Paul and Lisa's first sight of each other at the party is marked by their shared white clothing, while Glendon is depicted in a separate shot, dressed all in black, indicating the alignment that will pan out through the remainder of the film.

The split forces of Christian order and unruly nature suggested by the missionary's previous warning continue as a party guest exclaims about the carnivorous Madagascar plant with its queerly eroticized furry centre and aggressively wriggling tentacle-like leaves, "Bringing a beastly thing like this into Christian England!" Christian values, specifically "English" ones, are shown to be in opposition to Glendon's questing nature, and desire for the strange in the natural world. Crucially, the stranger Dr. Yogami arrives unexpectedly at this moment, and responds to the guest, "Nature is very tolerant sir – she has no creed." Approaching Glendon, he adds, "Evolution was in a strange mood when that creation came along... It makes one wonder just where the plant world leaves off and the animal world begins." Yogami, with his Japanese-sounding name, played by a Swedish-born actor, known at the time for playing Charlie Chan, emerges from outside Christian England and, drawing on the peculiar twists of Darwinian evolution, introduces a world where categories blur and the 'natural' is thrown into confusion. The subtext of a homosexual rapport between Yogami and Glendon, noted by Harry M. Benshoff (1997: 47, 48), and explored in depth by Spadoni (2010, 2011), is brought further to the surface when, after Glendon asks if they have met before, he affirms they have, but only once "for a moment ... in the dark." It transpires that Yogami is, like Glendon, a student "of nature and plants" and there is a physical closeness between them as they walk on together, through a succession of partitions between the garden and conservatory until Yogami holds back behind a transparent partitioning door. They are face to face, separately spaced—either side of the glass—identically dressed in a black suit, with white buttonhole and handkerchief in the top pocket. Yogami is suddenly a *doppelgänger*, an uncanny replica of Glendon, familiarly strange—a reflection of Glendon's repressed nature (see Fig. 5.5).

While Glendon is resistant to Yogami's approach, significantly it is Glendon who calls Yogami—by name—back round to his side, suggesting an unconscious desire for him to be near. They stand extremely close to each other in sharp contrast to the divide between Glendon and his wife earlier, as he asks again about meeting in Tibet. In the living room, an intimate moment is interrupted when, as Yogami explains the bite on Glendon's arm, Lisa arrives, lightly reprimanding, "There you are Wilfred!" There is an allusion to Glendon's secret desire when he fights and kills Yogami, significantly within the private space of his laboratory. Earlier Yogami had warned: "The werewolf seeks instinctively to kill the thing it loves best." So much is made of Glendon's attempts to avoid killing his wife through the final stages of the film that the fact that he

Fig. 5.5 Encountering Dr. Yogami—confronting the self—*Werewolf of London* (Stuart Walker, 1935)

kills Yogami and not his wife could pass almost unnoticed, but it adds a further layer to the extra-marital complexities of the film.

While strict boundaries are thus represented between the diurnal and nocturnal worlds, the fears brought about by the werewolf realm are shown to coincide with an irrational attraction towards it. This is mirrored in Ettie's excitement at the garden party to see the exotic carnivorous plants brought from foreign lands, as she squeals, "Oh how revolting!" Similarly, while the first scenes of the film cast Lisa and her husband at opposite poles from each other, at the same time there is a strategic paralleling as they each simultaneously begin to embark on new, secret reunions. Glendon's close encounter with Yogami is cross-cut with a scene in which Paul and Lisa privately reminisce about their childhood, with Lisa continuing the horse metaphor begun by Paul to describe their unruliness: "Yes, a wild pair we were weren't we… high headed, hard at the bit, quick with the heels… how we used to fight – remember?"

The scene ends with Lisa telling Paul that the fight in her disappeared the night they broke things off.

Werewolf of London's spotlight on Glendon's obsessive attempts to control and artificially shape nature could be read as a statement to let nature take its course. The transgressive potential of this is substantial considering the gay subtext. Spadoni (2011) proposes it is not homosexual activities that are condemned by the film but rather society's restrictions. As he argues, the film highlights that "living successfully in the modern world demands taming, or repressing, the archaic beast within" (Spadoni 2011: 9). Societal and legal constraints on what was deemed acceptable were tightening up during the 1930s, when many Americans thought the Great Depression following the stock market crash in 1929 had been provoked by the hedonism of the 'Roaring Twenties,' and the activities and behaviours of associated characters, particularly homosexual men, became strongly policed. As Jennifer Terry (1999: 23) asserts, "Municipal efforts to stem a purported tendency among homosexual men to roam city streets and prey upon innocents led to the involvement of forensic psychiatrists in the development of a special diversion program that targeted homosexual men for psychiatric rehabilitation." As Terry explains, although this intervention was based on the notion that homosexuals were "fundamentally maladjusted," it tended to be seen as a "benevolent alternative" (but not a strong counter) to the homophobic panic and strict laws at the time (1999: 23). To return to Yogami's words, exotic plants that defy categorization prove that nature "has no creed." Nature is fluid, rather than fixed, especially when freed from institutional control. The film must speak its message in coded terms, but societal repression is its central feature.

The film's progressive edge extends only so far. The film closes with a conventional heterosexual coupling, when Glendon is shot by a policeman, freeing up the potential for Lisa and Paul to be together legitimately. Glendon's werewolf facial features are not so different from his human ones, to the point that he is recognizable by his wife, who attempts to placate him before he is killed. Despite this, Glendon has not been viewed particularly sympathetically by critics or audiences. Spadoni (2010: 66) attributes the lack of sympathy to him uttering his last lines "*as a werewolf*" and because, having fallen downstairs, he is framed upside down. J. Robert Craig comments that Hull's depiction of Glendon "as the film's focal character does little to create audience identification with, and sympathy for, his plight, because the good doctor comes off as a stuffed shirt" (2005: 78). Glendon's stiff Englishness clearly contributes to this. The heterosexual burgeoning romance between Paul and Lisa is perhaps made all the more palatable, and innocent, because of Paul's relaxed and open panache—a key attribute he seems to have gained from living in America. When they first meet, Glendon belittles Paul's carefree mood that asks "nothing more of life" than running his flying school. Entrepreneurial, rather than academic, Paul provides a match for Lisa, whose childlike fighting spirit returns when she spends more time with him. When Glendon tries to stop her from riding out late with Paul during the full moon, she tells him, "I'll promise you nothing of the sort. I shall ride tonight, tomorrow night, the next night – in fact every night of the moon. Come on Paul." While the film ventures into the recesses of Glendon's dark, locked laboratory, it ends with a small aeroplane flying between the sunlit clouds, to the resonances of a light orchestral score. The image transforms into the Universal Studios plane circling the globe and 'THE END' signalling that Lisa and Paul fly off to a new life in America.

Larry Talbot (Lon Chaney Jr.), the central protagonist in Universal's *The Wolf Man* (George Waggner, 1941), is often viewed more sympathetically than Glendon.[25] The film centres on Larry's return to his father's British estate, following his brother's untimely death. Having spent 18 years away in America, there is justification for Chaney Jr.'s soft American burr to come through as he delivers Talbot's chat-up lines to the attractive Gwen Conliffe (Evelyn Ankers) as she works in her father's antiques shop. Larry is refreshingly brash in approaching Gwen who he has glimpsed through a telescope from his father's observatory.[26] However, it is Larry's persistence that brings about his downfall, when he insists on taking Gwen to the wooded outskirts of town to get their fortunes read, and he encounters Bela (Bela Lugosi), the gypsy fortune teller, in wolf form. Having managed to kill the wolf, he escapes but does not escape being bitten, meaning his fate like Glendon's is set as the next werewolf. As in *Werewolf of London*, the curse seems to originate from the margins of society, and gypsy traditions are posed in contrast to

---

[25] Spadoni (2010: 66) says the ending never aroused the sympathy that Boris Karloff's monster or Lon Chaney Jr.'s Larry Talbot had, saying that critics saw him as stiff. Edwards (2005: 152) comments that Talbot is "likeable," unlike Glendon.

[26] The film was billed under his famous father's name, Lon Chaney; "Lon Chaney as The Wolf Man" appears on the opening star profiles, and the closing credits.

the rituals of the Christian church, as highlighted when the priest takes exception to Bela's non-Christian burial.

While Talbot's tragedy takes centre stage, Gwen's significance within the narrative is foregrounded at the start of the film when she points out to him as he purchases the cane with the silver wolf-head that 'Little Red Riding Hood' was a werewolf story. Later, Gwen comes under attack when the neighbourhood rushes to the shop with a gush of vitriol, blaming her for the death of her friend, saying she had abandoned her to cavort with Larry. The film's identification with Gwen's position provides a critique of the blame often placed on Little Red Riding Hood and of Perrault-style warnings to young girls not to invite men to their parlors. At the film's close, Gwen is shown recoupled with her fiancé, the bland alternative closer to her own class, meaning that she must abandon her wayward dreams. However, her final utterance of Larry's name suggests that her physical desire for him is not completely tamed.

Generational, and specifically paternal, tensions are evident in the relationship between Sir John Talbot (Claude Rains) and his son, Larry. Talbot attributes his son's claims to be a werewolf to "another form of schizophrenia," a psychological rather than a physical affliction, brought on by the stories he has been told by the gypsy woman, Maleva (Maria Ouspenskaya). He is sure the condition can be cured. His pride revolves around his son's future inheritance of the Talbot estate, and he is insistent that Larry must stay to face his responsibilities just as the succession of male Talbot heirs have always done. Talbot hires a psychiatrist, intent on booking Larry in for shock treatment. The night of the werewolf hunt, when Larry tells his father that if the men cannot get into the house, he will get out to them as the affliction takes hold, Talbot ties Larry to a chair. The film concludes with the father beating the werewolf to death using the cane Larry has given him, unwittingly killing his own son, until the gentle transformation back to human form at the point of Larry's death. As Craig (2005: 81) asserts, "The film's voice of rationality, Sir John is fated to discover there is more to lycanthrophobia than its manifestation as a mental problem, for it is he who is fated to kill Larry during the climax." Barbara Creed (1993: 26) looks into the "murderous father–son relationship" in some depth, alluded to in *The Curse of the Werewolf* in which Alfredo, who has adopted the role of father figure, shoots the son, but clearly marked in *The Wolf Man*. Creed (1993: 26) suggests that Larry, attracted to the gypsy camp in the forest, "retreating into a world of totemism and taboo," rejects the father's (rational, civilized) world (of law, and the Church) in favour of the mother's world, symbolized by Maleva, the gypsy woman. In killing the son, the father reinforces paternal law. However, the film also casts some doubt on the perpetuation of paternal order, and the notion that certain conditions can or should be cured with shock treatment. The torturous precautionary measures resorted to by the father represent the restraining techniques of a repressed patriarchal society keen to perpetuate the façade of normality.

While nominally British, *The Wolf Man* was filmed on Universal's stock European village, meaning the setting is an amalgam of medieval-style houses and horse-drawn carriages, interspersed at other points with modern-day cars and telescopes. However, a landmark werewolf film in which the specific qualities of a northern British landscape and London's cityscape are spectacularly present is the British-American coproduction *An American Werewolf in London* (John Landis, 1981).[27] The film portrays two American young men, David Kessler (David Naughton) and Jack Goodman (Griffin Dunne), who are backpacking across Europe, beginning their trip in Britain. They do not make it to the rest of Europe. They are attacked on the moors of northern England during a full moon; Jack is mauled to death, and David is severely wounded, waking up in a London hospital, attended to by nurse Alex (Jenny Agutter) and visited by the reanimated corpse of Jack, who tells him he died an unnatural death and must now walk the Earth in limbo until the werewolf curse is lifted. The wolf's bloodline must be severed and David, the last remaining werewolf, must be destroyed.

The dual (comedy–horror) tone is a vital feature of *An American Werewolf in London*. Its postmodern parodies that pay homage to gothic and fairytale traditions at some points detract from or defuse the horror. For example, there are overt nods to the use of red in fairy tales, and specifically 'Little Red Riding Hood.' The film is rich with red clothing, including: David's puffer coat, checked shirt and the woman's coat he borrows; the coat of one of the two giggling girls outside Alice's house; the girls' coats in the photograph at the doctor's office, the boy's and girl's blazers at Trafalgar Square and the woman's clingy

---

[27]Two other werewolf films were released the same year (1981), *The Howling* (Joe Dante) and *Wolfen* (Michael Wadleigh, John D. Hancock [uncredited], Rupert Hitzig [uncredited]).

dress on television just before David's transformation.[28] In addition to the increased saturation of bright blood as the film progresses, the city itself also makes a fitting setting with its splattering of red buses and telephone boxes, common features of London at the time, but acquiring an accentuated iconicity within the otherwise muted city palette. Many of the locations also pay homage to werewolf movie mores. The London Zoo location, for instance, where David wakes up naked, is inspired by a tradition of zoo locations in werewolf films. We might recall *Werewolf of London*, in which Glendon in werewolf form frees the wolves of London Zoo before launching an attack on the woman canoodling with the married zoo attendant, and *Legend of the Werewolf*, in which Etoile bears an endearing affinity with the enclosed wolves he oversees at the zoo, seeming to communicate with them, attacking boys for throwing stones at them and undergoing a violent transformation after reluctantly obeying the order to kill them. The daytime, public settings expose David's nakedness drawing attention to his awkwardness, articulating his vulnerability, but the concept of humanity stripped bare is very literally, and ludicrously, played out, drowning out the underlying commonality between humans and animals, as he runs around hiding behind bushes. While *An American Werewolf in London* might seem to present a showcase of empty motifs without the thematic, underlying concerns that are central to fairytale and gothic horror, I suggest that there is a greater complexity to the film. While the humour is often an antidote to the horror, it also provides a means to tackle difficult subject matter obliquely, and works alongside the horror to examine central concerns of human maturation, tragedy and sudden brutality, as a close analysis of the opening helps to unpack. At a counterpoint to the horror, Bobby Vinton's upbeat version of 'Blue Moon' plays over the opening shots of the vehicle immersed in the landscape.[29] The accent of the farmer who drops David and Jack off seems to locate them in the Yorkshire Moors.[30]

---

[28] The girls are uncannily reminiscent of the 'twins' in Stanley Kubrick's *The Shining* that came out the year before. The girl in red outside Alex's flat has a dog that barks at him (its canine instincts clearly sensing his lupine interior). This animal sixth sense is a staple of the werewolf film, for example: Aunt Ettie's dog in *Werewolf of London*, growling at Glendon while still physically in human form.

[29] Notably, *The Shining* had a not too dissimilar opening visually but the ('Dies Irae') music casts a grave tone.

[30] These scenes were actually filmed in Wales. The Yorkshire Moors works, both as a tourist destination and a place that in its remoteness can be threatening.

The backpackers are sitting in the back of a truck with the sheep. As Landis (the director) laughs, "They are dead from the first frame!" ('Beware the Moon,' 2009) Furthermore, when they arrive at the pub 'The Slaughtered Lamb,' Jack questions why the sign is a wolf rather than a lamb. These unsubtle symbols—embedded in the set-design— form an overt homage to generic and fairytale traditions and motifs.

When David and Jack step into the crowded pub, the cacophony of voices and movements, as the last dart lands on the dartboard, suddenly stops. There is silence as the locals turn round to look at the newcomers. This is emphasized by sharp cross-cutting between separate shots of small groups or pairs of locals and shots of the two Americans. The film was made by an American director, but under the British Quota System at the time—whereby the producer got a share of the British box office, in place to encourage production in the UK, meaning it had to have a British context and contain mainly British actors.[31] This entrance into the Slaughtered Lamb pub has become one of the most referenced film moments in popular culture and discourses. The phrase, 'It was like walking into the Slaughtered Lamb,' has become a shortcut to saying we have entered an inhospitable place. We identify with David and Jack as outsiders in this community. As Landis (2009) states, it recalls the cinema cliché—borrowed from classic Westerns—of entering the saloon and the music stopping. While this scene is located within a very specific place, the scenario is also familiar (generically) with a broad global reach. The sequence foregrounds the urban / rural divide of entering an insular space where people have a shared indecipherable understanding, uninterpretable by the 'outsider.' However, the shots also accentuate David and Jack's alien-ness as Americans within the rural British setting. They are clearly absurd-looking in their bright puffer jackets, zipped up to the top, with their backpacks clipped ready to do Europe. David in particular stands out, in his red coat, as different from the locals in their brown and green tweed and parkas. David will after all be the central figure of the film; he is to some degree Little Red Riding Hood. Later that night, despite having been warned by the farmer and by someone at the pub ("Go – stay on the road – keep clear of the moors"), it is David who is on the side of the track next to the grass when they stray onto the moors, leading them to the lair of the werewolf.

---

[31] Amongst the crowd is a young, up-and-coming Rik Mayall who Landis had seen doing stand-up in London and asked semi-jokingly to come along in the morning.

The actor who plays David would have been recognizable both sides of the Atlantic as the singing and dancing figure from the Dr. Pepper commercials airing at the time and his star persona must have contributed to the image of a fresh-faced, wholesomely naïve young American, at least at this stage of the film. Jack wanted to go to Rome, the comedy being they begin here instead in this rain drizzled void of civilization. The beast they encounter seems to originate from here, the tragedy being that it is David that made them come here first. The American connection helps to partition off this section of Britain at the time as a remote, forgotten part of Europe, a place that werewolves might just still inhabit.

An American Werewolf in London was remarkable at the time of its release for locating the horror within a contemporary London setting. The shock of David's decomposing friend Jack, mentally unchanged, appearing to him suddenly in the bathroom mirror of Alex's flat (just after David and Alex have become lovers) is Shakespearian in its sense of foreboding, but based on an abject humour that is intensified by the everyday setting. Later, David is beckoned by his now virtually skeletal friend to enter a cinema in Piccadilly where the pornographic film *See you Next Wednesday* is being screened[32] (Landis' reference to a phrase used at the end of Stanley Kubrick's *2001 A Space Odyssey*) and they sit chatting together in the cinema auditorium, amongst the other animated corpses David 'killed' during his werewolf spree the night before. Freshly blood-splattered, the decomposing bodies discuss ways that David could take his own life, a sure means to break the curse, much to Jack's disgust—showing his dogged loyalty to their friendship.

David's big transformation takes place amidst the everyday items of Alex's front room while she works into her night shift. David is shown to be in agony and horrified, as the beast from within is born out of himself, as hair sprouts and his face and hands extend. The sequence has been much praised for its boldness. For example, James B. Twitchell (1985: 217) marvels that "this seamless metamorphosis happens in no breakaway before our unbelieving eyes, almost as if the wolf is enfolding outward *through* the skin of a man." The transformation is not masked behind obstructing parts of the decor nor staggered via multiple cuts and fragmentations as it has been in previous films, such as *Werewolf of London* and *The Wolf Man*. The single cut to the plastic Mickey Mouse is humorously,

[32] A poster for *See you Next Wednesday* is seen on the wall of the underground where the commuter tries to flee from the werewolf.

unsubtly foregrounded, highlighting that this sequence has no other cutaways. Plastic Disney figures were popular consumer items at the time, and the cutaway acts as a comical reminder that the transformation is taking place in an everyday contemporary British home. There is also a nudge (during this major transformation feat of special effects) to Disney as corporate conglomerate animator—made slightly ridiculous, framed in this static disposition. The amusing build-up of tension accelerates throughout the day, as David keeps checking his reflection and gets accidentally locked out of the house. The transformation is painful, like childbirth as Barbara Creed argues (1993: 125), but I suggest there is energy in it, and Sam Cooke's version of 'Blue Moon' sets an oddly chirpy soundtrack. After David was bitten on the moors, he formed a sexual relationship with Alex, as if the bite is a rite of passage, and the transformation is an unleashing of the beast within. David strips off naked and sweats for the change. Despite the labored horror, there is a huge relief of tension, as if David, akin to a naïve ingénue, who mocked Jack for his purely sexual interests in a girl at the start of the film, has grown up. Settings also help to create an acerbic social critique. There is some delight when the condescending dinner party host, Sean, meets his death gorily from the powerfully transformed David out the back of Sean's elegant Hampstead Heath home. There is a similar glee in the depiction of the commuter trapped on the London underground escalator, his briefcase spilling open below him, as the huge wolf emerges at the base.[33]

David is also a tragic hero. When they are about to enter the Slaughtered Lamb near the opening of the film, Jack says it is all David's fault if something goes wrong. David initially runs away when Jack is attacked, only to return too late and get mauled himself. As Angela Curran (2003: 56) argues, "This reconfiguring of the monster as in some way 'like us' moves the narrative from the realm of horror into the domain of Aristotelian tragedy, within which we are forced to confront aspects of our humanity that go unacknowledged or unrecognized until misfortune occurs." Troublingly, it is David's humanity, in returning to help his friend

---

[33] In 1981, polarities between rich and poor were broadening in Britain and America. In the UK, the miners' strike coincided with London bankers gaining more power internationally. Large car manufacturing unions were crushed in the USA. Right-wing leaders would gain force as the year progressed, with Ronald Reagan and Margaret Thatcher beginning to forge a nominally stronger US/UK 'special relationship' based on shared values.

(albeit late), that seals his fate. Thus, moral codes of punishment and reward are disturbed. The young Americans' life assurances—playing baseball, taking a 'gap year' in Europe, university—are turned to dust when they find themselves on the moors, and David lands up dying in a London alleyway at the film's close. A past sense of direction is permanently upset.

Darker moments underlie the film. While still in hospital, David has a sudden fevered nightmare of Nazi zombies killing his family in front of him, while he is sat doing homework at the dining room table, and his younger siblings watch television; the zombies ravage everything with machine guns, set fire to the house and then slit his throat. The horror is preceded by Miss Piggy on the television talking about the violence in Punch and Judy shows, in a comical nod to *The Muppet Show*'s Frank Oz who appeared in the hospital playing the suspiciously officious Mr. Collins from the American Embassy. Waking suddenly, David tells Alex he has had a nightmare, but when she opens the curtains another Nazi zombie appears and stabs her repeatedly with a knife, blood flooding across her white nurse uniform, as nightmare and 'reality' become fused.[34] Prior to this, we learned that David is Jewish, when a nurse alludes to him having been circumcised. And it is important to note that Landis—himself Jewish—has discussed the Holocaust undercurrents of *The Wolf Man*, which was written by the screenwriter (Curt Siodmak), a Jewish émigré who fled the Nazi regime. Later, David tries to slit his wrist with his penknife in a London telephone box after he has called home to say he loves his family, managing only to get his ten-year-old sister, who in some strange event has been left home alone. What seems to be stressed here is the unreliability of authority, the instability of belonging, and the horror and terror of unexpected violence, in an everyday setting.

With regard to gender, there is a hint of Alex's untamed desires, as well as David's. Alex is not a central figure like the heroine of *The Company of Wolves*, nor does she join the wolves as Rosaleen does.

---

[34] This sequence also seems to strike a chord with the World War II German–American encounter 'deeply engraved in the American mind' that captivated the imagination of popular culture: "the story of the German 'werewolves,' Hitler's last underground fighters, who challenged the occupying armies in the war's closing months" (Christina von Hodenberg 2008: 71). Hodenberg suggests that the fears of a Nazi insurgency (in which American G.I.s were warned that friendly German civilians might be 'wolves' in disguise) was greater than the threat but that it captured the imaginations of American genre movies (2008: 78).

However, Alex's attraction to David is expressed openly; she invites him to stay at her flat and she is unfazed by the werewolf at the end. In previous films explored in this chapter, there is some level of sympathy from werewolves' girlfriends and wives, either in listening to the man open up about his werewolf side (*Curse of the Werewolf*) or even when confronted with the werewolf face to face (*Werewolf of London*). However, Alex is a more vigorous figure, actively approaching the werewolf (as Beauty does the Beast in the classical fairy tale) despite the danger in the final alley scene. Nevertheless, she remains a supporting character, unlike the heroine in *The Company of Wolves* whose dreams and passions drive the film. Rosaleen alone witnesses the huntsman's transformation, standing before him as he changes. The spectacle of the transformation, climaxing with the wolf's nose pushing through the huntsman's face, saturates the sequence. As Carole Zucker (2000: 69) argues, it is "unmistakably sexualised": "His back heaves, he sweats, his morphing body bursts through his clothes." While the hyper-masculine transformation takes centre stage, Rosaleen's lack of fear is noteworthy. When she shoots him, the wolf's wound incites her sympathy. Her agency endures, even though her own subsequent transformation to wolf occurs off-screen.[35]

The finale of wolves jumping through the portrait into the family house, as the dream streams into the 'real,' is a revolutionary inversion of the usual release of repression, which tends to be imagined as a bursting out rather than in. However, awakening to wolves crowding outside her bedroom door, the heroine screams piercingly (echoing Alice's scream at the start of the film) when a wolf comes crashing into her bedroom through the window. The heroine's scream is troubling and seems to be indicative of the lingering tensions within the film. In a Channel 4 television interview on *The Company of Wolves*, transmitted the year the film was released, Carter (1984) is initially perplexed by Jordan's decision to include the scream, seeing it as an "extended homage to Hammer Horror films"—a regression to objectifying the female, as victim. However, she then suggests, "I guess that when the girl wakes up in a state of agitation she's perhaps thinking that some things are justifiably repressed...." When asked separately about the scream for the same programme, Jordan first

---

[35] Carter's radio play *A Company of Wolves* is a more radical rewriting of the fairy tale. The heroine removes her clothes first, and almost has to make him do the same; once the heroine expresses her desires, the werewolf has difficulty articulating his. The radio play is not contained by opening and closing sections like the film is.

posits it as "an orgasmic thing... both joy and terror at the same time" like on a rollercoaster. However, later (on the 2005 DVD commentary) he retracts, saying that he should have had the heroine welcome the wolves rather than scream in terror at their intrusion to be more in keeping with the film's celebration of burgeoning female sexuality.

The ending is a sticking point as it is clearly a departure from the words that close Carter's story 'The Company of Wolves': "Sweet and sound she sleeps in granny's bed, between the paws of the tender wolf" (Carter 2007: 139). These are also the final words spoken by the narrator at the end of the radio play (Carter 1997: 83).[36] Carole Zucker asks whether the film thus authorizes Granny's "vision of the terror of sexuality," but she goes on to suggest that it can be read as a "reflection of the terror she finds in becoming a woman, and in finding herself deprived of the sense of power she experienced in her dream" (Zucker 2000: 70). On one level, the ending seems to deny the heroine's dream, in the face of everyday reality, reinstating repression's terror of the dream world encroaching without the necessary codes of civilization. However, on another level, it could be argued that the film warns of the dangers of over-repression. When Rosaleen becomes a wolf in the dream, the only way to survive is to leave (to become an outcast permanently on the move as the gypsies are in *The Wolf Man*). The wolf that invades the heroine's bedroom could be the transformed Rosaleen, making this a vision of the wolf-self overriding the tamed self—the dream overpowering the 'real' (repressed). It speaks of the dangers of growing up bringing with it an over-repression of desire, with the only outlet being outlawed as an external threat on internal 'safety.' In this sense, the film can be read not as a denial of the repressed but a warning against over-repression, gaining inspiration from the gothic inclination to embrace the wild side within everyday life.

However, ultimately, the film is open to multiple interpretations, and seems to discourage a single reading. The voice-over narration of a translation of Perrault's *verse moral* to 'Little Red Riding Hood,' spoken over

---

[36]The screenplay aimed for an ambitious ending, of Alice diving into the floor (in the screenplay, Alice is the heroine within the contemporary frame, who witnesses her own death in the dream, with Rosaleen her younger sister taking over). Alice bounces on her bed, then springs off "as if on a diving-board," then "plummets": "The floor parts. It is in fact water. She vanishes beneath it" (Carter and Jordan 1997: 244). A he- and she-wolf enter the remaining room "half-forest, half-girl's bedroom" nosing Alice's items (1997: 244). It was never screened due to the technical difficulties it would cause at the time.

the end credits, does seem to be a final nail in the coffin for female liberation: "Little girl, this seems to say / Never stop upon your way… " However, the female voice provides a compellingly ironic tone. The heroine is voice-less in the contemporary opening and ending frames, apart from the scream, making the final words of verse all the more haunting. In her caution, "Wolves may lurk in every guise" and "Sweetest tongue has sharpest tooth," she could be referring to herself (watch out, she seems to say, the wolf might be me).

Nature–culture tensions within humanity touch us at every level, crushing boundaries of class, gender or nationality. As Glen Duncan (2013: 29) asserts, the werewolf figure in all its forms and guises "exploits our duality in the baldest possible way, reminding us that for all our rarefied consciousness, the evolutionary umbilical remains uncut: the wild animal sleeps only ever lightly, and sometime comes spectacularly wide awake." Nevertheless, specific boundaries that separate humanity have often been underlined in werewolf movies, reinforcing societal fears within specific cultures at a given time. Enhanced masculinity and exaggerated rage have become central to cinematic representations of the transformation to werewolf, creating a masculinized monster, indicated by titles such as *The Wolf Man*.[37] Coinciding with this development, as is evident in *The Curse of the Werewolf*, for example, are the attacks on female victims, dividing women into fixed virtuous / disposable types. *The Company of Wolves* goes to considerable lengths to break with traditions that have frozen the figure of Little Red Riding Hood either as endangered prey or catalyst of danger, presenting instead a complexly layered coming-of-age tableau. Even though the heroine's dreams drive the narrative, tensions accelerate as the film progresses. The (male) werewolf's spectacular transformation to some extent overshadows the heroine's own, and the closing frame envisions the wolves' return as a catastrophic collision with the constraints of contemporary life. This is foreshadowed by the magazine special issue 'The Shattered Dream' lying on the heroine's pillow at the film's start. Nevertheless, while all of the films explored in this chapter are on some level inescapably inhibited by containment, societal repression comes under close scrutiny. The werewolf fantasy maintains its radical potential, releasing the unsayable into the public domain, calling for a cultural embrace of estranged nature, marginalized identities and repressed traumas.

---

[37] Paul Naschy (famed for Mexican werewolf movies since the 1960s) also had a similar physique.

References

Benshoff, H.M. (1997). *Monsters in the Closet: Homosexuality and the Horror Film* (Manchester and New York: Manchester University Press).
'Beware the Moon', 'Special Features', *An American Werewolf in London* DVD, Disc 2, 2009 Universal Studios.
Bourgault du Coudray, C. (2006). *The Curse of the Werewolf: Fantasy, Horror and the Beast Within* (London and New York: I.B. Taurus).
Buscombe, E. (1976). *Making* Legend of the Werewolf (London: British Film Institute).
Carter, A. (2007). 'The Company of Wolves', in *The Bloody Chamber And Other Stories* (London: Vintage Books), pp. 129–139.
Carter, A. (1997). '"The Company of Wolves" Radio Play', in A. Carter (1997) *The Curious Room: Collected Dramatic Works* (London: Vintage), pp. 61–83.
Carter, A. and Jordan, N. (1997). '"The Company of Wolves" Screen Play', in A. Carter (1997) *The Curious Room: Collected Dramatic Works* (London: Vintage), pp. 185–244.
Creed, B. (1993). 'Dark Desires: Male Masochism in the Horror Film', in S. Cohan and Ina Rae Hark (eds.), *Screening the Male: Exploring Masculinities in Hollywood Cinema* (London and New York: Routledge), pp. 118–133.
The Company of Wolves (transmitted 17 October 1984). Channel 4 Visions series, Episode 2, https://www.youtube.com/watch?v=EokEcGmWJ3U [last accessed 28 July 2017].
Craig, J.R. (April 2005). 'The Origin Story in Werewolf Cinema of the 1930s and 40s', *Studies in Popular Culture*, 27: 3, 75–86.
Curran, A. (2003). 'Aristotelian Reflections on Horror and Tragedy in *An American Werewolf in London* and *The Sixth Sense*', in S.J. Schneider and D. Shaw (eds.), *Dark Thoughts: Philosophical Reflections on Cinematic Horror* (Lanham, Maryland and Oxford: The Scarecrow Press, Inc.), pp. 47–64.
Duncan, G. (2013). 'The Werewolf', in J. Bell (ed.), *Gothic: The Dark Heart of Film* (London: BFI), p. 29.
'Elder, J.' (Hinds, A.) (August, 1960). *The Curse of the Werewolf* 'Shooting Script', Hammer Film Productions Ltd.
Endore, G. (1933). *The Werewolf of Paris* (Paris: Farrar and Rinehart, Incorporated).
Edwards, E.D. (2005). *Metaphysical Media: The Occult Experience in Popular Culture* (Carbondale: Southern Illinois University).
Greenhill, P. (2008). '"Fitcher's [Queer] Bird": A Fairy-Tale Heroine and Her Avatars', *Marvels and Tales (Erotic Tales)*, 22: 1, 143–167.
Hallenbeck, B.G., and Van Genechten, J. (November 2001). 'The Making of... *The Curse of the Werewolf*', in R. Klemenson (ed.), *Little Shoppe of Horrors* ('*The Curse of the Werewolf*' Special), 15, 38–94.

Harper, S. (1998). 'The Scent of Distant Blood: Hammer Films an History', in T. Barta (ed.), *Screening the Past: Film and the Representation of History* (Westport, Connecticut: Praeger).
Hopper, K. (Fall, 2003). 'Hairy on the Inside: Re-visiting Neil Jordan's *The Company of Wolves*', *The Canadian Journal of Irish Studies*, 29: 2, 17–26.
Hutchings, P. (1993). *Hammer and Beyond: The British Horror Film* (Manchester and New York: Manchester University Press).
Jackson, R. (1991, reprinted version). *Fantasy: The Literature of Subversion* (London and New York: Routledge).
Jordan, N. (2005). 'Commentary by Director Neil Jordan', 'Special Features', *The Company of Wolves* DVD, Granada Ventures Limited.
McCann, S. (2010). '"With redundance of blood": Reading Ireland in Neil Jordan's *The Company of Wolves*', *Marvels & Tales*, 24: 1, 68–85.
Murphy, M. (December 1999). '*The Curse of the Werewolf*', *Dark Terrors*, 17, 7–9.
Newsom, T. (September–October 1992). '"Letters" section', *Film Comment*, 28: 5, 80.
Perrault, C. (2009). '"Little Red Riding-Hood" (1697)', in C. Perrault (2009) *The Complete Fairy Tales*, translated by C. Betts, with illustrations by G. Doré (Oxford and New York: Oxford University Press), pp. 99–103.
Orenstein, C. (2002). *Little Red Riding Hood Uncloaked: Sex, Morality, and the Evolution of a Fairy Tale* (New York: Basic Books).
Spadoni, R. (2010). 'Strange Botany in *Werewolf of London*', *Horror Studies*, 1: 1, 29–71.
Spadoni, R. (Winter 2011). 'Old Times in *Werewolf of London*', *Journal of Film and Video*, 63: 4, 3–20.
Terry, J. (1999). *An American Obsession: Science, Medicine, and Homosexuality in Modern Society* (Chicago and London: The University of Chicago Press).
Teverson, A. (2013). *Fairy Tale: The New Critical Idiom* (London and New York: Routledge).
Twitchell, J.B. (1985). *Dreadful Pleasures: An Anatomy of Modern Horror* (New York: Oxford University Press).
Verdier, Y. (1997). 'Little Red Riding Hood in Oral Traditions', *Marvels & Tales*, 11: 1/2, 101–123.
von Hodenberg, C. (2008). 'Of German Fräuleins, Nazi Werewolves, and Iraqi Insurgents: The American Fascination with Hitler's Last Foray', *Central European History*, 41: 1, 71–92.
Zipes, J., ed., (1993, second edition). *The Trials and Tribulations of Little Red Riding Hood* (New York and London: Routledge).
Zipes, J., ed., (2000). 'Little Red Riding Hood', *The Oxford Companion to Fairy Tales* (Oxford: Oxford University Press), pp. 301–302.
Zucker, C. (2000). 'Sweetest Tongue Has Sharpest Tooth: The Dangers of Dreaming in Neil Jordan's *The Company of Wolves*', *Literature/Film Quarterly*, 28: 1, 66–71.

CHAPTER 6

The Horror in *Pan's Labyrinth*: Beneath the Rhetoric of Hope and Fear

The elaborate interlacing of the fantasy and 'real' world in Guillermo del Toro's *El laberinto del fauno/Pan's Labyrinth* (Mexico, Spain, USA: 2006) makes it an important film for exploring the various functions of fairytale and gothic horror on screen.[1] This chapter investigates how horror related to the rhetoric of hope and fear seeps between worlds in *Pan's Labyrinth*, as a fantasy or visionary world is intertwined with scenes depicting traumas caused by fascism immediately after the Spanish Civil War. I consider the film's treatment of the horrors endured during Francisco Franco's domination in Spain, and the hope and fear related to specific historical actualities. Key to this investigation is the journey of the young pre-pubescent heroine, Ofelia (Ivana Baquero), as she faces extreme terrors and responds to the fantasy and 'real' world in a creatively defiant way. To some extent, *Pan's Labyrinth* reinforces some of the patriarchal fears and assumptions associated with the female role and body, often rooted in gothic horror as well as fairytale traditions. However, beyond this, the film questions the rhetoric of hope and fear that underlies dictatorship and the blind following of orders. I suggest that in this respect Ofelia functions as an empowering, progressive young female hero. Fairytale themes in the film—fears of 'otherness', rites of

---

[1] An earlier, shorter version of this chapter was previously published: Laura Hubner (2010). 'Pan's Labyrinth, Fear and the Fairy Tale', in Stephen Hessel and Michèle Huppert (eds.), *Fear Itself: Reasoning the Unreasonable* (Amsterdam and New York: Rodopi Press), pp. 45–62.

© The Author(s) 2018
L. Hubner, *Fairytale and Gothic Horror*,
https://doi.org/10.1057/978-1-137-39347-0_6

passage—are interwoven with the historically specific, to address traumas caused by dictatorship and male brutality. I explore the roles Ofelia adopts and the choices made available to her that reverberate back on the 'real' life massacres associated with her stepfather's violent regime.

From the outset, it is clear that the fantasy world, strongly associated with Ofelia and her vision (of a different way), should be read on a level equivalent to its 'real' counterpart. The transitions between worlds are multiple and complex, developing the template of an outer 'real' frame that unfolds into dream that inspires films as diverse as *The Wizard of Oz* (1939), *Rebecca* (1940) and *The Company of Wolves* (1984), to the point that residues between fantasy and real worlds become interwoven, and the two worlds inform each other, adding new layers of meaning. While in *Pan's Labyrinth* we witness Ofelia venturing into the fantasy world—and it is clearly a world that she is driven to explore—fantasy creatures and spaces emerge within and out of the landscape, as if they exist just beyond the borders. The labyrinth itself exists within the 'real' setting, but its function as a portal to the Underground World belongs to the magical, fantasy realm.

Despite the fluidity between the two worlds, I argue that the more rigid, simple character types dwell in the 'real' world, making it resemble a classical fairy tale, while much greater uncertainty thrives in the realm of fantasy. I suggest that because the brutality of the subject matter of the 'real' world is difficult to speak of, exploring historical atrocities that still resonate, fairytale simplicity is used to convey the 'real' world and the characters that function within this realm. Furthermore, fairytale structures, roles and narratives are utilized to help universalize the specific, bringing attention to key tensions for broader appeal, while at the same time drawing on the fairy tale's capacity to address unspoken about and taboo subject matter. In turn, while the fantasy realm does contain elements of a fairy tale (the three tasks, for example), its overall tone effuses gothic uncertainty, raising as many questions as it answers, and opening onto a world in which moral certainties are challenged. I argue that the gothic qualities of the fantasy world help to shed new light (or shadows) on events that take place in the 'real' world, complicating both the events themselves, and the characters' actions, outcomes and the effects of their choices and actions.

Pan's Labyrinth is set in 1944, five years after the end of the Spanish Civil War. Events take place in a remote hamlet within woodlands in the north of Spain close to the French frontier. Vidal (Sergi López), a captain in Spain's Civil Guard, has been posted there to purge the area of the *maquis*, the republican resistance movement. Crushed in the Civil War, a small number of the Resistance continue to fight a campaign against Franco's regime. *Pan's Labyrinth* is a bold and challenging film, at least as far as it faces head-on the horrors of human brutality and terror, positioning them within a specific historical context. The difficulty of confronting such terror is a deep-rooted and complex issue:

> Repression was certainly not the only characteristic of the Franco regime, but it had been stamped through blood and fire onto the memory of the Spanish population. The trauma of the civil war, after which so many vowed to 'never again' go through such an experience, tended to paralyse active opposition against the dictatorship, even during the country's transformation into democracy. (Campos 2004: 352)

While the Spanish Civil War and Franco's regime are traumatic periods that have received considerable (though sporadic) attention in the history of post-Franco filmmaking, close inquiry into specific ideological and political proceedings has been sparse, suggesting a wariness, or fear, of re-treading and negotiating past events. Spain's recent history has provided Spanish filmmakers in particular with a wealthy source of material. Barry Jordan and Rikki Morgan-Tamosunas (1998: 16) calculated that more than half of the nearly 300 historical films produced since the 1970s were set during the Second Republic, the Civil War and Francoism. The oppositional film-making of the 1970s was quick to subvert Francoist idealism. However, as David Archibald argues: "This initial move to debate the central political concerns of the Civil War was followed by a move away from detailed historical political analyses" (2004: 76).[2] Perhaps this is because, along with other real-life atrocities like the Holocaust and Hiroshima, there has been a numbness stemming from deep-rooted subjection, trauma and fear. As Archibald argues, this tendency of Spanish films to elide the political and historical detail

---

[2] Archibald cites as an example *La lengua de las mariposas / Butterfly's Tongue* (José Luis Cuerda, 1999). He suggests that the film depicts Republican Spain with "rose-tinted spectacles," consigning the Civil War to the past: "The stress that *La lengua de las mariposas* places on the transformative powers of education suggests that in contemporary Spain, with a generation of young people brought up free from the constrictive dictatorship and educated in the world of liberal democracy, it is a nightmare that need no longer haunt contemporary Spanish society" (Archibald 2004: 81).

"is reflective of a more widespread tendency in Spanish society itself" (2004: 77). What Archibald refers to is the haunting silence, noted by historians, such as Paul Preston (2000: 21):

> Since the return of democracy to Spain, commemoration of the Civil War has been muted. The silence was partly a consequence of the legacy of fear deliberately created during the post-war repression and by Franco's consistent pursuit of a policy of glorifying the victors and humiliating the vanquished. It was also a result of what has come to be called the *pacto de olvido* (the pact of forgetfulness). An inadvertent effect of Franco's postwar policies was to imbue the bulk of the Spanish people with a determination never to undergo again either the violence experienced during the war or the repression thereafter.

Rob Stone (2002: 130) argues that this silence rose up again when, following a widespread disillusionment with socialism, the right-wing Partido Popular ('People's Party') were voted into power in 1996: "Since then, Spanish film-makers have barely touched on contemporary social issues or even a political theme."[3] Jonathan Ellis and María Sánchez-Arce locate a split in Spanish society between an older generation who still remember the Spanish Civil War and are cautious about resurrecting old wounds and a new generation who are too young to remember and are eager to learn about it (2016: 185).[4] Prior to *Pan's Labyrinth*, an increasing tendency to either glorify the present

---

[3] One of the few exceptions, noted by Stone, *Sé quien eres / I Know Who you Are* (Patricia Fereira, 2000), can be seen to reflect on the dualities and complexities of Spanish identity. This romantic thriller centres on a female psychiatrist who locates the traumas connected to her patient's loss of memory, by unearthing the hidden violent episodes of history blotted out by an entire nation. As Stone (2002: 131) argues, "Thus, in this film's honest look back at recent Spanish history, there is, perhaps, the beginning of a cure for social amnesia and a recognition of its necessity."

[4] Ellis and Sánchez-Arce (2016: 216, footnote 1) elaborate, "The gaze of the grandchildren no longer respects the pact of oblivion. While Spain's political class remains cautious about breaking the silence, a significant section of civil society is ready to remember the past and restless to tell and be told its almost-forgotten stories. Since the new millennium a series of civil pressure groups, most notably the Association for the Recovery of Historical Memory, has petitioned the government for financial assistance to locate and recover the bodies of all those who were killed by Franco's forces both during and after the Civil War." The Civil War remains a talking point in current disturbances including those related to the violent intervention by Spanish police attempting to suppress the independence referendum held in Catalonia on Sunday, 1 October 2017 on the grounds that it was not legal.

by distancing or satirizing the past or keep the focus away from central political scrutiny is evident.⁵

Thus, the graphic level of detail used in *Pan's Labyrinth* to represent the carnage resulting from Franco's power is significant, making it a very hard film to watch and listen to. We see, for instance, a starving father and son (who are out hunting rabbits) slaughtered by Captain Vidal, who assumes that they are resistance fighters. He smashes the son in the nose and face repeatedly with a metal truncheon until he is dead, in the father's presence, and then he shoots the father in the throat. Within the frame, the specks of blood fly. When Vidal finds the skinny dead rabbit afterwards, he curses the men who found the father and son for wasting his time, thus valuing his time above everything else. He shows no regret for his savage murders, and takes the rabbit back for dinner.⁶ We also see Vidal's brutal torture of "the stuttering man." He tells him that if he can count to three without stuttering he will go free. The scene, shown in a long take and in close-up, lingers to capture the blood flowing from the man's mouth, his every breath clear on the soundtrack as he fails to say the number three. These are just a few examples of the graphic realism afforded the many violent acts.

This close engagement with specific acts of violence to capture the horrors of Franco's regime makes *Pan's Labyrinth* distinctive within contemporary cinema. However, the film's representations of brutality echo the severe violence exposed beneath the regime's veneer in many of Spain's post-Franco oppositional films of the 1970s, such as José Luis Borau's *Furtivos* (1975). Indeed, the function of the rural woodland setting in *Pan's Labyrinth* can also be related back to the 1970s oppositional films. Jordan and Morgan-Tamosunas (1998: 46) suggest that in contrast to official Francoist cinema's depiction of a rural idyll to convey Franco's vision of Spain as a timeless forest, oppositional writing and films:

---

⁵ *El Bosc/The Forest* (Óscar Aibar, 2012) is a noteworthy Spanish film set in the 1930s about the ravages of the Spanish Civil War on a family, as factions struggle for territory. Close to the family's farmhouse, strange lights shine as an entrance to another world. The difficult and ambivalent relationship with the past is something that is also relevant to Mexican culture. In addition, Mexican cinema has a rollercoaster history controlled by varying levels of censorship.

⁶ This is all the more brutal due to Vidal's complete lack of empathy for the father–son relationship, despite the concept of the male bloodline being crucial to his own sense of identity. Time is clearly valued over human relationships.

...appropriated the rural context for the elaboration of a critical discourse which established rural Spain as the spatial representation of stasis and repression. The rural came to be represented in terms of its material deprivation and anachronistic repressive structures.

A similar emphasis is evident in *Pan's Labyrinth*. In addition, the film recalls the tendency of Spanish filmmaking in the 1970s to mythologize the individual fighters of the Resistance and their brave supporters in rural communities. For example, *Los días del pasado* (Mario Camus, 1977), the first film to focus on the previously banned subject of the *maquis*, pays close attention to the characters, their lifestyles, their interminable waiting and lack of supplies. As Jordan and Morgan-Tamosunas (1998: 47) argue: "The isolation and mystique of the rural setting contribute to the elevation of these figures to the level of myth." The ending of *Pan's Labyrinth* raises Mercedes (Maribel Verdú), her brother and his companions to this level of myth. Moreover, the film's rural setting of dark undergrowth and woodland helps to enable a blurring between 'reality' and fantasy that is also reminiscent of these earlier representations of the *maquis* in Spanish cinema.

José Arroyo (December 2006: 66) suggests that, plot-wise, the physical setting in *Pan's Labyrinth* provides the resistance movement with a "potential escape." The woods certainly offer a space for Outlaw existence, but the Resistance aim to fight rather than to escape. As Captain Vidal observes:

> The guerrillas are sticking to the woods because it's hard to track them up there. Those bastards know the terrain better than any of us.

The woodlands can be liberating for those who know how to navigate them. To the villain Vidal, they represent his fears, of the unknown 'other,' of all that is uncivilized and less easily controlled. His intention is to starve the 'creatures' out, commanding his forces to block all access to food and medicine.[7] In this way, the wild wood also becomes a threat to the Resistance. Its remoteness from civilization leaves them hungry and trapped. A single trail of smoke viewed by Vidal through binoculars

---

[7] In this sense, the treatment of the fighters is reminiscent of abandonment in fairy tales, such as 'Hansel and Gretel.'

Fig. 6.1 The Resistance are spotted, framed by Vidal's binoculars—*Pan's Labyrinth* (Guillermo del Toro, 2006)

confirms the existence—and signals the whereabouts—of the resistance fighters (see Fig. 6.1).

The binocular frame represents the confines of Francoist vision, containing and suppressing the lives of those who continue to fight within the wild and uncompromisingly severe northern borders. As Arroyo suggests, "Generically, the setting allows for the dense woodlands, darkness, rain and damp traditionally associated with horror" (December 2006: 66). With the relentless slaughter of the Resistance, the wooded mountains become what Carol Clover (1989: 101) calls the "Terrible Place," in which the victims at some point find themselves in the horror movie, symbolically here the dark, amoral side of the human psyche, invaded by the monstrous dictatorship.

In this respect, we should note horror's homage to fairy tale as a forum for critical engagement with taboo subject-matter. Parallels can again be made with Spanish filmmaking since the 1970s where, as Jordan and Morgan-Tamosunas (1998: 50) argue, "the use of legends and [fairy tales] as provocative correlatives of reality" was often integral to the narrative form. Jordan and Morgan-Tamosunas discuss, for example, three major films by Julio Medem, a key arthouse director of Basque cinema—*Vacas* (1992), *La ardilla roja* (1993) and *Tierra* (1995)—revealing that all three films emphasize "the disruption of the pastoral and spiritual tranquillity of the rural context by violence in its various forms of war, rivalry, jealousy and madness, again forging a link with this darker aspect of both fairytale fantasy and rural genres" (1998: 51–52). These are central elements in del Toro's filmmaking, and we should also note *Pan's Labyrinth*'s homage to fairytale ambivalence, where wild woodland can be both threatening and dangerously appealing. This ambivalence is evident in the shift of representation in Spanish cinema from forest as repressor in the 1970s towards the reincarnation of its nostalgic appeal from the 1980s onwards, where wild woodland again becomes a source of charm. Wild woodland functions in *Pan's Labyrinth* as both oppressor and liberator; it offers Ofelia a temporary form of escape and defiance, as is made clear from the start of the film.

The film opens with the sound of the faint melody. It is the film's theme tune, sung by Mercedes to soothe Ofelia later in the film. Mercedes is Vidal's maid, secretly helping the resistance fighters. The melody is accompanied by Ofelia's breathing. White words on a black background explain the context. We then see a close-up of Ofelia's face looking towards the camera but slightly off-frame, blood streaming from her nose. The camera rotates to reveal that her face is on the ground, her left hand out towards the corner of the frame; the sound of her breathing becomes louder. It becomes apparent that the shot is being played in reverse as the blood starts retreating back into her nose. She adjusts her gaze to look directly at the camera as the voice-over starts up.

We might note some of the complexities of the film even at this stage. Del Toro (2007) states that *Pan's Labyrinth* is a "female movie." The close-up on Ofelia's face identifies her as central to the tale, and the Brechtian break with naturalism as she stares into the camera suggests that we become aware of her position and perspective within the political events of the film. However, the male voice-over narrating the tale of a princess who fled to our world from her magical kingdom only to die, leaving her father yearning for her return suggests a further perspective is a masculine authorial voice. The film returns to the close-up of Ofelia's face at the end, but the final images of a flower opening and an insect are accompanied by the same male voice-over. The authorial voice-over helps give meaning to the images, but there is also a reflexive awareness throughout the film suggesting that meanings are more complex than the sum of simply one narration or voice; multiple stories and interpretations are possible.

After initial shots of the young princess leaving the dark underworld and running up the spiral staircase to the bright circle opening to the human world, the main narrative begins with Ofelia, travelling with her mother, Carmen (Ariadna Gil), to join her new stepfather, Vidal. The first shot is of Ofelia's hand turning the page of a book containing fairy tales. There is a cut to a close-up of the page. Next to the words, we see an illustration of a girl in a floating dress, surrounded by four fairies flying around her. A cut to medium shot reveals mother and daughter side by side, and the woodland outside Ofelia's window. The mother grasps her stomach, her other hand holding a tissue to her mouth as she tries to stave off the sickness of late pregnancy. The sharp distinction between the adult world and the fantasy world of the child is depicted in the relationship between mother and daughter. For instance, when they stop the car for Carmen to relieve her sickness and Ofelia ventures into the woods, an insect, somewhere between a dragonfly and a mantis, flies around her face. She is called to return to the car by her mother, who is standing with a military official of the Civil Guard:

Ofelia: I saw a fairy.
Carmen: Just look at your shoes!

In this short scene, it is clear that the woodland is the place that ignites Ofelia's imagination and it is the place that the first fantasy world sequences emanate from. As Ofelia and her mother return to the car, the camera is positioned behind the insect watching them leave. This is notably a moment that underlines the importance of the fantasy world, beyond the bounds simply of Ofelia's imagination. When the insect moves around the tree to the other side, the camera follows it to view the vehicles (the two shiny black cars followed by the luggage truck) as they continue on the journey in an ordered line. The viewpoint suggests that magical agents watch over the everyday world. The insect follows them. Fantastical viewpoints helping us to see and authenticate Ofelia's visions, such as this single moment and later when she crawls into a hole between roots of a tree, act as a further reminder of Julio Medem's work. For example, naturalism is extended in *Vacas* (1992) when the camera assumes the viewpoint of cows or is swallowed into a magical hollow tree trunk. In *Tierra* (1995), we see the insects busily working underground, as they affect the local wine production.

From the opening of *Pan's Labyrinth*, the magical world associated with Ofelia's is one that we are invited to share. Within the new woodland context, Ofelia begins to be lured to the magical fantasy world. The otherworldly clicking sound of the insect switches to the orderly ticking of Vidal's pocket watch, shown in close-up before there is a cut to the captain looking up, uttering "15 minutes late." Ofelia sees the insect again after her first meeting with Captain Vidal, suggesting a powerful rejection of his world. The insect takes her to the labyrinth, an old ruin within the woods, not far from the old mill and their new home. Mercedes, who becomes her friend, warns, "Better not go in there. You may get lost."

Much of the film's action revolves around the tensions brought on by disobeying orders and warnings. Mercedes' caution to Ofelia is motivated by her concern for the girl's safety, but narratively it functions in line with what Vladimir Propp (2008: 26) terms the necessary "interdiction." The fairytale hero disobeys the interdiction, and thus initiates the quest or journey. Going into the labyrinth opens up the Underground fantasy world of the faun (Doug Jones). While there are clearly many different ways of interpreting this, Eric White's reading of the insect as a means to explore Ofelia's unconscious is compelling. As "an emissary from the id," the insect leads Ofelia "into a world at once perilous and marvellous, the mysterious 'Underground Realm' of her own psyche" (2008: 373). I suggest that rather than denying the importance of the fantasy world, this reading adds further layers; the insect opens the door to an alternative world as vital and complete as the 'real' world, running concurrently with it. During the night, the insect returns to Ofelia, transforms itself into the fairy in her book and leads her to the labyrinth, where they descend through the circle into the underworld shown at the start of the film. Deep within, she encounters the faun who tells her that she is the lost Princess Moanna, whose father is King of the underworld, and that the labyrinth is a portal to the Underground Realm (her original home). He declares that if she completes three tasks before the advent of the full moon she can reclaim her rightful place in her father's realm. In order that she can carry out her tasks, he gives her a "Book of Crossroads," which is supposed to make it clear to her "what must be done." The "Cross" denotes Christian conceptions of death and resurrection, together with the knowledge that Spain (and most of the globe) is at this moment in history (1944) at a point of crossroads. However, since the pages are blank, the tasks and rules are open to Ofelia's

Fig. 6.2 Words and pictures flood Ofelia's body and the walls—*Pan's Labyrinth* (Guillermo del Toro, 2006)

imagination. As White (2008: 374) argues, "Only when she stares intently at its pages and unleashes her own powers of visionary projection will they fill with words and images pertaining to the task at hand." She thus plays a key role in the narratives of these pages, as writer, hero, reader and interpreter, and the images fill the frame via a long dissolve merging with the everyday setting (see Fig. 6.2).

The meanings of the words and images are open to interpretation, in keeping with the film's resistance to following blindly a single set of rules. Ofelia seems to be physically drawn to the labyrinth, and to the dark wild wood, creating and tackling tasks by trusting intuition and imagination.

Woodland signifies a space in-between, its liminality a pointer to something once seemingly understood as primeval, prior to discourse, providing an insight into an archetypal understanding of human behaviour. Through the course of western history, diverse fairy tellers (e.g., Marie-Jeanne L'Héritier, Charles Perrault, Wilhelm and Jacob Grimm and Walt Disney) have used woods and forests to warn children against straying from the path. Jack Zipes argues, for instance, that Perrault and the Grimm Brothers transformed 'Little Red Riding Hood' from "an oral folk tale about the social initiation of a young woman into a narrative about rape in which the heroine is obliged to bear the responsibility for her violation" (2006: 28). While there have been multiple modifications of this tale making it difficult to assess an original ('true') folktale, Zipes demonstrates the point that fairy tales are subject to social, cultural and moral shifts, and that meanings interpreted by authors and readers are ideologically positioned. As a warning against revolt, woodlands can be a symbol of repression, as much as a symbol of escape, pointing finally towards a return to civilization, a sanitized norm governed by societal law and order, as part of a necessary rite of passage for those between the age of childhood and adulthood. Paradoxically, the attractions of fear and the pleasures of the tale lie also in the possibilities of straying from the path, and of the need for active disobedience. Due to recent shifts in attitudes towards gender and sexuality, writers (such as Marina Warner, Angela Carter and Vicki Feaver) have investigated the fantasy of straying, and of actively desiring to stray, as a possible voice for female identity through emerging womanhood. Despite multiple retellings and re-workings of fairy tales, the fears associated with burgeoning female adulthood and the female body remain a controversial talking point that is never finally resolved.

Del Toro (2007) states that it is important that Ofelia is not mature sexually, that she is still a girl. He acknowledges the film's homage to fairytale conventions in which pre-pubescent girls pass through a rite of passage, "blooming into womanhood" or "independence." He states that, while most people can identify Ofelia with *Alice in Wonderland* and Dorothy in *The Wizard of Oz*, the tradition is much older.[8] However, while Ofelia is approaching the transition to adulthood, burgeoning womanhood is encoded with slightly conventional, essentialist symbolism.

To claim that *Pan's Labyrinth* is conventional gives a misleading and incomplete picture, particularly bearing in mind its head-on confrontation of the horrors of human brutality following on from the Spanish Civil War, and the graphic level of detail used to represent the carnage, as discussed earlier in this chapter. However, to some extent there is a sense that the film functions, ostensibly, according to a rather "simple" essentialist understanding of gender and sexuality. Indeed, del Toro uses the word "simple" when discussing the character types that appear

---

[8] Presumably here del Toro refers to young heroines in fairy tales like 'Little Red Riding Hood,' 'Snow White' and 'Rapunzel.'

in the film, drawn from fairytale traditions. The film's use of polarized archetypes to distinguish gender is also a conscious authorial decision; del Toro claims that, while fascism is a "boy's game," the film centres on the "11-year-old girl's universe." Ofelia's innocence is linked with her gender, placing boundaries on her insight and capabilities. At the end of the film, the fatherly (Godly) male voice-over tells us that Ofelia returns to the realm of her father. Gender roles are divided to the extent that the females are more inclined towards caring roles, possess magical powers and intuition, and although Mercedes severely attacks Vidal, she does not kill or imprison him, leaving him at large to shoot Ofelia. By contrast, Vidal is presented as naturally evil. The (male) voices of the priest at the funeral, the faun, the father (Father) and the final voice-over preach a law (akin to that of the Catholic Church) that one must suffer pain to receive transcendence.

The mise-en-scène emphasizes the sharp gender distinctions between Vidal's world and Ofelia's fantasy world. The rounded interiors of the labyrinthine monster worlds contrast with the sharp phallic angularity of Vidal's world; we might take as examples the long columns of cars and men with guns, and the scene where Vidal is stood beside his extended table, planning their attack. These serve as iconic references to an international history of war genre movies, labelling Vidal as instantly recognizable fascist villain. Vidal symbolizes Franco, who in 1944 was still making his victory over the republicans absolute, crushing any remaining instances of resistance, executing thousands of prisoners.[9] What is perhaps most striking about Vidal, though, is his reductively typed behaviour that visibly defies ambiguity or depth of character. He is pure evil from the moment he castigates Ofelia for holding out the wrong hand to greet him at their first meeting. His acute precision as he shaves with a sharpened blade connotes a masculine identity as rigid as the rules he follows; he resembles a comic-book figure of evil destined to provoke terror. The only reason that Carmen has been made to travel the long

---

[9] Franco wore the uniform of a Captain General (a rank reserved for royalty), seeing his position as assigned by God, and he ruled with a conservative, authoritarian conviction. However, his vision was far from ideologically coherent, forged out of an amalgamation of what Campos (2004: 348) sees as "two contradictory ideological and nationalist agendas" (a National-Catholic agenda meeting a fascist one): "Having long debated the nature of Francoist ideology, historians now tend to agree in their assessment of the Franco regime as a National-Catholic one, whether one views that label as referring to an ideology or a mentality."

distance is because Vidal demands that his son is born close to him (not for loving, caring reasons, but because the bloodline must be clear). Even though Vidal's motivations are ostensibly driven by a hope for the future and a firm belief that he is doing the right thing, so that (as he claims) his son can "be born in a new, clean Spain," the film makes it clear that his hopes are extremely misguided. Within the realm of the 'real' world, the blatant citation of Francoist rhetoric combines with the film's homage to war movie and fairytale binaries, seeming to stifle any indication of the complexities underlying historical events, as if it were possible to rid them of the terrors that provoked them. The insight into Vidal's hopes for the future casts considerable doubt on excessive trust in hope, asking us to question the ideologies we subscribe to. Hope as well as fear can lead to losing one's way. Nevertheless, there is scarcely the depth in Vidal's character to trigger a reflection on how real-life atrocities happen or the human characters involved in perpetuating them. In this sense, *Pan's Labyrinth* corresponds with a tendency common in previous decades to gloss over these events or to consign them safely to the past. The depiction of Vidal as a two-dimensional figure mirrors the representation of similar figures in 1990s Spanish films that attempt to distance the past, such as the immature and absurdly fanatical Francoist leaders in *La noche más larga* (García Sánchez, 1991). In this respect, *Pan's Labyrinth* seems to filter the past through a mask of caricature.

However, this reading would be to overlook the subversive potential of fairy tale. Del Toro (2007) discusses the film's debt to fairy tale, and recounts at some length his attempts to remain faithful to fairy tales' "simple" ingredients: "I always felt that the power of a fairy tale was that it was at the same time very simple and very brutal." He claims that the characters need to be types, and that today there is too much fear of simplicity. It is crucial, he argues, that Ofelia is innocent and good, incapable of violence against any living being. His words indicate that it is necessary to hold onto fairytale binaries, and he suggests that we might take the rebels in the woods as the woodsman who rescues Little Red Riding Hood, the Captain as the Big Bad Wolf and Ofelia as Little Red Riding Hood: "I believe that the hardest thing to pull off in art is actually simplicity"[10] (Del Toro 2007). He has a point in that devastating

---

[10] Del Toro does not go on to address the fact that the rebels are not able to finally save Ofelia from dying, at least within the 'real' world. However, it is worth noting that Ofelia's

subjects, silenced in other spheres, can be dealt with in the form of fairy tale. It is striking that, despite some blurring between the two worlds of the film, the strictest character types belong to the 'real' world whereas the ambiguous characters are reserved for the fantasy world. While there has been a tendency to presume that the fantasy world is the natural residence for fairytale qualities, I suggest that the 'real' world has a more conventional fairytale framework. Although there is some fluidity between the two worlds, the more rigid, simple character types inhabit the 'real' world, where extreme good is opposed to extreme evil as it is in the classical fairy tale, while more ambiguous characters thrive in the realm of fantasy. In other words, certain fairytale tropes are adopted in the 'real' world in order to convey more provocative subject matter in black and white terms, which the intervention of the fantasy realm helps to disturb.

Many theorists have pinpointed the centrality of simplicity for the functioning of fairy tale within diverse media and contexts. For instance, Millie Taylor examines fairytale archetypes as a means to understanding British pantomime:

> Good characters and evil characters are clearly separated and identified... There is no room for complexity or development of character because the tale is told through action and each character has a role in delivering the action of the story. (2007: 77)

Fairytale frameworks, by which the action revolves around good conquering evil, help to enforce structure and meaning, universalizing the local and specific. In *Pan's Labyrinth*, specific historic actualities are conveyed through timeless, universal conventions. As Michael Atkinson (2007: 53) suggests, "amidst the Fascists' tactics of summary executions, torture, and mutilations, Del Toro has found an evil that mythologizes itself in the eyes of the young—an ogre no one needs to imagine." Ogre-like humanity is given new meaning, while the narrative upholds a mythology of pure (simple) evil that is both linked to and is able to

---

actions and decisions recall the girl's disobedience and use of initiative in the early folk version of 'Little Red Riding Hood,' entitled 'The Story of the Grandmother' detailed in Chapter 5, in which the girl manages to outwit the wolf. The tale is reproduced in Jack Zipes (1993: 21–23).

be detached from the specificities of masculine dictatorship during this particular point in history.

However, reading the fairytale action often involves tracing darker and more complex roots embedded within the tale. The allegorical, fairytale framework allows *Pan's Labyrinth* to allude to the unspoken in terms of the actions of fathers and forefathers throughout this period of history. Troubling practices are transferred onto the evil stepfather (Vidal), rather than being allied with the natural father who has already passed away before the film's opening. That Ofelia's natural father (a simple tailor) no longer lives means that she can remember him as unblemished. By incorporating the stepfather as the villain, cruelty and brutality exist only outside Ofelia's natural bloodline; good and evil remain at distinct poles, undamaged and straightforward. Thus, fatherless and then orphaned when her mother dies in childbirth, Ofelia conforms to the traditional fairytale hero. The assignment of malevolence onto the stepparent is a civilizing, classical fairytale tradition. As Maria Tatar (2003: 37) has illustrated in her study of the Grimm brothers' many modifications through the different versions of *Children's and Household Tales* (1812–1857), one clear way of making a mother's cruel behaviour tolerable for readers and listeners of the tales was to turn her into a stepmother. Once reconfigured as 'stepmother,' there need be no constraints on her spiteful thoughts and activities:

> Thus the heartless mother who leaves her children to starve so that she and her husband might live and thrive becomes a wicked stepmother, and the evil queen driven by sexual rivalry to do away with her daughter slips easily into the role of the jealous stepmother who plots the murder of her beautiful stepdaughter. In each case, Wilhelm Grimm recognized that most children (along with those who read to them) find the idea of wicked stepmothers easier to tolerate than that of cruel mothers. (Tatar 2003: 37)

While *Pan's Labyrinth* is targeted at a predominantly adult audience, fairytale codes of practice help address problematic subject matter linked to very recent events. Thus, although *Pan's Labyrinth* veers towards civilizing history by transferring atrocities onto the two-dimensional, wicked stepfather, appearing to evade notions of a more complex, morally uncertain or even angst-ridden father figure, it nonetheless begins to pave the way for considering a world in which the father figure can be conceived as menacing or mistaken, a notion that remains taboo.[11] This gesture thus offers testament to the fairy tale's residing ability to refer allegorically to concerns that are otherwise unmentionable.

One of the most striking aspects of *Pan's Labyrinth* is that the imaginary world associated with Ofelia is as dark as the 'real' one. Indeed the fantasy world contains opaque and ambiguous qualities that are lacking in the dimensions of its real counterpart. The fantasy world gives direct expression to the dualities and taboos of human nature, reminiscent of the subversive functions that Rosemary Jackson (1991: 4) attributes to fantasy literature: "The fantastic traces the unsaid and the unseen of culture: that which has been silenced, made invisible, covered over and made 'absent.'" Although '*Pan*'s Labyrinth' (my emphasis) is the film's formally recognized international English title, del Toro (2007) is clear that the faun is not Pan, and that 'Pan' conjures up misleading connotations; he is "too dangerous a character to put in a fable like this."[12] The faun's ambiguous and duplicitous characteristics make the reactions and decisions Ofelia has to make in response to his tasks all the more difficult. The way to a single, true course is obscured, and it is never finally confirmed explicitly whether the choices she makes are morally correct.

Gothic as well as fairytale sensibilities are evident in the fantasy scenes associated with Ofelia. Gothic elements extend beyond the decadent excesses of the setting, pervading the obscure figures that Ofelia encounters, fundamentally upsetting the core of her identity. Lisa Hopkins' definition of 'gothic' exposes its dual function as not only a source for creating but also upsetting polarities such as 'good' and 'evil,' so that "things which appear to be opposite can actually be frighteningly, uncannily similar" (2005: xii). The fantasy world within *Pan's Labyrinth* creates this kind of destabilizing effect. Ofelia's extreme innocence and youth contrast with the faun's extreme power and age. However, a number of factors break down these absolutes and allude to a less than

---

[11] Although the stepmother is much more common in the fairytale canon than the stepfather, *Pan's Labyrinth* is not the first to split the father in two. William Shakespeare's *Hamlet* and Ingmar Bergman's film *Fanny and Alexander* (1982) (which bears similarities with *Hamlet*) serve as two examples of this divide between the good 'real' father and the wicked stepfather.

[12] Del Toro (2007) speaking on 'The Power of Myth,' *Pan's Labyrinth* 2 Disc DVD set, Optimum Home Entertainment, Disc 2. 'The Labyrinth of the Faun' is less concise and perhaps less memorable than 'Pan's Labyrinth.'

straightforward gothic doubling. The fantasy is associated with Ofelia and she is curious about it. The faun is ambivalently good and evil and Ofelia is surprisingly untroubled by the monsters. Links might be traced between Vidal and the faun; the captain's more ambiguous features are displaced onto the faun. We might even see a doubling between Ofelia and the faun. However, it is beyond the film's moral scope to envisage any conclusive parallels between Ofelia and Vidal. The fantasy world's gothic elements nevertheless function as compelling allusions to some of the real-life dualities and confusions that contributed to the rise of Francoist fascism.

Ofelia is remarkably unfazed in the wonderland of monsters. She confronts face-to-face the visions of the faun tearing off raw flesh with his teeth. On her second task, she approaches "the Pale Man" (Doug Jones), an ancient human-like creature with loose hanging flesh, whose eyeballs rest on the table alongside the dripping red fruits of the banquet in front of him. Curious as Lewis Carroll's Alice, Ofelia picks up and looks at his eyeballs. She then looks up at the ceiling paintings of the Pale Man monstrously killing babies, to the faint sound of babies crying. In one painting, he bites into a baby's head. In another painting, he has impaled a baby's chest with a sword. The paintings recall Francisco Goya's 'Saturn Devouring His Sons' (circa 1819–1823). The God of Time ate his children, so overcome by fear that they would overthrow him, a haunting sign of things to come, as Vidal will murder his stepdaughter at the end of the film.

Ofelia is disturbed if bemused by the images, but continues to look—now down towards the direction of a pile of worn shoes, a shocking moment that speaks to the film's audience, as an image that has become iconic in the aftermath of the Holocaust, but would clearly make no sense to Ofelia. Revulsion also lies in the knowledge that, in 1944, the horrors of the death camps were happening concurrently with events in the film's 'real' world. The camera pans up and past a large fire place in the distance. In a horrific, uncanny moment, we register that the sound of the crackling fire was audible earlier, and alongside the babies crying, but it is only now that we witness Ofelia stood between the pile of shoes and the semi-circular fireplace flaring like a large open mouth with a barbed iron jaw, that the full horror of the connection emerges.[13]

---

[13] A number of authors note that the pile of shoes is a reference to the Holocaust. See, for example: Atkinson (2007: 3); Walter Rankin (2016: 85); Ellis and Sánchez-Arce (2016: 200),

A further uncanny shudder is provided by the realization, on repeated viewings, that there are a great number of shoe piles resting at each pillar of this cathedral-like underground heaving belly of a hall. I suggest these tend not to be noticeable on first viewing; it is only when the camera elects to make significance of one of the piles, through Ofelia's gaze, that the knowledge is awakened, a gesture perhaps to the retrospective revelations of the full-blown atrocities that took place in death camps at this point of history. The Pale Man, blinded to the scene (having left his eyes on the table) sits with his back to the fire, the sumptuous feast in front of him, as Vidal has previously sat at the head of his table for the feast of stolen rabbits.

Ofelia, hungry because she missed her father's dinner having got her "princess" dress covered in mud, gazes at and moves towards the opulent fruit pile. She flicks away one of the fairies that gestures against touching the fruit. Turning back to check on the lifeless Pale Man, and flicking away another fairy, Ofelia plucks a succulent purple grape-like fruit and pops it into her mouth. This act awakens the Pale Man, who inserts the eyeballs into his palms, and holds up his hands to his head, fingers out-stretched, emulating the appearance of the faun (notably played by the same actor). Ofelia takes another grape, pulls off another fairy and eats the grape, pausing to chew for a moment and savour the delicious taste. The Pale Man grasps the fairies and bites their heads off messily. As the creature then places his hands in the position of the faun, Ofelia runs off. She only just manages to escape by drawing a door with chalk on the ceiling and hauling with all her might her dangling body upwards, back into her mother's bedroom.

As well as paralleling the faun, the Pale Man functions as a double for Vidal, and Franco's regime. Moreover, there is a strong allusion to Catholicism, or the Church as institution, whose involvement with Franco's regime and, in the union of Church and State, with fascism more broadly, is represented as equivalent to turning a blind eye at best, or drawing the blood of innocents at worst. As White points out, the Pale Man "neither samples the banquet he cannot see laid out before him nor permits anyone else to partake of life's bounty" (2008: 375).

Christopher Hartney and Sarah Penicka (2016: 227). Barry Spector (2009: 83) additionally observes, "The piles of children's shoes, the semicircular fireplace, and the date (1944) all evoke the Holocaust."

More generally, the slaughtering of babies is also a comment on the Civil War's devouring of its own people and "how the decision of elders to go to war can eat an entire generation of youth" (Hartney and Penicka 2016: 229). The duplicitous nature of Ofelia is explored when, Eve-like, she tastes the forbidden fruit.[14] She is liable for her actions, as Walter Rankin argues: "By giving into temptation and eating the grapes, Ofelia partakes in the history and culpability of Franco's Spain, losing two fairies in the process" (2016: 85). The effect of Ofelia's actions is horrific, but in the longer term to disobey the order not to eat or drink anything seems to enable a progression from this initiation into the next trial. Although Ofelia seems not to know the full gravity of what she does, her slightly spoilt rebuttal of the rules, even faced with the threat of a creature that massacres innocents, shows a bravery that is absent in the complying Vidal. To question and rebel rouses the dormant monster. As Ellis and Sánchez-Arce (2016: 198) argue, "The *maquis* successfully steal from Vidal but at the cost of several lives and blowing Mercedes' cover." Ofelia's entrance into this task equipped with a knife also anticipates Mercedes' own trial in which she bravely stabs and slashes Vidal. Mercedes' possible mistakes through the film (accidentally exposing to Vidal that she has a spare key, and using a knife against him but not killing him) inadvertently, and tragically, lead to Ofelia's death, but some small progress is made against the dictatorial regime by the end of the film. The sequence thus adds further layers to the actions and characters of the 'real' world, ambivalently advocating the importance of disobedience while at the same time acknowledging complicity in brutality on a monumental scale.

In Proppian fairytale terms, Ofelia's sequential trials and ongoing journey befit a hero on a quest, rather than a passive princess, but her strange encounters with these decadent, grotesque images of ageing and decay move into gothic horror territory, suggesting a much more complex, shadier understanding of the world. Ofelia's ability to make decisions and act upon them, sometimes in defiance, is empowering. As Kira Cochrane (2007) argues:

---

[14] Spector (2009: 83) observes that Ofelia resembles Persephone, who ate Hades' pomegranate; like the Greek queen who was forced to spend half her time in the Underworld and half her time with the gods, Ofelia is also a resident of two worlds.

In a contemporary landscape in which many young girls aspire to a dull, passive version of princesshood, Ofelia offers something different, something complex, something uniquely powerful. She is a strong antidote in a sea of blandness.

For Cochrane, what makes Ofelia stand out as a female hero is that she is represented as having "a clear certainty, self-absorption and objectivity, which make her far from simplistically vulnerable."[15] Cochrane (2007) also argues that "the sexual themes are far less pronounced than usual, and Ofelia's creativity is presented at face value." She suggests that the celebration of the female does not rest solely, as it does in so many pre-pubescent fantasy tales, on "our ability to reproduce."

I would agree that the sexual and reproduction themes are less pronounced, but only to a point. On the one hand, the film's overt lack of attention to the specific (gendered) concerns of a young female that are often at the centre of fairytale and gothic horror narratives is potentially a progressive move. We have only to think of *The Exorcist* (William Friedkin, 1973) and *Carrie* (Brian de Palma, 1976). Women's creative power lies in their biology, and the female body is depicted as a hideous, 'other,' to be feared, out of control, without limit and regressively linked with witchcraft. As Barbara Creed argues:

> Menstruation was also linked to the witch's curse – a theme explored in *Carrie*... Historically, the curse of a woman, particularly if she were pregnant or menstruating, was considered far more potent than a man's curse. A 'mother's curse', as it was known, meant certain death. (1993: 74)

The convention of working through fears of the female body, the menarche, the menstrual cycle, female sexual desire and childbirth all take as their inspiration a combination of folk/fairytale and gothic traditions (note the punishment of the female sexual deviants in, for example, *Jane Eyre* and *Rebecca*). With respect to childbirth, we might also consider films like *Rosemary's Baby* (Roman Polanski, 1968) and *The Hand that Rocks the Cradle* (Curtis, Hanson, 1992). In this respect, it is possible to argue that *Pan's Labyrinth* is refreshing, in the sense that it is an

---

[15] Cochrane (2007) suggests that in this respect Ofelia is rather like Rosaleen from *The Company of Wolves* (Neil Jordan, 1984) adapted, as outlined in the previous chapter, from Angela Carter's short story.

initiation film, in which gender (overtly, at least) seems less important than a universal understanding of humankind. *Pan's Labyrinth* examines in close proximity the role of the child in relinquishing fear and making challenging decisions through a rite-of-passage journey between childhood and adulthood, navigating between rational or allegedly 'civilized' choices and less clearly signposted pathways. Parallels can be made with del Toro's previous film *El espinazo del diablo / The Devil's Backbone* (2001), centring on the heroic determination of a young boy and his male friends at a deserted orphanage during the Spanish Civil War. Indeed, del Toro has often stated that these two films are linked together, that *Pan's Labyrinth* is the "sister movie" to *The Devil's Backbone*, which he sees as the "boy's movie."[16] It might be argued that an even more profound horror underlies *The Devil's Backbone* with its uninhibited slaughter of so many children at a deserted orphanage during the Spanish Civil War. However, both films feature a child visionary, or hero, who is daring enough to enter a confused abyss, and would risk death to save the lives of others. This humanist confidence in the individual's role within the collective stimulates both films.

On the other hand, there is a certain awe surrounding the female body in the uterine imagery of Ofelia's fantasy world, the infinite circular archways and interiors and the shots of Ofelia's baby brother in the womb.[17] Sexual themes are often couched in a more stylized symbolism in the plethora of fairytale literature and films. For example, there is the indelible icon of red (Little Red Riding Hood's cloak) or red on white (the three drops of blood on the snow/milk in 'Snow White' and the pricking of the finger in 'Sleeping Beauty') to symbolize emerging womanhood, sexuality or the loss of innocence. And traditionally, this tends to be a symbol of fear, of something to be kept in check. To a certain extent, *Pan's Labyrinth* perpetuates some of the fears associated with the female role, in relation to sex, death and childbirth, often rooted in gothic horror as well as fairytale traditions. In one scene, Ofelia watches as red ink blotches fill the pages of her fairytale book like blood on cloth. She rushes from the bathroom to find her mother bent double, blood spilling around her white skirts below the waist. Carmen's pregnancy takes a turn for the worse after she throws the mandrake root Ofelia has

---

[16] See, for example, Del Toro (2007).

[17] As suggested earlier, these rounded interiors contrast with the sharp phallic angularity of Vidal's world.

been keeping under the bed into the fire. Carmen eventually dies after giving birth to a baby boy. Thus, the female body is linked with death, magic and witchcraft. The thematic use of red and white demonstrates the film's dependence on the imagery surrounding the mystique of the female body in transition.

Nevertheless, as Cochrane argues, there is evidence that the film also resists nature and biology when Ofelia responds to Mercedes' caution that "having a baby is complicated" with "Then I'll never have one." Indeed, Ofelia and Mercedes form a resilient alliance. As Paul Julian Smith suggests, if "horror comes from knowing both sides of the story, then those two sides (victim and heroine) are distributed by del Toro to his twin active female protagonists" (2014, 75). Mercedes survives, having slashed Vidal across the mouth as swiftly as gutting a pig—part self-protection, part-revenge. Women (as evidenced by Carmen's position) had few rights under Franco's regime, bar the traditional mother/ daughter roles contained within the domestic domain. Home financial management was passed down from fathers to husbands, leaving wives financially as well as legally unable to leave abusive relationships. As Mercedes points out to Vidal, it is precisely because of her female invisibility that she has been able to carry out such a tapestry of tasks that resist his power, right under his nose, feeding and helping her brothers in arms. Vidal is only left alone with Mercedes as he embarks on her torture because, as he reassures Garces, his second in command, "For God's sake, she's just a woman." We are invited to question such assumptions about female limitations early in the film; for example, with the close up on Mercedes' hands, foregrounding the quick ease with which she tucks the sharp kitchen knife into her apron. A couple of the women who work under Mercedes in the kitchen look concerned for her safety and an older woman smiles to herself. The women notice but never mention her activities; this is bravery without bravado.

While Mercedes is finally rescued from the encircling army by the arrival of her brother and the *maquis*, the many parts she plays are a colossal feat of ingenuity in aiding resistance. Although she tells her brother that she feels guilty for having served Vidal day after day, the many roles she plays—as housekeeper, informer/spy for the Resistance and carer for Ofelia—put her in a position that is at least as dangerous as that held by resistance fighters out in the woods, as she has to confront close up the regime in all its guises, carrying out her mission in plain sight. Ofelia's movement between two worlds reflects on the necessary precariousness of Mercedes' life as she moves swiftly between the mill and the woods. By the end of the film Mercedes, her brother, and his companions are raised to heroic levels, indicating how individual choices and bravery lead to collective enterprise. And Ofelia is certainly no passive victim.[18] In a powerful way, she disobeys throughout the film: she defies Vidal and refuses to call him 'father,' she ventures into the woods and returns to the labyrinth. Finally she disobeys her stepfather and steals her baby brother, she disobeys the faun by not handing over the baby and she says 'no' to Vidal after he takes the baby.[19] From Vidal's perspective, Ofelia stands alone with the baby by the labyrinth—no faun in sight. That Vidal does not see (cannot share) the vision Ofelia sees suggests either that it is in her imagination or that he lacks the vision to see beyond surfaces—or the courage to question what he sees. The doctor, who shows a deep humane concern for Carmen's long journey, is daring enough to see beyond boundaries imposed by ideologies. Because he helps and gives relief to the resistance fighters, he brings about his own death: "To obey without thinking—just like that. Well—that's something only people like you can do—Captain."[20] He is shot in the back by Vidal, who is protected from the rain by his attendants' umbrellas, on a bleak rain-drenched, unremarkable day—observed in long shot to stress the regime's lack of human feeling. Dropping the case of medicine bottles that have given his game away, he manages a few more steps before sinking forwards head first into the mud. A lone woman in the distance turns round to look but continues on her way. Seconds later, women come to tell Vidal that his wife is in labour.

Biology and the (male) bloodline are undercut at the end of the film. Vidal appears from the labyrinth holding his baby son, having shot Ofelia. He realizes that he faces death as he turns the corner to find the resistance fighters waiting for him, the mill he has been living in ablaze behind them. He walks up to Mercedes and Pedro, handing over the

---

[18] It is worth noting that the female network is a strong feature of a number of films by Pedro Almodóvar, who significantly worked as one of the producers on del Toro's *The Devil's Backbone*.

[19] Unlike Abraham's agreement to hand over his son Isaac to God, in the Bible, Ofelia's refusal to sacrifice the baby is evidence that she has passed the test by showing initiative.

[20] The mass suppression of republican sympathizers, leading to death or enforced departure, meant that Spain lost a huge number of its professionals (including doctors, nurses, lawyers, teachers and artists) in the aftermath of the Civil War.

baby. He takes out his pocket watch to crush it at the time of his death, a tradition handed down from his father. When he says, "Tell my son—Tell him what time his father died—Tell him that I," Mercedes interrupts with, "No. He won't even know your name." This scene directly subverts the codes and conventions of official Francoist cinema made during the 1940s, whereupon violence is glossed over and the deaths of fascist heroes are glamorized as they sacrifice themselves for Spain and for their God. Vidal's words echo the words of Pedro Churruca in *Raza* (José Luis Sáenz de Heredia, 1942): "When death calls, one must go proudly, ... such was your forefathers' beautiful death." *Pan's Labyrinth* reverses the heroic figures, and emphasizes instead the violence at the hands of the fascist villains. In addition, Mercedes' refusal to let Vidal's son know his paternal lineage inverts the usual affliction faced by children of the republicans. As Mar Diestro-Dópido argues, "This line clearly alludes to the fact that around 30,000 children of 'Reds' killed or imprisoned were adopted by Franco supporters. With no knowledge of their past, they became the other disappeared, living for years under identities far removed from their real ones" (2013: 77). Although Mercedes' line carries its own potential problems, perpetuating the avoidance of acceptance and discussion in future generations, its specific function at this point of the film is crucial in foregrounding such repression of republican children's identities. Implicitly referring to long-held knowledge about the repressed, the film goes some way toward bringing attention to silenced voices and stifled memories.

At the end of the film, Ofelia's body shines white in the light of the full moon, blood floating from her mouth, to some degree reinforcing essentialist fairytale (red-on-white) colour schemes. A golden light marks her transcendence into the realm of her father, where emerging wearing bright red boots, more durable versions of the red slippers worn by Dorothy in Oz, she inhabits the womb-like red golden palace of her father's kingdom. This new birth comes as a result of great pain, a sacrificial journey seemingly endorsed by the male narrator's sermon-like summary, linking Ofelia's emerging sexuality with death.[21]

[21] Del Toro (2007) attributes this sense of transcendence emerging out of pain to his Mexican roots. He relates it to the mythology of the Mexican people's awareness and acceptance of death as a cyclical process and to his status as 'lapsed Catholic.' Speaking to Mark Kermode, 'Guardian interview at the National Film Theatre with Director.' The film embodies some of the tensions and ambivalences of 'lapsed Catholic' identification, challenging the Catholic Church as an institution, and for its complicity, while aspects of religion's creed seep into the film's imagery and sentiment.

While in actuality, the resistance fighters at this point of history would be immediately quashed, Ofelia's rebirth offers something of a future hope:

> Most Spaniards would live in abject poverty and terror from 1939 until 1975. And yet, Ofelia's rebirth in the underworld of the imagination (where Time Stands Still) also predicts the rebirth of Spanish democracy. (Spector 2009: 89)

However, the route she has taken is treacherously ambiguous, and even should we see the final vision as one of hope, the film makes it clear that future stability is not achieved by sticking stolidly to the decreed path. While Vidal is concerned throughout the film with strict time-keeping, following orders and bequeathing his identity through the male lineage, Ofelia, whose choices might be seen to guide the film's moral heart, has the strength to disobey and to retrace a pathway towards an identity she has lost. Parallels can be traced with the country's own lost identity, as del Toro asserts: "The essential conundrum of the princess is that she does not remember that she is one. And the pre-Celtic and pagan ancient myths remind us who we are. ... I love the idea of a primal myth that shakes everyone into remembering who they really are" (Diestro-Dópido 2013: 84–85).[22] The image of Ofelia lying dying at the film's close repeats the shot of her at the beginning when, as the film reverses, blood trickles back up her nose, thus effecting within the narrative a return to the beginning. The ending seems to offer a cyclical return to the fairytale realm of the father, but the historical actuality lingers. The concept of the princess who forgot who she was relates directly to the ongoing memory-loss imposed by the Spanish Civil War, aggravated during Franco's long dictatorship, and continuing after the restoration of democracy. Many of the true horrors and associated taboos causing and emanating from Franco's regime remain.

The image of Ofelia dying also resembles a shot at the end of the Colombian film *La vendedora de rosas / The Rose Seller* (Víctor Gaviria, 1998) of a young girl, Mónica, in her red jacket lying dead on the

---

[22] The theme of rediscovering the true path via a return to the real self that has been forgotten or lost can be seen across many Latin American folklore and fairy tales. This theme is evident in, for example, some of the recent incarnations of Brazilian folktales (folclore) in the series of short-film animations sponsored by the Rio de Janeiro City Council, called 'Juro que vi' ('I swear I saw it'), which won national awards, such as the Grand Cinema Award of Brazil (2010) under the category of short film animation.

ground, a symbol of the plight of the many homeless girls caught up in the underworld of Medellín's destructive drug culture. As the camera tracks downwards, a tiny red gash becomes apparent on the side of her mouth, similar to the trickle of blood from Ofelia's nose; it is the only sign of the brutal violence she has been subjected to. *The Rose Seller* ends with a gentle dissolve from Mónica's body to the full moon, next to white words on a black background stating that 150 years ago, Hans C. Andersen wrote a similar tale about 'The Little Match Girl.'[23] Alluding to the fairy tale revitalizes (if only temporarily) the wonder of the Little Match Girl's final ascendance to join her grandmother in heaven, and the importance of her belief in the vision. While reference to the fairy tale could be seen to provide a formulaic ending to appease mainstream audiences, the ending seems to be more ambivalent than this, presenting both the magic restoration of faith and the 'real' tragedy (the death of the innocent child alone on the street—the thousands of unrecorded deaths like this). The blatant truth is that nothing has changed, either in contemporary Medellín or more universally since Andersen's tale; there was no single solution to the situation at the time of the film's release. Such a self-conscious, reflexive return to the fairytale resolution destabilizes the security of the fairytale end in any original form. It is present both to restore belief, for those who need it, and to reinstate the political message that society must collectively help to confront the shared problem of child poverty, abuse and abandonment.

I suggest that *Pan's Labyrinth* draws similarly on the concept of a transcendent ending, drawing both on the hope that it offers while at the same time remaining conscious of the lingering horror, and the need for a collective investment in change. Earlier in the film, Ofelia tells her own story to her unborn brother in her mother's womb about a rose on a mountain top that could grant immortality to anyone who plucked it, but no one attempted this because of its toxic thorns.[24] People spoke

---

[23] This citation provides both an authorial reference to mid nineteenth-century Denmark and a universal quality, for home and international audiences. The association with Andersen's fairy tale helps to extend the specific to a more timeless realm. The particular political issues of drug trafficking, prostitution and homelessness in Medellín are thus given a more universal understanding.

[24] It is worth noting Ofelia's similarity with the teenage heroine Rosaleen, in *The Company of Wolves* (Neil Jordan, 1984), who also tells her own story (about the wounded she-wolf), providing insight into her visions, as explored in Chapter 5.

of their fear of death and pain, rather than the promise of eternal life, until the rose finally wilted. The vision of eternal life suggests that, in sacrificing her own life by not giving over her baby brother, Ofelia has surpassed the fear governing most people, achieving an immortality associated with carrying out a moral deed, and bringing about an end to the perpetual cycle of fear. Even though the way is not clear, and the baby seemed only to bring her trouble, and is Vidal's son, she refuses to hand her brother over, suggesting there is a humanity that can be trusted if only it can be remembered, a kindness and hopefulness that sees beyond self-interest in the face of violent demands.

In the Underground Realm, Ofelia receives not only her parents' approval, but also a round of applause and a standing ovation from those in the pews either side of the grand cathedral-like building. It is a vision of hope, and of recognition for choosing the correct, ethical path, that all the pain and blood loss has been worth it. However, there are also signs that there might be shortfalls in this vision; as Sue Short (2015: 129) points out, the former fairy self, Princess Moanna, was not happy in the opening scenes of the underworld, "longing to escape its darkness and evading her 'keepers' to do so, begging the question of why her father was so intent on keeping her captive." Ofelia smiles, but faintly on the soundtrack, we can hear her final gasps for air, at the same time as the rapturous applause, as the shot fades to a blinding gold and returns to the image of her lying on the ground in close-up, blood streaming from her nose, still breathing and her eyes still open. She smiles briefly, confirming that what we have seen was her vision, and then her mouth drops, and there is a cut to Mercedes crying, looking down on the dead girl. Ambivalently, Ofelia's hope merges with the stark reality of her death. Weeping, Mercedes embraces Ofelia, now covered in blood, as the camera pans to a high angle looking down on the two female protagonists, and an orchestral variation of Mercedes' melody rises on the soundtrack. The male voice-over says:

> And it is said that the princess returned to her father's kingdom. That she reigned there with justice and a kind heart for many centuries. That she was loved by her people. And that she left behind small traces of her time on earth, visible only to those who know where to look.

The camera pans across the woodland setting arriving at the shot of a white flower opening on a dead tree, improbable but not impossible, with the insect watching on (see Fig. 6.3).

Fig. 6.3 A white flower opens as the insect looks on—*Pan's Labyrinth* (Guillermo del Toro, 2006)

The final male authorial voice tells us how to read the image, just as the image of the flower remains an open signifier. The insect points to our desire for beauty and tranquillity. It is a reminder that new life continues, of the magic surrounding us, if we care to look, even amidst devastation, and where least expected. But it does not make up for the horror. It is both an escape from the atrocities of war and a memorial of it, an icon of peace.

There remains an ambiguity over whether to see Ofelia's transcendence with the hope that Ofelia seems to, or whether to interpret this as her final fantasy. However, as Jennifer Orme (2010: 224) suggests, the film stamps out the very concept of a single overruling narrative: "neither the mimetic world of fascist Spain nor the magical Underground Realm is more real than the other; this juxtaposition of congruent realities produces critiques of monologic totalitarian discourses and endorses stories of magical transformation as forms of resistance and vehicles of hope." The transcendent realm of the magical world offers a sense of hope—for eternal life or an expectation of a longer term peace. However, despite the grim outcome of Ofelia's death, there also exists a sense of hope in the 'real' woodland setting as Mercedes and her brother seem to achieve victory, however short-lived this might be. The enclosed woodland context intensifies the victory as Vidal has a prominence in the film similar to Franco himself, making it seem at this point as though the Resistance can only rise further. While this was far from the case historically, it helps to build a montage of possibilities that resists time and history. Rather than presenting a tragic loss, or suggesting the glimpse of a bright future for the next generation, we are left somewhere in-between. As Allison Mackey (2010: 181) argues, "Recovering and rearticulating hope in the face of neoliberal cynicism involves an understanding that the future is not yet decided and that history is, in fact, open and unfinished..." In the same way that it explores multiple realities, narrations and narratives, the film advocates the importance of questioning the rules, and of making decisions based on ethical and humane ways forward moment to moment, eyes open to the tragic pitfalls of obeying blindly. The horror bleeds through the film, and beyond it. The final image of the flower does not eradicate the brutalities depicted in the film or the 'hidden' horrors that could only be alluded to through the realm of fantasy.

References

Archibald, D. (2004). 'Re-framing the Past: Representations of the Spanish Civil War in Popular Spanish Cinema', in A. Lázaro-Reboll and A. Willis (eds.), *Spanish Popular Cinema* (Inside Popular Film) (Manchester and New York: Manchester University Press), pp. 76–91.

Arroyo, J. (December 2006). Review of *Pan's Labyrinth*, *Sight and Sound*, BFI, 16: 12, 66–68.

Atkinson, M. (January–February 2007). 'Moral Horrors: In Guillermo del Toro's *Pan's Labyrinth*, the Supernatural Realm Mirrors Man's Inhumanity to Man', *Film Comment*, 43: 1, 50–53.

Campos, I.S. (August, 2004). 'Fascism, Fascistization and Developmentalism in Franco's Dictatorship', *Social History*, 29: 3, 342–357.

Clover, C.J. (1989). 'Her Body, Himself: Gender in the Slasher Film', in J. Donald, (ed.) *Fantasy and the Cinema* (London: BFI), pp. 91–133.

Cochrane, K. (Friday 27 April 2007). 'The Girl Can Help It', *Guardian Unlimited*, http://film.guardian.co.uk/features/featurepages/0,,2066034,00.html [Last accessed 28 September 2017].

Creed, Barbara. (1993). *The Monstrous-Feminine: Film, Feminism, Psychoanalysis* (London and New York: Routledge).

Del Toro, G. (2007). 'The Power of Myth', Disc 2, *Pan's Labyrinth*, 2 Disc DVD set. Directed by Guillermo del Toro. (Spain, Mexico and USA: Optimum Home Entertainment).

Diestro-Dópido, Mar. (2013). *Pan's Labyrinth* (London: Palgrave Macmillan).
Ellis, J. and Sánchez-Arce, M. (2016). '"The Unquiet Dead": Memories of the Spanish Civil War in Guillermo del Toro's Cinema', in D. Olson (ed.), *Guillermo del Toro's The Devil's Backbone and Pan's Labyrinth: Studies in the Horror Film* (Colorado: Centipede Press), pp. 185–206.
Hartney, C. and Penicka S. (2016). 'The Fantasy of High Art and History: del Toro's El Laberinto del Fauno', in D. Olson (ed.), *Guillermo del Toro's The Devil's Backbone and Pan' s Labyrinth: Studies in the Horror Film* (Colorado: Centipede Press), pp. 207–242.
Hopkins, L. (2005). *Screening the Gothic* (Austin: University of Texas Press).
Hubner, L. (2010). '*Pan's Labyrinth*, Fear and the Fairy Tale', in S. Hessel and M. Huppert (eds.), *Fear Itself: Reasoning the Unreasonable* (Amsterdam and New York: Rodopi Press), pp. 45–62.
Jackson, R. (1991, reprinted version). *Fantasy: The Literature of Subversion* (London and New York: Routledge).
Jordan, B., and Morgan-Tamosunas, R. (1998). *Contemporary Spanish Cinema* (Manchester and New York: Manchester University Press).
Mackey, A. (Spring 2010). 'Make it Public! Border Pedagogy and the Transcultural Politics of Hope in Contemporary Cinematic Representations of Children', *College Literature*, 37: 2, 171–185.
Orme, J. (2010). 'Narrative Desire and Disobedience in *Pan's Labyrinth*', *Marvels & Tales*, 24: 2, 219–234.
Preston, P. (2000). *Comrades! Portraits From the Spanish Civil War* (London: HarperCollins).
Propp, V. (2008, revised second edition,). *Morphology of the Folktale*, translated by L. Scott (Austen: University of Texas Press).
Rankin, W. (2016). 'Defusing the Mythology of World War II: Fairies, Fighters, Ghosts, and Bombs in Guillermo del Toro's *Pan's Labyrinth* and *The Devil's Backbone*', in D. Olson (ed.), *Guillermo del Toro's The Devil's Backbone and Pan' Labyrinth: Studies in the Horror Film* (Colorado: Centipede Press), pp. 69–87.
Short, S. (2015). *Fairy Tale and Film: Old Tales with a New Spin* (Basingstoke and New York: Palgrave Macmillan).
Smith, P.J. (2014). *Mexican Screen Fiction* (Malden, USA: Polity Press).
Spector, B. (Summer 2009). 'Sacrifice of the Children in *Pan's Labyrinth*', *Jung Journal: Culture and Psyche*, 3: 3, 81–86.
Stone, R. (2002). *Spanish Cinema* (Inside Film) (Harlow, England: Longman).
Tatar, M. (2003, expanded second edition). *The Hard facts of the Grimms' Fairy Tales* (Princeton and Oxford: Princeton University Press).
Taylor, M. (2007). *British Pantomime Performance* (Bristol: Intellect).
White, E. (2008). 'Insects and Automata in Hoffmann, Balzac, Carter, and del Toro', *Journal of the Fantastic in the Arts*, 19: 3 (74), 363–378.

Zipes, J., ed. (1993, second edition). *The Trials and Tribulations of Little Red Riding Hood* (New York and London: Routledge).

Zipes, J. (2006). *Why Fairy Tales Stick: The Evolution and Relevance of a Genre* (London and New York: Routledge).

CHAPTER 7

Afterword: Uncanny Transformations in Film

This study was motivated by the fluctuating and distinctive effects conjured as fairytale and gothic horror converge, clash or combine in cinema in transformative ways, adding new depths of meanings as they collide or share qualities and find new expression. The bringing together of diverse fairy tales and fairytale versions creates new connotations that the gothic adds to in intricate and haunting ways. By identifying with protagonists, defeating or facing demons and returning to rational order, we are licensed to face the shadier, or hidden terrors that linger beyond civilized confines. But it is the tension or tenuous balance between disorder and order that keeps gothic pulsating. Many of the films explored through this study interact with fairy tales' universal, timeless and flexible settings, enabling insight into unspeakable or repressed scenarios of abuse within the home, abandonment, rape and murder. The films also find access—through diverse means—to fairytale and folkloric emphasis on the necessity of strategy and initiative as a means to survive, or to open up a dialogue for change and transformation. Added to this, the gothic has a transgressive capacity, involving a lingering of the past within the present, and the notion that horror emerges from within—razing boundaries between self and 'other.' Strict oppositions, such as good and evil, or dread and desire, are driven by similar impulses. Gothic horror is propelled (in a cycle of repression) by a return of the repressed, often in turn bringing about a return of repression. While order is to some extent restored at the film's close, the subversion of norms and securities is never finally forgotten.

© The Author(s) 2018
L. Hubner, *Fairytale and Gothic Horror*,
https://doi.org/10.1057/978-1-137-39347-0_7

Throughout the case study chapters, I have focused on the films, first and foremost, applying and building on the theoretical and methodological approaches established earlier on. This process allowed for detailed analysis of the texts—providing insight into various manifestations of fairytale and gothic horror. The films selected for close critical analysis in this study have enabled the conceptual and contextual frameworks to be explored in some depth, but this is just a starting point. Often a wider scope has been indicated, especially when arguments relate to a larger cultural field, and there is scope for similar processes to be applied to other films (and cultural texts)—both those that are given only scarce attention in this book and those that are missing completely. This study allows for links to be made between the central framing films *Rebecca* (Alfred Hitchcock, 1940), *The Company of Wolves* (Neil Jordan, 1984) and *El laberinto del fauno / Pan's Labyrinth* (Guillermo del Toro, 2006) as rite-of-passage narratives whose dream or fantasy worlds surround the films in complex ways, giving voice to an unconscious female desire that transgresses boundaries of restrictive patriarchy. However, analyzing each of these films in relation to a much broader range of (related) films has also helped draw attention to specific effects and divergences at a given time, providing due consideration to the importance of cultural and historical context.

Gothic tendencies merge with fairytale frameworks and elements in horrifying ways in *Rebecca*—the film that seemed to trigger a spate of 'persecuted wife' or 'Bluebeard' Hollywood movies, as the unexpressed tensions brought about by World War II began to have an effect. The many hallmarks of a 'classical fairy tale' that give structure to *Rebecca*'s opening are gradually challenged as gothic instabilities take hold. While the 'confession' of the beach cottage revelation sequence activates a closeness between Maxim and the heroine that seems geared towards a fairytale ending, I argue that the interweaving of fairytale and gothic horror tendencies suggests a reading of the film that sees the heroine's sustained union with Maxim as an added repression of her desires and dreams. The intertwining of the fantasy and 'real' worlds in *Pan's Labyrinth* allows for an idiosyncratic functioning of fairytale and gothic horror. I argue that fairytale structures, roles and narratives of the 'real' world help to universalize historical actuality (the brutal dictatorship that immediately followed the Spanish Civil War), while the gothic fantasy world—strongly connected to the young heroine, Ofelia—not only enables unspeakable or taboo subject matter to be addressed but also bears witness via allegorical means to the torturous confusions that contributed to the rise of Francoist power, together with the unspoken about actions of fathers and forefathers throughout this period of history.

The return of the repressed creates disruption in all the texts explored through the course of this book, and while order is to some extent restored, the subversion of norms and securities is never finally forgotten. Repression itself comes under close scrutiny, thus allowing vital insight into cultural and political restrictions and standards of morality—drawing attention to unconscious drives and fears, as secrets and dangers bleed into the open. The werewolf is a fitting metaphor for the wild creature within, embodying a cyclical uprising of repressed drives and desires. However, the tragic seeping of the tear from the werewolf's eye at the end of *The Curse of the Werewolf* (Terence Fisher, 1961) affords an uncanny lingering on the human within the beast, blurring distinctions between notions of the conscious and unconscious self. While strict boundaries are represented between diurnal and nocturnal worlds in *Werewolf of London* (Stuart Walker, 1935), the fear instigated by the werewolf realm bears a stark resemblance to an irrational attraction towards it, given further articulation in the film's gay subtext, suggesting that (British) repression can itself be dangerous. While the film ventures into the locked, hidden recesses of Dr. Glendon's London laboratory, it ends with Lisa and Paul flying off to a new life in America. Similar compulsions are evident in Larry Talbot's draw to the gypsy camp in *The Wolf Man* (George Waggner, 1941) followed by the complex tensions between father and son (repression and liberation), and are further explored in *An American Werewolf in London* (John Landis, 1981) through its dream depictions of sudden brutality in a familiar domestic setting, alluding to uprisings of violence that permeate European history. *The Company of Wolves* shatters essentialist traditions that have represented Little Red Riding Hood either as sexual siren or threatened victim. While the heroine's awakening scream at the end of the film seems to crush the freedom explored through her dreams, the film also cautions against the dangers of over-repression. Thus, despite the restoration of order and restraint that overtly cloaks the films, the horror of societal repressions remains a persistent point of contention.

The home (or self) is often at the root of the horror in the films examined in this study, and 'the uncanny' (like the gothic) is strongly aligned with style, tone and atmosphere, generated in distinctively cinematic ways. For example, in *Rebecca*, Maxim's restrictive control is conveyed through his manipulation of the home video of their honeymoon, when he freezeframes the past as an idealized vision of his marriage (and of his wife as the maternal figure), obliterating the heroine's own dreams. Visual repetitions abound, such as the final shot of the 'happy couple,' which presents an uncanny mirroring of the image of the couple's brief embrace after Maxim's revelation in the beach cottage, adding a disturbing further layer that undermines the romantic finale, implying that certain memories cannot be entirely eradicated. The burning of Rebecca's room (and pillowcase) at the end also reminds us that there are two 'Bluebeard' rooms in the film. It recalls the heroine's tentative crossing into Rebecca's territory in the grand West Wing overlooking the sea, in the sequence that displays, in abundance and excess, an extraordinary, and heavily coded, exposition of the heroine's repressed desires. At horrifying moments in *Rebecca*, awareness reaches out beyond the text, towards an alertness to the uncanny that is not shared by the characters on screen. There is a residing uncanniness in Maxim's scripting of the narrative in the beach cottage revelation sequence, enhanced by Olivier's overblown performance style, and—as a play on the restrictions of the Motion Pictures Production Code—the cinematography used to vivify Maxim's monologue adds a further, unsettling layer to the words. The camera's hefty overtness is a near self-reflexive moment, creating awareness of the camera's presence—and Rebecca's absence—her words seemingly ventriloquized by Maxim but never actually validated or heard. The unwitting irony of the heroine's words used to reassure Maxim about Rebecca—"She can't speak... She can't bear witness"—resonate long after the film's ending. In *The Two Mrs. Carrolls* (Peter Godfrey, 1947) and *Secret Beyond the Door* (Fritz Lang, 1947), similar to the 'Bluebeard' moment of revelation, the new wife's realization that she shares identical features with the previous dead wife helps her confront, however uneasily, the threat that her husband poses to herself. However, the sense of the uncanny works differently in *Rebecca*, as the second Mrs. de Winter subsists simply by repressing knowledge, and Maxim's brutality is overshadowed by (Maxim's) emphasis on Rebecca's unspeakable sexual desires and deviancies. The rite-of-passage formula of strategy and initiative, befitting a fairytale hero, is denied the heroine, substituted by her seemingly self-assigned and self-perpetuated task to support and protect the husband. While the heroine fails to break the cycle, repressing her desire to identify with her predecessor, Rebecca's haunting return through the course of the film speaks of the threat posed upon generations of women who question the 'common sense' of patriarchal heritage and control.

Pan's Labyrinth explores multiple realities, narratives and modes of narration, promoting the importance of questioning the prescribed route. The film both draws on the hope of its transcendental ending while remaining ambivalently conscious of the residing horror, and the need for individuals to play their part in a collective investment in change. As the Pale Man doubles for Vidal, and in turn for Franco's regime, there is the further allusion to the Church's compliance with fascist decision making. The ending suggests a cyclical return to the fairytale realm of the father, but Franco's violence persists. We might recall that Ofelia's imagination is given visual expression as the blank pages of the 'Book of Crossroads' transform into vibrant images that take shape and transmute across the everyday setting. The meanings of the words and images are open to interpretation, demonstrating that the solutions to the tasks presented to her are ambiguous, in keeping with the film's caution against blindly following a preordained set of rules.

My motivation to write this book stemmed from an attempt to get closer to what it is about the films, and moments within them, that make me shudder. The findings of this study have suggested that it is repression itself rather than the return of the repressed that propagates the horror in the films examined. Although the transgressive potential of these films is not fully (or finally) realized, female agency and desire are given some degree of credence, if only through imagined worlds and fantastical visions. A residing hope runs through many of these films, as they ask us to act, to intervene and to make decisions based on humane considerations and marginalized dreams, choosing steps carefully, moment to moment, applying initiative with skilled dexterity—as a bridge to a transformed future.

Index

A
abandonment, 5, 164n7
abuse, 5, 19, 24
Adventures of Caleb Williams, The (Godwin), 61–2
advertising, 14, 22n8
Age of Enlightenment, 56–7
Alice in Wonderland (Carroll), 170, 176
Almodóvar, Pedro, 182n18
American film. *See* Hollywood
An American Werewolf in London (Landis, 1981), 9, 28, 147–53, 193
Andersen, Hans Christian, 5, 23, 29, 30–1
Anderson, Judith, 76, 110
Anecdotes of Painting in England (Walpole), 59
animals, 27
Archibald, David, 161–2
architecture, 55–6, 59
Ardilla roja, La (Medem, 1993), 165–6
Arroyo, José, 164
Atkinson, Michael, 173

Aulnoy, Baroness d', 32
Avery, Tex, 122n6

B
Bacchilega, Cristina, 100
Baquero, Ivana, 10, 159
Barbebleue (*Bluebeard*) (Méliès, 1901), 25, 104n38
Barker, Clive, 46
Barnville, Marie-Catherine Le Jumel de, 32
Barthes, Roland, 33, 47–8
Basile, Giambattista, 31
Bazin, André, 48
beach houses, 89–90
Beast Must Die, The (Annett, 1974), 135n21
beasts, 15, 20
   See also werewolves
Beaumont, Jeanne-Marie Leprince Madame de, 32
beauty, 15, 17, 20, 81
'Beauty and the Beast', 14, 27
Before the Fact (Iles), 97
Benshoff, Harry M., 142

Berenstein, Rhona J., 110
Bergese, Micha, 123
Bergman, Ingmar, 68n14
Bettelheim, Bruno, 20–1
Biffault, Louis and Francois, 16n3
Block, Robert, 46
Bloody Chamber, The (Carter), 31, 38
Bloom, Clive, 60
'Bluebeard', 8, 15, 19, 32, 81n10
 and films, 7, 25, 27–8, 75
 and marriage, 24–5, 85–6, 98, 100, 101, 102
Bluestone, George, 54
boat houses, 89–90
Boccaccio, Giovanni, 31
Botting, Fred, 6, 44, 45, 58n6, 66–7, 70
boundaries, 9, 155
Bourgault du Coudray, Chantal, 118, 119
Bram Stoker's Dracula (Coppola, 1992), 44
Breen, Joseph, 97, 108
Britain. *See* Great Britain
British Board of Film Censors (BBFC), 133–4
Bronfen, Elizabeth, 85, 104n36
Brontë, Charlotte, 78n6
Brontë, Emily, 44
brutality, 9, 10, 19
Bunnell, Charlene, 70
Butterfly's Tongue (*La lengua de las mariposas*) (Cuerda, 1999), 161n2
Byron, Glennis, 59

C
Cabinet des fées, Le (de Mayer), 16n4, 31, 32
Cabinet of Dr. Caligari, The (*Das Cabinet des Dr. Caligari*) (Wiener, 1920), 54

Cahill, James Leo, 48–9
camera devices, 6, 62
 and *The Company of Wolves*, 125, 126
 and *Pan's Labyrinth*, 167, 186
 and *Rebecca*, 80–1, 82, 87–8, 91–3, 95, 106–7, 113, 194
cannibalism, 19
Carrie (de Palma, 1976), 18n5, 179
Carter, Angela, 31, 32n17, 38, 45
 and 'The Company of Wolves', 123, 125n8, 153, 154
Castle of Otranto, The: A Gothic Story (Walpole), 59
catchphrases, 14
Catholicism, 177, 183n21
Caught (Ophüls, 1948), 11, 102
censorship, 133–4
 See also Motion Pictures Production Code
Chaney, Lon, Jr., 145
characterization, 16–17
childbirth, 17, 131–2, 151, 179, 180–1
children, 5, 13, 17, 18
 and fairy tales, 20–1, 33
 and *Pan's Labyrinth*, 180
 and Spain, 183
Children and Household Tales (*Die Kinder und Hausmärchen*) (Grimm), 30, 33, 122
Christianity, 33, 133, 139, 141–2, 168
 See also Catholicism
Christie, Ian, 46–7
'Cinderella', 14, 19, 20, 27, 32, 102
cinema. *See* film
circuses, 47
civilization, 4, 9, 14–15, 120, 130
 See also culture
class, 82, 138
Clover, Carol, 165
Cochrane, Kira, 178–9, 181
colonialism, 52, 53–4

colour. *See* red
comedy, 60, 138, 147, 148, 150–1
'Company of Wolves, The' (Carter), 38
Company of Wolves, The (Jordan, 1984), 3, 9–10, 119, 125–8, 193
   and 'Little Red Riding Hood', 37–8, 120, 123–5, 154–5
   and scream, 153–4
   and sources, 36
Contes de ma Mère l'Oye (Perrault), 32
Coppola, Francis Ford, 44
Craig, J. Robert, 144
Creed, Barbara, 146–7, 151, 179
cruelty, 15, 19
culture, 118, 119–20, 125–6
curiosity, 4, 15, 16
Curran, Angela, 151
Curse of the Werewolf, The (Fisher, 1961), 128–35, 193

D

Deacon, Desley, 110
death, 4, 47–50, 117–18
Decamerone (Boccaccio), 31
Del Toro, Guillermo, 20, 166, 170–1, 172–3, 183n21, 184
   See also Pan's Labyrinth
Delarue, Paul, 16n3, 121
Demons of the Mind (Sykes, 1972), 135n21
Dent, Jonathan, 57
desire, 15, 66–7, 105, 110–11, 152–3
Devil's Backbone, The (*El espinazo del diablo*) (del Toro, 2001), 180
dialogue, 93–5
Días del pasado, Los (Camus, 1977), 164
dictatorships, 10, 159, 160
   See also Franco, General Francisco
Diestro-Dópido, Mar, 183
disguise, 15, 16

Disney, Walt, 18, 26n10, 150–1, 169
Doane, Mary Ann, 78, 93, 94
dogs, 125–6, 127
domestic abuse, 5, 19, 24, 84–5
Don't Bet on the Prince (Zipes), 22
doppelgängers, 6, 62n10, 63, 65n12, 66
Dracula (Bram Stoker), 60, 61
Dracula movies, 44, 46
Dragonwyck (Mankiewicz, 1946), 84n12, 102
dreams, 4, 9–10, 123, 127–8, 155
dress, 81–2
Du Maurier, Daphne, 46, 52, 53, 75
Duncan, Glen, 155
Du Plessis, Michael, 104

E

editing, 6, 11
Edwards, Emily D., 138
Ellis, Jonathan, 162, 178
'Emperor's New Clothes, The' (Andersen), 30
endings, 2, 5–6, 15, 43–4, 102–3
   and *The Company of Wolves*, 153–5
   and *Pan's Labyrinth*, 184, 185–8, 195
   and *Rebecca*, 77–8, 79, 106–7, 112–13
Endore, Guy, 129
entrapment, 84
Equal Franchise Act (1928), 83
evil, 1–2, 5, 15
   and *Pan's Labyrinth*, 171, 173–4, 176
evolution, 118, 142
excess, 6, 45, 60
Exorcist, The (Friedkin, 1973), 64n11, 179
Experiment Perilous (Tourneur, 1944), 102, 103

F
'Fairy Tale Route', 30n14
fairy tales, 1–3, 4–6, 13–14, 191–2
  and children, 20–1
  and classical, 14–17, 19–20, 33–5
  and female roles, 21–2, 23–4
  and film, 25–6, 27–8, 36–9
  and function, 22–3, 26–7
  and happy endings, 43–4
  and literature, 30–4
  and *Pan's Labyrinth*, 10, 159–60, 167, 170–1, 172–5, 185
  and *Rebecca*, 7–8, 76, 77, 105
  and red colour, 147–8
  and sexuality, 180
  and traditions, 17–19
  and uncanny, 70–1
  and versions, 28–30, 35–7
  and woodlands, 169–70
Fanny and Alexander (Bergman, 1982), 175n11
fantasy, 3, 6, 9, 28, 128
  and *Pan's Labyrinth*, 10–11, 159, 160, 167–9, 175–6
fascism, 159, 171, 177, 183
fathers, 33, 174–5, 182–3
fears, 4, 10, 38, 46–7, 66–7
  and *Pan's Labyrinth*, 159, 185–6
  and *Rebecca*, 53–4
Fell, John L., 19
female roles, 5, 10, 18, 21–2, 84–5
  and coming of age, 121
  and *The Company of Wolves*, 126–7
  and jealousy, 77–8
  and 'Little Red Riding Hood', 15–16
  and marriage, 23–5
  and *Pan's Labyrinth*, 166–7, 171, 179, 180–2
  and *Rebecca*, 81–3
  and violence, 23
  and werewolves, 155
  See also mothers; stepmothers; wives
feminism, 3, 5, 21–2

Fenton, George, 126
film, 2–4, 6, 191–2
  and 1940s Hollywood, 8, 24–5, 75, 84–5
  and death, 48–50
  and fairy tales, 15, 17, 18–19, 23, 25–6, 27–8, 29, 36–9
  and gothic, 44–7, 50–1
  and split self, 62–5
  and werewolves, 9
  and Woolf, 54–5
Fisher, Terence, 128–9
flashbacks, 76, 90, 91
Fletcher, John, 89, 107
folktales, 15–16, 121, 184n22
Fontaine, Joan, 7, 54, 76
foreignness, 24
Forest, The (*El Bosc*) (Aibar, 2012), 163n5
framing, 6, 11, 14, 27, 87, 128
France, 31, 32, 135–6
Francis, Freddie, 136
Franco, General Francisco, 10, 159, 161, 163–4, 181, 184
  and *Pan's Labyrinth*, 171, 172, 177, 178, 195
Frankenstein (Shelley), 52, 60, 61
Frankenstein movies, 46
Frayling, Christopher, 49
Freud, Sigmund, 6–7, 65–6, 70–1, 100, 111
  and unintentional return, 102, 106
'Frog Prince, The', 27
full moon, 117, 137–8, 183
Furtivos (Borau, 1975), 163

G
Gallafent, Ed, 81–2
Gaslight (Cukor, 1944), 84n13, 102
gender, 170–2, 179–83
  See also female roles; men
Germany, 30n14

giants, 15
Godwin, William, 61
good, 1–2, 5, 15, 173, 176
gothic, 1, 2–3, 5–7, 14, 191–2
  and definition, 43–5
  and everyday life, 51–2
  and fears, 66–7
  and film, 45–7, 50–1
  and history, 55–60
  and literature, 59–62
  and *Pan's Labyrinth*, 10–11, 175–6, 178–9
  and *Rebecca*, 7–8, 53–4, 75, 76
  and werewolves, 119
Gothic Revival, 56
Goths, 55
Goya, Francisco, 176
Gramsci, Antonio, 34n20
grandmothers, 124–5
Great Britain, 9, 118–19, 148–50
  See also London
Great Depression, 144
greed, 4, 14, 15, 19
Greenhill, Pauline, 105
Griggs, Yvonne, 109
Grimm, Jacob and Wilhelm, 15, 16, 29, 30, 169
  and 'Little Red Riding Hood', 122
  and rewriting, 33
Groom, Nick, 55, 59
gypsy traditions, 145–7, 193

H
Hallenbeck, Bruce G., 129
Hamlet (Shakespeare), 175n11
Hammer Films, 128, 129, 130, 134
Hand that Rocks the Cradle, The (Hanson, 1992), 179
Hannon, Théo, 49
'Hansel and Gretel', 19, 22, 25n9, 33, 164n7
Hanson, Helen, 91, 93–4

happy endings. *See* endings
Harbord, Janet, 77
Harper, Sue, 129, 130
Harry, He's Here to Help (*Harry un ami qui vous veut du bien*) (Moll, 2000), 62–3
Héritier, Marie-Jeanne L', 169
heroes, 15, 19, 101, 102, 183
Hinds, Anthony, 129, 134, 136
Histoires ou contes du temps passé (Perrault), 32, 120
Hitchcock, Alfred, 75, 84n14, 90–1, 96
  See also Rebecca
Hoffman, E.T.A., 65
Hollywood, 8, 119, 129, 137
  and Production Code, 95, 96–7, 108, 194
  and werewolves, 119, 137
Holocaust, the, 152, 176–7
home, 7, 8, 193
homosexuality, 107–10, 112, 142, 144, 193
hope, 159, 172, 183–4, 186–8, 195
Hopkins, Lisa, 69
Hopper, Keith, 127
horror films, 6, 18n5, 23, 28, 75
  and fairy tales, 165–6
  and historical, 128–9, 130
  and influences, 46–7
  and werewolves, 148
Hughes, William, 57
Hutchings, Peter, 130–1

I
I Know Who you Are (*Sé quien eres*) (Fereira, 2000), 162n3
Iles, Francis, 97
illustration, 17, 24, 25
initiation tasks, 5, 18, 120, 168–9
innocence, 17, 20
insects, 167, 168, 186–7
Italy, 31

J

'Jack and the Beanstalk', 14, 27
Jackson, Rosemary, 5, 28, 43, 61, 128, 175
Jane Eyre (Brontë), 78n6, 179
jealousy, 4, 14, 15, 19
Joan of Arc, 105
Jones, Doug, 168, 176
Jordan, Barry, 161, 163–4, 165–6
Jordan, Neil, 123, 153–4
  See also *The Company of Wolves*
Judaism, 152
'Juniper Tree, The', 27

K

King, Stephen, 46

L

Laberinto del fauno, El. See *Pan's Labyrinth*
Ladybird Well-Loved Tales, 21
Landis, John, 149, 152
Lansbury, Angela, 123
Leff, Leonard J., 90
Legend of the Werewolf (Francis, 1975), 64n11, 135–6, 148
Let the Right One In (*Låt den rätte komma in*) (Alfredson, 2008), 67–70
Lewis, M.G., 61
Light, Alison, 78n7
liminal zones, 4, 11, 118
literature, 2, 3, 18, 30, 54
  and adaptations, 97
  and gothic, 52, 58, 59–62
  See also fairy tales
'Little Ida's Flowers' (Andersen), 30n15
'Little Match Girl, The' (Andersen), 185
'Little Mermaid, The' (Andersen), 14, 23, 30

'Little Red Riding Hood', 9, 14, 15–16, 26, 146
  and *The Company of Wolves*, 37–8, 123–5, 154–5
  and versions, 29, 120–3, 169–70
  location, 17–18
  and werewolves, 118–19, 128–9, 137, 147–8, 148–9
London, 9, 137, 138, 147–8, 151
López, Sergi, 10
Louis XIV of France, King, 32
love, 4, 15
Lovell-Smith, Rose, 24–5
Luckhurst, Roger, 47
Lumière, Auguste, 49, 50n2
Lumière, Louis, 46, 49, 50n2
Lüthi, Max, 20

M

McCann, Sharon, 127
Mackey, Allison, 188
magic, 27
Magic (Attenborough, 1978), 63–5
magic lantern, 47
Maltby, Richard, 96–7
marketing, 132–3
marriage, 23–5
  and 'Bluebeard', 85–6
  and *Rebecca*, 78–84, 87–9, 108
  and remarriage, 102–3
  and violence, 84–5
  and *Werewolf of London*, 139–41
  See also wives
masks, 16
Maturin, Charles, 59, 61
Medem, Julio, 165–6, 167
media, the, 14
  See also social media
Méliès, Georges, 25, 47n1
Melmoth, The Wanderer (Maturin), 59
melodrama, 75
men, 8, 21–2, 84–5

See also fathers; patriarchy
menace, 109–10
menstruation, 17, 179
Millien, Achille, 16n3
Modleski, Tania, 92, 111
monstrosity, 45, 176
morals, 14–16, 19–20, 69, 120
Morgan-Tamosunas, Rikki, 161, 163–4, 165–6
mothers, 33, 103, 167, 174
  and *The Company of Wolves*, 124–5, 126
motifs, 14, 17, 147–9
Motion Pictures Production Code, 95, 96–7, 108, 194
Moulin Rouge (Houston, 1953), 136
mummies, 48
murder, 5, 8, 19, 24, 99–100
  and *Rebecca*, 95, 96
  and werewolves, 138–9, 142–3, 146–7
music, 81, 87, 148, 151
  and *The Company of Wolves*, 126, 127
  and *Pan's Labyrinth*, 166, 186
myths, 14, 22, 30n13, 33–4

N

nature, 15, 52–3, 144
  and culture, 118, 119–20, 125–6
  See also wilderness; woodlands
Nazism, 152
New Fairy Tales (Andersen), 30–1
Noche más larga, La (García Sánchez, 1991), 172
novels. *See* literature
Nugent, Frank S., 109–10

O

O'Connor, Pat, 21–2
ogres, 15, 21–2, 173–4
Olivier, Laurence, 7, 76, 91, 93–5, 194

oral storytelling, 29–30, 32, 34–5, 121–2
Orenstein, Catherine, 15
Orme, Jennifer, 187
otherness, 45

P

Pan's Labyrinth (*El laberinto del fauno*) (del Toro, 2006), 3–4, 10–11, 20, 22–3, 28, 159–61
  and ending, 185–8, 195
  and fairy tales, 172–5
  and fantasy, 167–9
  and father figure, 33n19
  and Franco, 163–4, 177–8
  and gender, 170–2, 179–83
  and gothic, 175–6, 178–9
  and the Holocaust, 176–7
  and hope, 183–4
  and narrative, 166–7
  and the past, 57
  and Spain, 192–3
  and woodland, 164–5, 166
pantomime, 173
Paris, 135–6
past, the, 6, 7, 11, 60
  and *Rebecca*, 8, 76–7, 79–81, 82–3
patriarchy, 8, 21–2, 98
Patterson, Sarah, 120
Peeping Tom (Powell, 1960), 133
Pentemerone (Basile), 31
Perkins, V.F., 11
Perrault, Charles, 15, 29, 32, 169
  and 'Bluebeard', 85–6, 112
  and 'Little Red Riding Hood', 120, 121, 122
Persona (Bergman, 1966), 68n14
'Petit Chaperon Rouge, Le' (Perrault), 120
"Phantasmagoria", 47
photography, 47–8
Piacevoli notti, Le (Straparola), 31

Picture of Dorian Gray, The (Wilde), 52, 137
Poe, Edgar Allen, 46, 62n10
posters, 132–3
princes, 15
'Princess and the Pea, The' (Andersen), 14, 19, 30
princesses, 15
private space, 7
Propp, Vladimir, 18–19, 101, 168
props, 92
prostitution, 131, 136, 138n24
Psycho (Hitchcock, 1960), 133
psychoanalysis, 3, 20–1
public space, 7
'Puss in Boots', 32

R
Radcliffe, Ann, 61
Rankin, Walter, 178
rape, 19
'Rapunzel', 19
Raza (Sáenz de Heredia, 1942), 183
Rebecca (Du Maurier), 52–3, 75, 179
 and film changes, 77–8, 95, 97
Rebecca (Hitchcock, 1940), 3, 7–8, 25, 29n11, 58n7, 75–84
 and confession sequence, 86–96, 97–8, 100–2
 and desire, 110–11
 and doubling wives, 105–6
 and ending, 106–7, 112–13
 and gothic, 53–4, 192
 and homosexuality, 107–10
 and patriarchy, 34n21
 and repression, 111–12
 and *Secret Beyond the Door*, 104
 and uncanny, 66, 193–4
 red, 147–8, 149, 180, 181
 and white, 17, 24, 131–2
Red Hot Riding Hood (Avery, 1943), 122n6

'Red Riding Hood' (Perrault), 32
'Red Shoes, The' (Andersen), 23
Redgrave, Michael, 103n34
Reed, Oliver, 130, 132–3, 134–5
religion, 56, 109, 121–2, 126
 See also Christianity; Judaism
Renaissance, the, 55–6
repression, 6, 7, 191, 193, 195
 and gothic, 45
 and *Rebecca*, 8, 77, 105, 111–12
 and Spanish Civil War, 161
 and werewolves, 9, 10, 118, 119, 138
Resistance, 10, 11, 161, 164–5, 188
Reyes, Xavier Aldana, 50–1
rites of passage, 18, 23, 120, 121, 170
rivalry, 4, 19
Romain, Yvonne, 133
romance, 3, 60
Rose Seller, The (*La vendedora de rosas*) (Gaviria, 1998), 184–5
Rosemary's Baby (Polanski, 1968), 179
'Rotkäpchen' ('Little Red Cap') (Grimm), 122
Rousseau, Jean-Jaques, 32
Russia, 18–19

S
Sánchez-Arce, María, 162, 178
'Sandman, The' (Hoffman), 65
'Saturn Devouring His Sons' (Goya), 176
science, 56
Secret Beyond the Door (Lang, 1947), 8, 25, 99–100, 112, 103–4, 194
Selznick, David O., 75, 90, 108
sentimentalism, 44, 60
setting. *See* location
sexuality, 23, 136, 180
 See also homosexuality
Shampan, Jack, 135–6
Shelley, Mary, 46, 52, 61, 62

Sherwood, Robert E., 91
Shining, The (Kubrick, 1980), 25–6, 148n28–9
Short, Sue, 2, 23–4, 28, 186
Shrek (Adamson/Jenson, 2001), 13
Silence, The (*Tystnaden*) (Bergman, 1963), 68n14
silver, 117
Siodmak, Curt, 152
'Sleeping Beauty' (Perrault), 19, 27, 32, 34n22, 48, 102
Smith, Andrew, 57
Smith, Paul Julian, 181
'Snow White', 14, 16–17, 19, 27, 102
social media, 51, 52
socialism, 162
Spadoni, Robert, 140, 142, 144
Spain, 10–11, 128–9, 160–4, 165–6, 192–3
and republicans, 182n20, 183
Spanish Civil War, 159, 161–5, 170, 177–8, 184
split self, 6, 16, 62–5, 66, 118
Spooner, Catherine, 45, 50
Squelette joyeux, Le (Lumière, 1898), 46
Stage Fright (Hitchcock, 1950), 91n19
stepfathers, 174, 175n11
stepmothers, 14, 15, 33, 83, 174
stepsisters, 15
Stevens, David, 55
Stevenson, Robert Louis, 46, 52, 118
Stone, Rob, 162
Storytelling. *See* oral storytelling
Strange Case of Dr Jekyll and Mr Hyde, The (Stevenson), 52, 118, 137
Strangers on a Train (Hitchcock, 1951), 62
Straparola, Giovan Francesco, 31
straying, 169–70
Suspicion (Hitchcock, 1941), 97

symbolism, 20

T

Tale of Tales, The (*Lo cunto de li cunti*) (Basile), 31
Tales, Told for Children (Andersen), 30
Tatar, Maria, 2, 27, 33, 85, 104, 174
and *Rebecca*, 95–6, 98
Taylor, Millie, 173
television, 49–50
Terry, Jennifer, 144
Teverson, Andrew, 23, 30–1, 35
theatre, 46, 173
theatricality, 94–5
'Three Little Pigs, The', 26
Tierra (Medem, 1995), 165–6, 167
'Tinderbox, The' (Andersen), 30
Tolkein, J.R.R., 29, 38–9
'Tom Thumb', 32
tourism, 30n14
Townshend, Dale, 59
transformation, 15, 18, 27
and werewolves, 117–18, 137–9, 150–1, 153
transgression, 6, 7, 44, 45
Travers, P.L., 23
Twilight (Hardwicke, 2008), 51
Twitchell, James B., 150
Two Mrs Carrolls, The (Godfrey, 1947), 8, 84, 99, 100, 102, 194

U

uncanny, the, 4, 6–7, 50, 65–6, 70–1
and *Rebecca*, 100, 102, 111, 193–4
'Uncanny, The' ('Das Heimlich') (Freud), 6–7, 65–6, 100
unconscious, 118, 119
Universal Studios, 119, 129, 137
Uses of Enchantment, The (Bettelheim), 20–1

V

Vacas (Medem, 1992), 165–6, 167
Van Genechten, Jan, 129
vanity, 14, 15
Vasari, Giorgio, 56
ventriloquism, 63, 93–4
Verdier, Yvonne, 121
villains, 15, 101
violence, 9, 11
  and 'Bluebeard', 24–5
  and censorship, 133
  and marriage, 84, 89
  and *Pan's Labyrinth*, 183
  and werewolves, 136, 137
  and women, 23
  See also brutality; domestic abuse; murder
visual imagery, 17, 46
voice, 93–4, 166

W

Waldman, Diane, 85, 103
Walker, Michael, 76–7, 82, 104
Walpole, Horace, 59
Walsh, Andrea S., 84
Walters, James, 47, 50
war movies, 171, 172
Warner, Marina, 24, 32, 36, 105n40
Werewolf of London (Walker, 1935), 9, 63, 117n1, 137–45, 148, 193
Werewolf of Paris, The (Endore), 117n1, 129
'Werewolf, The' (Carter), 38
werewolves, 4, 8–10, 27, 117–20, 148–9
  and *The Company of Wolves*, 123, 124, 125, 153–4
  and curses, 130–1
  and humanization, 133–5, 151–3, 193
  and 'Little Red Riding Hood', 120–1
  and location, 128–9
  and marketing, 132–3
  and transformation, 137–9, 150–1
  and violence, 136, 137, 142–3, 145–7
Wilde, Oscar, 52
wilderness, 4, 9, 11, 15, 17–18, 52–3
'William Wilson' (Poe), 62n10
witches, 15, 33, 78, 83
Wittmann, Anna M., 58
wives, 7–8, 23–4
  and 'Bluebeard', 85–6
  and persecuted, 75, 84n12, 99–100, 112
  and *Rebecca*, 77, 87–9, 98, 105–6
Wizard of Oz, The (Baum), 170
Wolf Man, The (Waggner, 1941), 9, 117n1, 145–7, 152, 193
wolves, 15–16, 17, 26, 123, 124–6, 127
  See also werewolves
Woman in the Moon and Other Tales of Forgotten Heroines, The, 22
women writers, 32
women's rights, 83, 181
Wood, Robin, 6, 62, 80n9, 96
woodlands, 17–18, 125, 164–5, 166, 167, 169–70
Woolf, Virginia, 54–5
World War II, 8, 84–5, 112, 152
  See also Holocaust, the
Wuthering Heights (Brontë), 44

Z

Zipes, Jack, 14–15, 22, 29–30, 31, 33–5, 36–7
  and 'Little Red Riding Hood', 121, 122, 169–70
zombies, 152
zoos, 148
Zucker, Carole, 153, 154

CPI Antony Rowe
Eastbourne, UK
November 26, 2019